In the Wake of Disaster

In the Wake of Disaster is the first book to seriously engage with the everyday state through a devastating disaster in Pakistan. It explores post-disaster politics in the aftermath of large-scale flooding of the Indus River that affected millions of people in 2010 and 2011. The way this disaster was lived, experienced and politically constructed tells a vivid and illustrative story about the social contract between the state and its citizens and Islamists in Pakistan. This book tells that story.

It sets out to examine a seemingly simple question: what is the responsibility of the state to its people in the aftermath of a natural disaster? Along the way it delves into rich detail about people's everyday encounters with the state in Pakistan, uncovers post-colonial discourses on rights of citizenship and dispels mainstream understanding of Islamist groups as presenting an alternative development paradigm to the state. Based on detailed ethnographic fieldwork, it forces the reader to look beyond narratives of Pakistan as the perennial 'failing state' falling victim to an imminent 'Islamist takeover'. It shifts the conversation from hysteria and sensationalism surrounding Pakistan to the everyday. In doing so it transforms our understanding of contemporary disasters.

Ayesha Siddiqi is Lecturer in Human Geography at Royal Holloway, University of London. She holds a PhD in War Studies from King's College London and has contributed to various UN and other policy forums on disaster risk reduction.

In the Wake of Disaster

Islamists, the State and a Social Contract in Pakistan

Ayesha Siddiqi

CAMBRIDGE
UNIVERSITY PRESS

University Printing House, Cambridge CB2 8BS, United Kingdom

One Liberty Plaza, 20th Floor, New York, NY 10006, USA

477 Williamstown Road, Port Melbourne, vic 3207, Australia

314 to 321, 3rd Floor, Plot No.3, Splendor Forum, Jasola District Centre, New Delhi 110025, India

79 Anson Road, #06–04/06, Singapore 079906

Cambridge University Press is part of the University of Cambridge.

It furthers the University's mission by disseminating knowledge in the pursuit of education, learning and research at the highest international levels of excellence.

www.cambridge.org
Information on this title: www.cambridge.org/9781108472920

First published 2019

Printed in India by Avantika Printers Pvt. Ltd.

A catalogue record for this publication is available from the British Library

ISBN 978-1-108-47292-0 Hardback

For my parents who made this
(and every other) journey with me.

Contents

Figures, Boxes and Tables

Figures

Box

Tables

Acknowledgements

This book germinated from the doctoral work I did at King's College London (KCL) in the early 2010s. At a time when most reports on Pakistan fell into one of two categories – representing it as the world's 'most dangerous' country, or one that would soon be falling in the hands of the Taliban – I was working on the problem of flooding of the Indus River. All the while being based at a department that studies war and talking about how, occasionally, the state in Pakistan managed to get things 'right'! My interest in this subject did not make sense to many at the time, but I am extremely grateful that it did to the AXA Research Fund, who funded the study. I owe my largest debt of gratitude to the people in Thatta, Badin and Tharparkar for opening their doors and welcoming me into their homes and their lives. They are the reason this work was even possible. At KCL, Anatol Leiven, Daanish Mustafa, Rudra Chaudhuri, Theo Farrell and Thomas Rid were all exceptionally generous with their time and support. I am also very grateful to Jeroen Warner and Matt Nelson, for providing me with such incisive and critical comments that helped shape future drafts.

While the journey may have started there it continued with me to my next institutional home at the University of Bath and then to the Department of Geography at Royal Holloway, University of London (RHUL). Both departments provided the kind of engaging and stimulating intellectual environments I needed to finish the book. I would especially like to thank Jenny Kynaston at RHUL for the maps in this book.

Along the way I have also been very fortunate to find mentors in Haris Gazdar and Marie Lall who not only helped me develop my unstructured thoughts into sound ideas but also made me believe in my work. I am also very grateful to a number of people who gave me their input over the years. This is undoubtedly a better and richer project because Martin Bayly, Amiera Sawas, Sarah Ansari, Ayesha Jalal, Mark Pelling and Humeira Iqtedar were so generous with their time and their advice.

Parts of this book have been published as papers in *IDS Bulletin* and *Contemporary South Asia* and I am thankful to the reviewers for their very helpful comments. This work has also benefitted from feedback on papers presented at British Association of South Asian Studies (BASAS), Association of American Geographers (AAG) and International Studies Association (ISA) conferences. I am also particularly grateful to have had the opportunity to engage in incredibly fruitful conversations with colleagues at the Climate Change and Environmental Pressure: Building Adaptation and Resilience of Local Communities in the Hindu Kush–Himalaya workshop in Hamburg and the International Conference of the Consortium for Comparative Research on Regional Integration and Social Cohesion (RISC) in Mexico City.

From the very beginning Qudsiya Ahmed and the team at Cambridge University Press have been a dream to work with. With a masterful blend of patience and drive they have shepherded me across the finish line despite all my fieldwork and teaching related delays, and I am immensely grateful to them all. I also want to acknowledge Christopher Deyer at Michigan University Press for his support and enthusiasm for the book. Despite going another way, I found the three excellent anonymous reviews on the book to be most incisive and helpful.

For the fact that an Urdu-speaking, ethnically Punjabi individual, who grew up in Karachi, could so readily find herself at 'home' in Thatta, Badin and Tharparkar I owe a debt of gratitude to my 'team' in the field. Mumtaz *bhai*, Zahid *bhai* and Zubair *bhai* left their homes and their families, and allowed their lives to revolve around my fieldwork schedule. My friends at LHDP (Laar Human Development Programme) and Samo *sahab* in Badin, and my friends at Plan Pakistan and Wazir *bhai* in Thatta provided me with far more help than I could have ever imagined and I am immensely grateful to them all.

There were many, many tea and coffee breaks, particularly during the dark and lonely times in writing, and I am grateful to have been able to share those with Dave Parker, Anna Knapps, Olivier Schmitt and Eduardo Peris. For being able to survive broken bones and continue writing important chapters, I am incredibly blessed to have had found family in Hiba Sameen, and in East London. As for my other family – Ali, Feline, Ignazio, Lucia, Giulia and Fizza who have all, at various points, edited my work, cooked my dinners and given me more support and warmth than I probably deserved – I have few words except a very insufficient thank you. None more so, perhaps, than Ammara, and by default Matt, who have taken on roles from friends and confidants to mentors and career counsellors and everything in between.

Finally, I am very aware of how unavailable I have been to people in my life as this book consumed more and more of my life, particularly to my family and friends in Pakistan. I am very grateful to have had Munir and Allahbuksh reminding me where home is. For putting up with me and being supportive of my less conventional decisions through the distance, and the years, I am incredibly grateful to Madiha, Ismat, Sonia, Nabah, Amina, Unaiza, Maliha, Leena, Amina and Bushra and very fortunate to call them my friends. I am incredibly fortunate to have found nothing but support and encouragement from Auntie Zeenat and Uncle Gamma along the way. My sister is my inspiration and helps to ground me in what is important. I am able to be me because of her. For being my fiercest critic and biggest fan and enabling me in only the best ways possible, I am immensely grateful to Salman.

My parents are the reason I have been able to follow my path and they have made this journey with me, sometimes from half a world and other times from half a country away. This book is dedicated to Mama and Abu.

Introduction

Setting the Scene

In the aftermath of a large-scale flooding disaster that affected Pakistan in 2010 (and again in 2011), *The Lancet* published a paper on the crisis in the country that wrote about a family affected by the disaster in the following words:

> *The family had received no medical help – or any other help for that matter – after the floods hit their village nearly two weeks ago. Aid never seemed to arrive, and in its absence, he feared his children's health would continue to deteriorate at an alarming pace.* (Solberg 2010, 1039)

And then about the wider crisis, the article stated the following:

> *On the ground, flood victims are becoming ever more desperate.*
>
> *Into the aid vacuum steps other, more controversial players. Unable to cope with the crisis, the Pakistani authorities are alarmed to find radical Islamic organisations with ties to militant groups handing out aid and providing medical care in the flood affected areas.* (Solberg 2010, 1040)

The message in this article was clear. The state in Pakistan was failing to reach out to affected citizens in the aftermath of the flooding disaster to provide a basic level of human security. This flooding disaster was unusual; in terms of people affected and the sheer scale of area submerged under water, it was undoubtedly the worst that post-1971 Pakistan had ever seen. But the idea that this had 'damaged' relations between the state and its citizens because of 'the government's shambolic aid efforts' (Shah 2010), 'fracturing' the social contract, was neither new nor novel (*BBC News* 2011; Ellick and Shah 2010; Rashid 2010).

Pakistan was created as an independent state carved out of British India in August 1947. The state and its citizens are still widely seen as being unable to build a lasting relationship with each other in the seventy years since its creation. Their interaction is regularly referred to as fraught, fragmented or simply non-existent. The absence of a meaningful relationship between the state and its citizens has been the subject of much scholarly and political analysis. Ayesha Jalal's work, for example, highlights some of the cleavages in the state–citizen relationship, particularly with regard to the confusion in understanding nationhood, statehood and identity in Pakistan. Her work suggests that for this relationship to move forward, a 'sustained debate on citizenship rights, accompanied by a reapportioning of responsibility for the construction and dissemination of ideas and knowledge between state and civil society' is needed in the country (Jalal 1995, 87).

This negotiation between the state and regular people to define the terms of their relationship, and establish certain rights of citizenship, is underway in Pakistan. In fact, as this work will illustrate, at certain political moments, such as in the aftermath of a large-scale flooding disaster in the southern part of the country, this citizenship struggle has also been pushed along in the right direction. This relationship between the state and its people is based on progressive ideas of citizenship but also reflects aspects of an older, more established political order – caste, kinship and hereditary relations. Despite the existence of these social and hereditary relationships, the state is the central social and political entity, one that is called upon by its citizens to deliver in the face of challenges such as the climatic disaster in 2010 and 2011. The state, for its part, also reaches out to people directly, to address their demands as citizens of Pakistan. This book goes beyond the more conventional ways of interpreting state–citizen relations that rely on substantial social determinism and injects new life into the citizenship debate on Pakistan.

A Social Contract in Pakistan

Pakistan's post-independence history has been marred by repeated civil, political and ethnic tensions and unrest – military coups, ethnic separatist movements, failure of democratic institutions and, most recently, the threat posed by Islamist militancy – and yet these are only some of the defining challenges facing the South Asian state. Most accounts that discuss the underlying factors contributing to this instability and conflict emphasise the very distant relationship between the state and its citizens in Pakistan. This is particularly highlighted in discussions on the country's powerful military establishment and the way it manipulates this distance to maintain power (Haqqani 2005). The distance between the state and the citizens is, therefore, considered to be a defining fault line that has manifested in a serious crisis of governance in the country.

When looking at the social contract, I follow in the tradition of writers such as Keating, who argue that the post-colonial social contract is 'real' in its structuring of political and social relations; it is not fixed but rather one 'in which the actors negotiate and rewrite the terms and conditions of democratic governance' (Keating 2007, 5). This makes it possible to interpret various forms of state–citizen interactions as part of this social contract framework. Broadly, my examination of this relationship between the state and its citizens is an ethnographic one. I use the works of scholars such as Gupta (1995) and Corbridge et al. (2005) to elucidate the nature of this social contract in Pakistan. Normally, such a contract between the state and its citizens is understood to be one where citizens are part of a social and political collective in order to be provided a basic level of human security by the state. In the case of Pakistan, an additional feature of the social contract has also been its consistent absence when theorising political society in the country.

The state has, instead, mostly been analysed as one that fails to provide basic services to its people. It is also regularly emphasised that the state in Pakistan prioritises funding a security–military establishment over building a developmental state for the people (Kabeer, Mumtaz and Sayeed 2010). All of this is often connected to 'feudal politics' and patronage networks that have come to define state functions and to posit the failing or near absence of a social contract between the state and its citizens. These explanations on state–citizen relations are well documented in the literature on Pakistan, with significant evidence from the province of Sindh (Kabeer, Mumtaz and Sayeed 2010; Kabeer et al. 2012; Lall 2012a, 2012b; Lyon 2002).

One group of scholars has consistently argued that there is no relationship between the Pakistani state and its citizens (Lall 2012a, 2012b; Dean 2005). Their studies have shown that state and society operate parallel to each other but with no relationship between them. Their central thesis is that there is no social contract between the state and its citizens in Pakistan that enables this parallel functioning to occur. It has been categorically stated that 'the problem in Pakistan today is that throughout history its governing elite, feudal, political and those with economic power, have failed to create a sense of citizenship across the nation, creating a political vacuum where governing structures operate in parallel to society, yet without much linkage'. The failure to build a relationship between the state and its citizens is not only a 'political failure' but also the 'biggest fault line' in Pakistani society (Lall 2012b, 270). The argument presented by these scholars is that there is no framework for building citizenship in Pakistan, and no language for society and state to speak to each other. These authors not only observe that there is currently no meaningful relationship between the two but also that it is unlikely one will develop at some point in the future.

A second group of scholars extends this analysis somewhat further and argues that this absence of a meaningful relationship between the state and its citizens is due to an overdeveloped society (Kabeer, Mumtaz and Sayeed 2010; Lyon 2002; Lieven 2011). Their work suggests that a fragmented social structure deeply divided along class (primarily 'feudal' land relations), ethnic and kinship lines has made it difficult for any kind of citizenship to exist outside of these dominant social relations. They see the social contract as entirely mediated through powerful power brokers. These types of fissures in society make the Pakistani state unable to establish a meaningful relationship with its citizenry. The bonds of citizenship are fragmented and there is a 'large distance' between the population and the state. One study based on 'rural Sindh' in Pakistan – the same geographical region that is the focus of this book – goes so far as to say that 'the government is largely conspicuous by its absence' in the villages where their fieldwork was done (Kabeer et al. 2012, 13). They further emphasise that the non-governmental organisation (NGO) they were working with in Sindh 'had to work in a context where the state was largely absent' (Kabeer et al. 2012, 56). This appears to provide further evidence to the idea that the state is 'absent' or far removed from the political imagination of its citizens, who have limited understanding and even more limited experience of a social contract between themselves and the state.

The inability of the Pakistani state to build a state–citizen relationship and a lasting social contract with its citizenry has, therefore, been discussed in significant amount in literature to date. This weak relationship has been attributed to a meddling military keen to seize political power, various development failures resulting from the state's inability to provide basic amenities to its citizens, and also a populace deeply divided along caste, kinship, 'feudal' and other lines. The people of Pakistan are, therefore, regularly cast as confused and unable to identify themselves as citizens of a functioning state. This dysfunctional state–citizen relationship is to a large extent seen to be the consequence of an imbalance, whereby enormous power is wielded by social institutions such as 'feudal' landlords and kinship groups (Mohmand 2011). As a result, 'what the citizens of Pakistan share as citizens, beyond their constitution, their flag, their national anthem and their defense force' is entirely unclear to them (Kabeer, Mumtaz and Sayeed 2010, 15). In regions of rural Sindh where the fieldwork for this book was conducted, citizens are seen to have no direct relationship with the state; rather it is the 'feudal' landlord, the head of kinship group, or some other individual at the top of the social and political hierarchy who defines the people's only understanding of a state.

Any contract between the state and the citizens outside urban metropolises is believed to be mediated by 'feudal' landlords. These 'feudal' lords are thought to be elected to political office by beleaguered masses, dependent on them for social and economic capital. At the same time 'feudal' lords are also able to maintain their position of dominance by dispensing patronage to their constituents and establishing a way for the latter to connect to the state.[1] This relationship between the state and its citizens is understood as being entirely mediated through social networks and patrons and is referred to by some scholars as the case of 'weak state and strong societies' in Pakistan. In fact, such work even asserts that the state–society disconnect works in Pakistan's favour, so that a strong society makes the broken state less relevant to people's lives, enabling it to carry on withstanding crises (Lieven 2011).

This book extends the debate beyond these constructions of the state in Pakistan as entirely subsumed by social structures. Instead, it illustrates that the politics of dispensing patronage through caste and kinship networks, using hereditary leaders such as *wadera*s and *pir*s, is an incomplete, and perhaps even a dated, understanding of the state–citizenship relationship outside of the metropolises in Pakistan. While these relationships are, of course, important they do not capture the full extent of people's interpretation of the state and citizenship in 'non-urban' Pakistan. In fact, there are other factors contributing to how people understand the state and their own relationship within it. While some forms of patronage remain important in contemporary Pakistan, the state is more than a myriad of *biraderi*s (Lieven 2011) or a myriad of feudal landlords (Lyon 2002) interacting with people through complex webs of patron–client relations. It is thereby providing a more developed and nuanced examination of state–citizen relations in Pakistan, not adequately explained by social structures and hereditary relations.

---

[1] See among others: Herring 1979; Alavi 1983; and Waseem 1994. I provide more detailed explanation and reference to literature in Chapter 3.

Based on the analysis of data collected from three districts of lower Sindh in southern Pakistan, I argue four things: first, that a relationship between the state of Pakistan and its citizens does exist; second, that social structures dispensing patronage are only one part of this state–citizen relationship, enhancing current scholarship beyond state–citizen conceptions that are primarily based on frameworks of *wadera*, *biraderi* and *pir*; third, that this construction of the state and its citizens beyond traditional conceptions is also based on rights and entitlements of citizenship and was pushed along in the aftermath of the disaster; and finally, that the narrative built around Islamists, such as the Jamaat-ud-Dawa, constructing themselves as alternatives to the state was emphatically incorrect. The idea of the state remained intact in the aftermath of the disaster.

The primary research question that this book, therefore, seeks to address is: *Do hereditary relations and social structures define the nature of the social contract between the state and its citizens outside Pakistan's urban metropolises?* The above question contains the following sub-questions:

1. Does a citizenship framework exist and is it understood and lived in parts of Pakistan such as lower Sindh?
2. Did the flooding disaster of 2010 and 2011 fracture the social contract between the state and the citizens?

The Political Construction of the Flooding Disaster

In the devastating flooding disaster in 2010, and again in 2011, the southern part of the country was seen to have made the 'biggest fault line' (Lall 2012b, 270) in Pakistani political society acutely and painfully visible. Between July and September of 2010, massive floods devastated the region along the Indus River and submerged one-fifth of Pakistan's landmass under water. The following year, in 2011, the period between August and September again witnessed devastating floods in the province of Sindh, with particularly serious impacts in the southern part of the province, known as lower Sindh. The political construction of these floods is relevant in illuminating key aspects of the state–citizen relationship in this region of Pakistan. This is because it was once again argued that the state was absent and that the people were left to fend for themselves, illustrating the extent to which the social contract between the state and its citizens is broken.

Scholars have often used disaster events as analytical windows that can help answer wider societal and political questions. Soekefeld's work on a landslide disaster in Attabad, Gilgit-Baltistan, in the far north of the country, for instance, asks, 'What, then do the politics of the Attabad disaster tell about political processes in Gilgit-Baltistan and Pakistan?' (Soekefeld 2012, 202). His answer includes an ideological divide between the political supporters of the Pakistan People's Party (PPP) and the *mir* (hereditary ruler) of the region. Additionally, he finds people to be ambivalent and unclear about the idea of government and notes that they often find state-led development and reform packages irrelevant in the area (Soekefeld 2012). By studying the politics around the landslide disaster Soekefeld developed a better and deeper understanding of governance and development in the region. In a similar vein but to a different end, Simpson studies the politics around the 2001 earthquake in Gujarat, India, to illuminate the ways in which cultural and religious icons and ideologies were naturalised into the political and physical geography of the region, emphasising that 'it is indeed the *aftermath* (of a disaster) that might reveal what is dear' to society (Simpson 2013, 50). Following in the tradition of such work, I examine the politics around the flooding disaster of 2010 and 2011 in order to extend the understanding of the state–citizen relationship in Pakistan.

The flooding disaster in 2010 and 2011 reinforced the narrative that the social contract in Pakistan is 'weak' or non-existent and that the state is 'absent'. It also magnified a perceived crisis of governance where it was being suggested that since the state had eschewed responsibility by way of not responding to the crisis, other political actors were ready and willing to do the government's job. After the floods of 2011, an international media report from the province of Sindh said:

> Correspondents say the perception is that for a second year running, the government in particular has failed flood victims. (*BBC News* 2011)

Also, reporting from Sindh, after the 2010 floods, a journalist described public opinion in the following words:

> The tented refugees offered scathing criticism of their local parliamentarian, who they said did nothing to help, and the government in general. (Walsh 2010)

The dominant political construction of the flooding disaster that emerged from the province of Sindh was one where the state had again failed its citizens by not providing disaster relief. The story further goes that by abandoning disaster-affected citizens in flood-hit areas, the state caused more damage to an already tenuous social contract with its people.

Further, the discourse around powerful 'feudal' or kinship group patrons mediating people's only interaction with a weak and largely 'absent' state was also able to encompass the post-disaster reality. For example, a study examining the political impacts of the 2010 floods in Karachi and 'interior'[2] Sindh concludes that 'local patrons in Sindh have faced serious erosion of popularity after the floods' (Haider 2010, 13). 'Feudal' landlords in particular were seen to be insensitive to the suffering of the masses and focused on saving their own lands instead (Jaan 2011, 54). It was, therefore, suggested that the evident tensions in this relationship, thought to define the very terms on which rural citizens interact with the state, would have further detrimental impacts on the tenuous relationship between the state and citizens in rural Sindh. Additionally, the anti-incumbency sentiment prevalent amongst Sindhi constituents disappointed by their local patrons was ripe for exploitation by alternative political actors, such as 'extremist groups' (Haider 2010). The floods in 2010 and 2011 were believed to further frustrate the problems evident within Sindh, primarily issues around state 'absence' and 'feudal' lords defining the terms of the social contract between the people and the state. This narrative prevailed well after the emergency of the disaster was over.

Since people in Sindh are assumed to understand the state only in terms of their connection to local patrons and the patronage that they dispense, the perceived gap between the patrons and the clients would become larger. This gap can easily be captured by Islamist groups providing state-like services in the aftermath of the disaster. Briefly then, this story around Islamist groups as alternative political agents, who were able to reach out to affected communities with greater efficiency and empathy than the state, was pervasive and widespread. It was used to declare the state as delegitimised in the eyes of citizens, thereby opening political space for other agents to mobilise around the disaster. Newspaper stories on the floods regularly featured headlines such as (Ellick and Shah 2010; Hasan 2010):

> Hard-line Islam Fills Void in Flooded Pakistan
>
> 'Hardline' Groups Step in to fill Pakistan Aid Vacuum

This 'void' or 'vacuum' left by the state in the aftermath of the flooding disaster in 2010 and 2011 being 'filled' by Islamist groups presenting themselves

[2] While this work challenges that assertion, traditionally most of the province of Sindh outside of its two urban centres, Karachi and Hyderabad, is seen to be rural and referred to as 'interior' Sindh.

as alternatives to the state gained significant traction in Pakistan and abroad. It soon began to influence Western policy decisions in the region, with US aid officials stating, within months of the 2010 floods, that more than US$50 million would be diverted from a different development package to flood relief. The explanation for this was that 'officials in Pakistan and its ally Washington are worried that militants could exploit the disorder caused by the floods, and the government's slow response, to gain recruits' (Anthony 2010). The ineffective and inefficient state, in the aftermath of the flooding disaster, was, therefore, not only damaging state–citizen relations further but also enabling opportunistic political agents to present themselves as challengers to state power. Evidence from Sindh also revealed trends similar to the rest of the country. After the Sindh floods of 2011, the Middle East–based *Al Jazeera English* famously aired a televised news report in which their Pakistan correspondent was on a Jamaat-ud-Dawa (JuD) boat, braving floodwaters; he declared into his microphone:

> The people of Sindh are in a desperate situation, they have not had any help from their government and the only help they have received is from the organisation, the Jamaat-ud-Dawa.[3]

The Islamist group known as the JuD is the charitable wing of the Lashkar-e-Taiba (LeT),[4] an Islamist militant organisation based in Pakistan, linked to the 2008 Mumbai terrorist attacks. Its roots trace back to Pakistani militants who joined the Afghan jihad against the Soviets in the early 1980s. There are published works on this group. For instance, Tankel's work published in 2011 discusses the evolution of this group from a small number of ambitious but insignificant militants in the early 1980s to the large, well-organised force that was capable of 'storming the world stage' with the attacks in Mumbai in 2008. Iqtedar's work (2011), also published at the same time, discusses how Islamist movements like the JuD, while being vehemently opposed to secularism, end up facilitating secularisation in urban spaces such as Lahore in Pakistan. Both these studies, especially the former, give details on why, how, when and where the JuD was formed and what it aims to do in the future.[5] The pitting of the

---

[3] *Al Jazeera English* coverage of the floods of 2011, available at http://www.youtube.com/watch?v=nlMrBmYV1ZU.

[4] 'Army of the Pure.'

[5] Since the Mumbai bombings of 2008, there has been a significant amount of interest in this group and there is a wealth of information available in English, Urdu and various vernacular languages on the JuD.

JuD against the state was no different to the way NGOs were constructed as 'alternative social and political organisation(s)' to the state in the aftermath of the Marmara earthquake in Turkey in 1999 (Pelling and Dill 2010, 25). In this construction, their specific religious ideology or level of Islamism is not important to the bigger story.

Rather, the JuD's significance here is a political one. In popular perception they were seen to be capturing a space left by a broken state and a fractured social contract between the state and its citizens. This narrative has been built on the assumption that the state was absent and had broadly retreated from public service in the aftermath of the disaster. Based on intensive fieldwork in the southern part of Pakistan known as lower Sindh, I deconstruct these ideas of the state as having receded from political imagination after the floods of 2010 and 2011 and illustrate that the reported scarcity of 'sightings of the state' (Corbridge et al. 2005) is unscientific and not based on scholarly analysis.

This study contends that these dominant constructions of state–citizen relations and of a failed *social contract* and collapsed *citizenship* in Sindh are either based on (*a*) works that have not been contextualised or historicised or (*b*) works of social structuralists who overemphasize social relations as the definition of state–citizen relations. Using unitary and exogenously constructed ideals around what it means to be a citizen, and naturalising these ideals to social and political processes of post-colonial states such as Pakistan, can help explain how the relationship between the state and its citizens is perceived to be broken. The lack of a vernacular vocabulary to speak about citizenship has resulted in survey-based, or less intensive (more extensive), studies which conclude that the state has failed to create a universal ideal around citizenship, indicating a failure in the state's ability to build a relationship with its people. Other studies extend social relations to encompass relations between the state and the citizens, concluding that there is no state outside of social structures.

This is now, however, reflective of the ground reality where people, in areas such as lower Sindh, have an understanding of the wider social and political entity of the state and see the provision of basic rights as part of the responsibilities of this state. They also have a lived understanding of their own place as citizens entitled to some basic provisions and express it as the 'job' or the 'duty' of the state to provide. Further, I illustrate that media stories and quick assessment reports in the aftermath of the flooding disaster accepted conventional wisdom around state failure and collapsed citizenship, making hasty generalisations that were not reflective of the complexity on the ground.

Additionally, such work seemed to suggest that the gap between the state and its citizens had increased because the state had failed its flood-affected citizens. This perception was widespread and pervasive and used sightings of Islamist groups in these areas providing disaster response activities as further evidence of a fractured social contract indicating that the state had left political space to be captured by these alternative agents.

Countering the Dominant Narrative: The Argument in Brief

This book examines the idea of an 'absent' and unresponsive state and people's inability to claim or exercise citizenship in Pakistan. It uses qualitative data and focuses exclusively on one region in Sindh. Using an in-depth approach, it argues that a bigger social and political entity, the state, exists in lower Sindh and that people have an acute sense of being citizens of this state regardless of whether they are able to articulate this sentiment in ways that can be commonly understood by those socialised in Western scholarly traditions. This study sheds light on the nature of this relationship, demonstrating that citizens make demands on the state, the most significant political actor. This relationship exists *despite* the existence of political patrons and influential families, and not *because* of it.

The flooding disaster of 2010 and 2011 in lower Sindh further shows that far from 'damaging' the social contract, the state and its citizens were able to use that political moment to strengthen their interaction with each other. The disaster, along with providing an analytical window to examine this interaction, also catalysed a moment that was utilised by the state to reach out to its citizens, who were also actively making demands on the state. The state, in its capacity, was trying to deliver on the basis of rights and entitlements, not patronage or kinship, thereby pushing a more progressive citizenship along.

Based on my research, I, therefore, argue that there exists a meaningful relationship between the state and its citizens in lower Sindh, though it includes some aspects of hereditary social relations and also other 'state effects' (Trouillot 2001). These effects include not only a number of universally recognised principles, such as service delivery and some basic rights, but also contextualised factors such as fragmented and individualised constructions of the entity of the state. My research into the state–citizen relationship in lower Sindh allows me to advance three main arguments:

1. *'Client-ship' and rights-based citizenship are not mutually exclusive and are simultaneously part of the social contract at a local level.* Powerful political

families may have risen to power through the use of traditional religious, kinship or land ownership power. These social relations, however, do not define the sum total of state construction at a local level. Despite popularly understood to be people's only idea of a state, functions and attributes of the state are not subsumed within the complex myriad of social relations. My evidence illustrates that the state is omnipresent and all-encompassing, and that political families can also sometimes be manifestations of this state or of wider political processes, such as political parties. The understanding of the state at a local level may be fragmented and not entirely coherent as one unitary actor, but it is considered responsible for providing its citizens basic rights in lower Sindh. Political families do not dictate the terms of the social contract people have with the state; those are determined socio-culturally or individually, but the political representatives can sometimes be expected to deliver on the terms of this contract as representatives of this state.

2. *The flooding disaster furthered elements of the social contract based on rights and entitlements of citizenship.* In the aftermath of the floods of 2010 and 2011, citizens demanded an interaction with a state that implemented policy solutions, not one that dispensed patronage along kinship (or other) lines. The state, for its part, responded with a universal, rather than a targeted, disaster response policy, also connected to the citizenship numbers of heads of households, making this a de facto right of citizenship. Demand-side push from citizens and supply-driven disaster response from the state helped a more progressive social contract along.
3. *Popular accounts that the Islamist group, the JuD, was able to rise to political prominence in the aftermath of the flooding disaster due to a paucity of the state and damaged social contract were emphatically incorrect.* What captured public imagination was that the post-disaster political landscape was often constructed as a JuD-versus-state in a battle to 'win the hearts and minds' of flood-affected masses. This was evidently a false dichotomy. The social contract between the state and its citizens was not broken in the aftermath of the flooding disaster in lower Sindh, and the JuD did not present itself as an alternative to the state. In fact, my evidence illustrates that had the state not reached out to citizens through large-scale public interventions, other political groups could have utilised this political momentum. It was an eventuality that did not occur largely due to state action and intervention.

On Methods and Approach

Ethnographic research methods

This study is based on qualitative research I conducted over seven months in three districts of lower Sindh in 2012–2013. My fieldwork sites included the southernmost districts of Thatta, Badin and Tharparkar, in the province of Sindh in Pakistan, and the data collection method was primarily ethnographic – including structured and semi-structured interviews, focus group discussions and participant observations. This was supplemented with data from other primary and secondary sources such as newspaper articles, government reports and other printed material. A detailed section on research methodology and philosophy is presented in the next chapter; at this point it is important to highlight why I chose this approach to address the main research question around the absent state and the broken social contract in Sindh.

My research project started out wanting to understand political transformation in the aftermath of a large-scale disaster. I was conducting this research within one to two years of the disaster taking place and, therefore, was not able to draw from fresh election or voting data. It was also not my intention to add to an already existing body of political economy work that establishes causal linkages between weather-related variables and changes in voting patterns in democracies. Rather, from the onset, I was interested in identifying and exploring various processes of change in the aftermath of the disaster. Additionally, once I was in the field, it became fairly evident to me that such a quantitative methodology, based on voting figures, would reveal relatively little in terms of the political impact of the flooding disaster. It seemed unlikely that people in flood-affected regions would change their voting preferences on the basis of just the one disaster. Rather, what became clear in the field was that flood-affected citizens in lower Sindh were, individually and within their communities, thinking and rethinking the issues around the state's 'responsibility to protect', disaster response and what political representatives were supposed to be doing during times of disaster. Hence, what the research was interested in illuminating was not causality between the disaster and voting preferences but the way in which the disaster was being politically constructed by the people most affected and what the wider impact of that was, something that can only be understood through analysing their stories and narratives.

Eventually, though, it became evident that this study was not simply telling the story of the politics that emerged in the aftermath of the flooding disaster in 2010 and 2011, but rather answering a bigger question about the nature of state–citizen relations and a social contract in this region of southern Pakistan. The post-disaster political narrative was important because it explains one piece of the bigger picture. In trying to understand the relationship between the state and its citizens, my study also started with the 'master narrative' of the absent state and the non-existent social contract in Pakistan, presented earlier. I refer to this body of work as the 'master narrative' because Bamberg identifies it as constitutive of '"frames" according to which courses of events can easily be plotted, simply because one's audience is taken to "know" and accept these courses' (2004, 360). Given that in popular discourse the flooding disaster in 2010 and 2011 only further reinforced ideas of a 'vacuum', 'breach' and 'void' in state–citizen relations, it is evident in this case that the expectation was that people 'knew and accepted' the course of the absent state and the non-existent social contract, making this the 'master narrative'.

I was keen to understand how the political space vacated by a failing state was being captured by alternative political agents in the aftermath of the disaster. In order to understand this post-disaster political space in lower Sindh and shed new light on this space, I had to employ in-depth qualitative research methods that addressed research questions that 'are often open-ended and exploratory, aiming to generate hypotheses rather than to test them' (Burke 2005, 238). The research project was, therefore, set up to be inductive in order to lead to novel and nuanced findings on post-disaster political space or indeed post-disaster state captured at a local level. It quickly became clear that this research on the flooding disaster in lower Sindh would help tell a bigger story on state–citizen relations and a social contract in Pakistan.

Why Thatta, Badin and Tharparkar?

This study is based on data collected in the three districts of Thatta, Badin and Tharparkar located in the lower Sindh region of Pakistan colloquially known as Laar. I choose these districts of lower Sindh as my field site because they were among the worst affected by the flooding disaster in 2010 and 2011. Thatta was devastated by floods that swept across Pakistan in 2010, while Badin and Tharparkar were badly affected by large-scale flooding in the province of Sindh the following year. A district-level breakdown of the impact of the disaster is presented in Table 4.1 in Chapter 4. When planning a research project that was going to engage quite seriously with some of the issues that emerged in the aftermath of the flooding disaster in 2010 and 2011, this region was the most obvious place to locate the field site.

I started my field research and data collection in the district of Badin but within weeks included Thatta and Tharparkar into my field site as well. To understand why, it is important to illuminate a few key aspects of this administrative unit known as a 'district'. The boundaries of the four provinces of Pakistan demarcate ethno-linguistic majority populations. Talk of any changes to these boundaries – for example, the addition of a new province, either for the Seraiki-speaking minority in the province of Punjabi-dominated Punjab or for the primarily urban Urdu-speaking minority in Sindh – have been politically contentious issues, often erupting into violence. Districts within these provinces, however, despite demarcating voting constituencies, have been regularly changed and are considered fairly fluid boundaries in most parts of Pakistan. Since 2002, a number of districts in Sindh have been bifurcated to create new districts for what are said to be primarily administrative, not political, reasons. When I worked in Sindh in the year 2006–2007 the province had 24 districts; today it has 28. In fact, Thatta, the district where I completed my fieldwork in March 2013, was spilt into two districts later in the same year, changing the boundary of the district (Mansoor 2013).

District boundaries are, therefore, fairly fluid in Sindh. This is administratively true because they are often being changed around and new districts are being added but this also results in people attaching limited importance to these boundaries. Most of my informants were quite unaware of where their district ends and where the next one begins. In terms of culture, language and a shared history it is almost impossible to differentiate between people from Thatta and Badin. Thar's Dhatki-speaking population, from the district of Tharparkar, has more distinct cultural idiosyncrasies, but those are primarily connected to their physical geography of living in a desert and the influence of the large Hindu population native to the district. They would, however, be indistinguishable from people living in desert areas of the districts of Badin or Umerkot, or even from the Hindu populations in Badin or Thatta. It is not easy to determine whether a village is located in Thatta or Badin, or Badin or Tharparkar, by simply looking at or talking to its residents. District boundaries almost seemed irrelevant in my early days of fieldwork.

While district demarcations in lower Sindh may be unimportant to people's cultural and social lives, they are an important part of the 'technologies of rule' (Corbridge et al. 2005) imposed by the state from above. Voting constituencies are divided based on districts and each district is allocated seats in the National and Provincial Assemblies based on population proportion. It was almost exclusively by asking people which individual they cast their vote for that I was able to identify which district their hamlet was situated in. This also made it necessary for me to include more than one district in my field site. In order to say something about the state–citizen relationship in lower Sindh and, in fact, argue that a social contract exists and was further strengthened in the aftermath of the flooding disaster, I wanted to illustrate that this was the case across this region and beyond just one voting constituency where the elected representative or political 'feudal' family was responsive and sympathetic to the needs of its constituents. This work illustrates that despite the difference in formal political representatives, or those seen to be 'feudal' patrons, my findings remain consistent across the three districts where I collected data.

Why qualitative methods?

The aim of qualitative research is not to generate generalizable findings but rather to answer the questions behind 'why' certain processes are playing out the way they are (Horsburgh 2003). This study is a detailed investigation into 'why', despite popular perception to the contrary, there is evidence that a social contract exists in the region of Pakistan that was studied. It postulates that doing so sheds light on local political and social processes that are extremely valuable in our broader understanding of Pakistan and state–citizen relations. Second, while the findings from this work will not support hasty generalisations, it is still possible to, carefully and with qualification, use these findings to illuminate key issues and nuances in the relationship between the state and its citizens at a local level in the South Asian context.

This methodology made it possible to see multiple meanings being assigned to the state. For instance, it was at times constructed as disjointed and fragmented but at the same time was also the omnipresent *sarkar* that was meant to provide basic rights and security to its people. Citizenship, too, was interpreted in multiple ways, some of which were contextual, others universal. Clientalism, in the form of, say, getting the Sheerazi Member of National Assembly (MNA) from Thatta to sign a *parchee*,[6] was something people relied upon in some contexts. In situations where something was seen to be an essential right, such as drinking water or a cash transfer from the state, it

[6] The literal translation would be 'a slip of paper'. In this context, any request for services from local authorities, endorsed by a local power-broker, is typically thought will be fast-tracked through the system.

was almost universally seen to be the state's job to deliver as an entitlement of citizenship.

More detail on this research process is provided in Box I.1. As the primary residential community of non-urban citizens in Pakistan, a *goth* (hamlet) is the most local and comfortable setting within which it was possible to get to know my informants and their views. Over seven months and across three districts, I was able to include data from a variety of different *goth*s that constituted a range of different local socio-political dynamics atypical of non-urban centres in both Sindh and Pakistan. Most hamlets or *goth*s had a majority Sunni Muslim (primarily of Ahl-e-Sunnat or Ahl-e-Hadis *fiqh*)[7] population, some in Thatta and Badin had a large number of Shia residents and, in all three districts, it was also common to find *goth*s with a large number of Hindu residents. In about thirty-four *goth*s of the total ninety-six I did research in, residential segregations along kinship (*biraderi*) lines was often practised. In just a few, only eighteen, *goth*s, residents were exclusively from one *biraderi*, and in the remaining *goth*s, no residential segregation pattern was clearly evident. It would not be a stretch to state that while the data was collected from *goth*s in three districts, these hamlets and districts constitute a microcosm of wider political society in non-urban Pakistan.

Overview of the Book

The next chapter discusses the analytical framing, particularly the conceptual foundations, of the book and the methodology followed to do this research.

Chapter 2 discusses local politics in the three districts of Thatta, Badin and Tharparkar where this study is based. While on the surface it may seem that families who control political power in these districts operate within the parameters defined by traditional social structures, upon closer inspection the evidence and analysis in this chapter explain that there is definitely more to the story. Sindh has been traditionally seen as a region of Pakistan almost entirely entrenched in patron–client relations between Sufi saints and/or 'feudal' landlords on the one hand and the 'rural' masses on the other, a general narrative that continues to prevail. This chapter, however, argues that the state and its politics on the ground is also autonomous and not entirely defined by

[7] In Sunni Islam, *fiqh* refers to the four schools of jurisprudence – Hanafi, Maliki, Shafi and Hanabli – based on the works of the Imams who systematized the science of Islamic jurisprudence between the 8th and 9th centuries.

these social traditions. While social relations are and remain important, people in this area also demand an interaction with a compassionate state, one whose political parties were expected to follow their ideological underpinnings and where those who have been voted into office must follow up on some of their responsibilities. Chapter 2 demonstrates how what was earlier described as 'client-ship' is but one part of the wider exercise of citizenship in lower Sindh.

Chapter 3 engages in more detail with this issue of what the state is and how it is interpreted in relation to the citizen at a local level in lower Sindh. This chapter constructs an ethnography of the state. It illustrates that beyond the social relations mentioned earlier, people have what sometimes comes across as a fragmented interpretation but a very clear idea of a bigger social entity of 'the state'. This bigger, almost omnipresent entity of the *sarkar* is responsible for providing developmental services and a basic amount of rights and security. While people may not always be able to express themselves in their vernacular vocabulary or construction as 'citizens', they have a lived experience of citizenship that includes ideas around rights and entitlements as well.

Chapter 4 shows how these ideas around rights-based citizenship were pushed along in the aftermath of the flooding disaster in 2010 and 2011. It blurs some of the neat divides in the citizenship literature discussed earlier, illustrating, instead, that the push in more progressive ideas around citizenship was both supply-driven from the state and demand-led by the citizens. In this case it was clear that individual- or community-level capacities to recover from the disaster were not enough and the wider social entity, the *sarkar*, had to be invoked. The *sarkar*, for its part, did reach out to affected citizens and, even if unintentionally, pushed citizenship along.

Chapter 5 further illustrates that a strong relationship between the state and its citizens exists in lower Sindh and the social contract was not fractured in the aftermath of the flooding disaster in 2010 and 2011, making accounts of 'Islamists' such as the JuD filling 'voids' or 'vacuums' left by the state emphatically incorrect. In fact, had serious entitlement failures occurred, the JuD might have been more successful in making a political impact, but my evidence shows that basic entitlement failures were a rare exception rather than the rule. Despite being one of the most publicly visible and well-connected Islamist groups, it dismisses the idea that the JuD had any interest in presenting itself as an alternative to the state. The increased interaction between the state and its citizens in the aftermath of the flooding disaster also meant that it was something they were quite unable to do.

The conclusion reiterates that a social contract beyond social structures including elements of rights and entitlements exists in lower Sindh and that it is possible to extend such analysis to other parts of Pakistan normally considered to be 'rural' and 'backwards'. The nature of the social contract might be relatively different but the ideas of rights, entitlements and the larger social entity of the *sarkar* have a role to play in the construction of state–citizen relations as well as notions of patronage. It is time that literature on citizenship in Pakistan went deeper and beyond what is immediately obvious to challenge some of these grand narratives on Sufi saints and 'feudal' landlords defining people's only interaction with the state.

Box I.1 The scale at which fieldwork was done

The district of Badin is administratively divided into five *taluka*s, which are further divided into union councils (UC). A UC is comprised of anywhere between 10–15 *goths* (hamlets) in a small UC to as many as 35 *goth*s in a large UC. Each *goth* is comprised of 25–30 households in a small *goth* and up to 100 or more households in a large *goth*. My fieldwork was done at the *goth*-level. After being introduced to a family or individual by my local contact, I would always be invited to their homes. Here, I would meet other members of their families, relatives and neighbours and be served tea or a meal. It would also normally be the time when I would conduct semi-structured interviews that had a loose question–answer format. After getting some basic information on the floods and the sources of assistance available to people in their community, it would stop being an 'interview' and would just be a conversation between my hosts and me.

In large *goth*s I would conduct more than one interview but then spend time over lunch, tea or, generally, to make observations and notes with the family of one of the interviewees. In smaller *goth*s, I would do one interview and then stay with the same interviewee family. It is important to point out, however, that my interviews were hardly ever with an individual in these communities. As is visible in the photograph at the beginning of the box, once I started talking to a person about their situation during and since the floods, more and more people would join the discussion; some would go home at lunch or dinner time, or to do chores, and then return later in the day. Hence, in each interview I was often able to capture the views of multiple individuals. This approach obviously has both advantages and disadvantages; however, given the social structures in rural Sindhi villages and the ease with which the *sehan* (front porch) is accessible to all neighbours and villagers, I did not see any way to avoid multiple people responding to me in the same interview.

The name of this village (typical of many others) was an individual's name and the name of the kinship group as well. Hence the village was called 'XYZ Leghari.' The village was relatively homogenous in terms of kinship, and residents were mainly Leghari; however, others such as Lund Baloch also lived there and, though some families married outside their kinship group and others did not, it seemed to be a family-level decision. Landholdings were typically '20 acres of land between five brothers', though some individuals also had bigger holdings and employed their own relatives to help with farming. They all admitted to voting for the main political family in the area, the Mirzas, because they believed in Bhutto and his party, the PPP, and the Mirzas were PPP candidates.

CHAPTER 1

A Social Contract

State–Citizen Relations and Unfolding Disasters

When theorising the state and its political processes in Pakistan, the story has undoubtedly centred on more structuralist modes of inquiry. In fact, scholarship on the post-colonial state of Pakistan as well as writings on the creation of Pakistan follow an academic tradition emphasising the structures that resulted in the formation of the state. Particularly notable in this regard are the influential publications of Hamza Alavi, one of the leading scholars on Pakistan. Alavi's eminent neo-Marxist thesis, which suggested that the Pakistani state had been created to preserve the economic interests of the *salariat* (salaried classes) of north India, was a valuable contribution to scholarship on the Partition of India and the creation of Pakistan (Alavi 1986). Subsequently, historians on Pakistan, such as Ayesha Jalal and Yunus Samad, reinforced these ideas in their respective works. Much of this literature, related to how Pakistan came into being, and, consequently, dealing with the workings of the independent state of Pakistan, follows this tradition of the Cambridge School of historians and pays special attention to economic interests and patron–client nexuses (Shaikh 2009). This approach has by and large dominated Pakistani historiography, and kept elites and their economic interests at the centre of the narrative (Ahmed 2013).

In particular, the argument that the post-colonial state of Pakistan continued its patronage of landed class interests long after the British had left, in exchange for the acquiescence of the 'masses', is a well-documented explanation of state and politics in Pakistan (see Alam 1974, Herring 1979, Gardezi and Rashid 1983, Gardezi 1991, Whaites 1995, Haqqani 2006 and Hasnain 2008). The political economy of agriculture, particularly agricultural land ownership and rural social structures in the country, are seen to be at the heart of this system. This is considered especially true in Sindh, referred to by Lieven (2011) as 'one of the most stagnant societies in Asia', which he avers is not capable of significant 'social and political' change. Economists have also supported the argument that where 'feudal' elites are particularly powerful, as in the provinces of Sindh and Balochistan, the state is unable to provide universal services such as education because these feudal elites find it convenient to perpetuate low literacy rates and keep the masses 'backward' (Hussain 1999). According to this literature, people living in areas such as lower Sindh in Pakistan have little understanding of the state or citizenship and are only able to interpret a social contract as emerging from social relations with these political patrons or 'feudal' landlords.

The argument I present in this book follows in the tradition of a different set of scholars from those referred to above. Authors such as Hasan (2009, 2013), Zaidi (1999), Gazdar (2008) and Mohmand (2011) have used empirical research, conducted in small towns and villages in contemporary Pakistan, to present two pertinent challenges to the body of scholarship which sees 'feudal' structures as solely significant. Primarily, two aspects are presented:

1. Economic changes such as capitalism and sociological changes such as increased urbanisation have resulted in significant change in the political relations described earlier.
2. While large landowners and social networks of caste and kin remain important in non-urban Pakistan, these relationships do not adequately encompass people's understanding or construction of the state.

The social contract in Pakistan is built on more than just social structures and increasingly includes an understanding (and, less often, a vocabulary) of rights and entitlements that are broadly constitutive of citizenship and are seen to be the responsibility of the state. These theoretical concepts, particularly the citizenship framework and its connection to a wider social contract, will be explored in this chapter before presenting the empirical evidence on the subject.

Citizenship, Client-ship or Both?

T. H. Marshalls, the British sociologist often credited with being the father of contemporary thinking on citizenship, is termed a 'civic liberal' (Jones and Gaventa 2002). His work on citizenship, published in 1950, included for the first time the 'social element', along with the political (the right to exercise and participate in political power) and the civic (the right to exercise individual freedom of thought, speech, faith, and so on), as a fundamental tenet of citizenship. The social element Marshall refers to is that, along with the right to economic welfare and security, citizenship should also include 'the right to share to the full in the social heritage and to live the life of a civilised being according to the standards prevailing in society' (1950, 11). This emphasis on a basic material minimum emerged in the post-war context of Britain's economic expansion, and the idea was that the state should protect the individual from economic and social uncertainties through the provision of welfare. In fact, in tracing the historical legacy of citizenship in Britain, Marshall himself argues that civil rights came first and were recognised under the first Reform Act in 1832. Political rights were next, and were not universally instituted till 1918, and social rights did not attain the same status as the other two in Britain till well into the twentieth century (Marshall 1950).

The construction of citizenship in these terms is quite unique to the context of Britain, and the British-ness of the Marshallian legacy on the concept of citizenship has been fiercely criticised over the decades. Turner addresses this issue in his work on citizenship and its historical evolution in the West, explaining that there is no 'single version of citizenship' and that 'different circumstances give rise to radically different forms of citizenship participation' (1993). In societies such as France or the USA, where a more revolutionary struggle for entitlements took place, an active and altogether different tradition of citizenship can be seen to have emerged. In Germany, by contrast, the failure of the bourgeois revolution in the 1840s, and the top-down development of a capitalist economy, resulted in a restricted environment for active and dynamic notions of citizenship (Turner 1993, 9). In fact, societies such as the USA and Switzerland that broadly followed the liberal strategy, much like Britain, still have remarkably underdeveloped ideals of social citizenship and it is their 'buoyant economies' that have historically insured citizens against a great deal of personal hardship (Turner 1990). Citizenship therefore emerges out of a social and political context and is not a unitary ideal but rather has a certain amount of flexibility built into what is essentially a contemporary idea.

In critiquing the 'monolithic' and 'unified conception of citizenship in Marshall', Turner offers particular insights into citizenship as passive or active, that is, whether it develops as a result of state action from above or, in opposition to it, from below. In Britain, this legal person, the citizen, emerged as a result of the constitutional settlement of 1688 in which the British citizen was also the British subject whose rights were given by a monarch sitting in Parliament. The subject-as-citizen paradigm clearly indicated the passive nature of citizenship in Britain. In France, on the other hand, the revolutionary struggles of the eighteenth century resulted in a highly articulate and active nature of citizenship, where Frenchmen ceased to be subjects and were bound together as citizens of a national entity (Turner 1990). The difference between the British and the French revolutionary traditions is epitomised in the discussion of citizenship by Edmund Burke in *Reflections on the Revolution in France* (1790) and Rousseau in *The Social Contract* (1762). The classical conservative tradition of Burke sees citizenship as a binding force, dependent upon the continued traditions of groups, institutions and the association between the individual and the sovereign power. For Rousseau, however, the exercise of genuine citizenship required the destruction of any institutions that separated the state from its citizens (Nisbet 1986).

In the sociological model of citizenship, the binary between the citizen as 'a subject of an absolute authority' and the citizen as 'an active political agent' has been a regular feature in interrogating this concept. Despite the contextual element that came to define these differences in citizenship, general prerequisites for the development of this ideal included 'universalistic' or equality-based notions of the subject and an erosion of 'particularistic' forms of kinship that were then 'pushed along' by varying social struggles. The advancement of this concept of citizenship required, in addition, a state that was caught between the struggle to ensure political rights and also to safeguard rights to wealth and property. As a final point, it is also important to note that citizenship has made significant advancements in situations of war, when 'subordinate groups' have been able to make more demands on the state (Turner 1990). While these categories of citizenship, and the context within which they develop, have illuminated key aspects of the state–citizen relationship and its historical development, it is important to look beyond the Occident. What Weber stated in 1966, that 'only in the Occident is found the concept of citizen,' while questionable then, certainly no longer holds true.

When 'rethinking "citizenship" in the postcolony' (Robins, Cornwall and von Lieres 2008), some scholars argue that to make the concept of citizenship relevant to the context of the post-colonial world, some of these neat boundaries between active and passive, revolutionary and traditional, and even liberal and paternalistic typologies of citizenship should be removed or blurred. This would allow inclusion of the vast majority of political participants who exist in societies where citizenship regimes are not defined as such but where it is still possible to find a tangible construction and exercise of rights of citizens.

In particular, they suggest that the 'pro-poor and developmental character of the state' should make its way into such a framework of citizenship because despite its illiberal and paternalistic aspects, the state in most developing countries is still 'the key vehicle for provision of services and resources'. To blur some of these distinctions between different types, forms and even histories of citizenship is important when seen in light of the fact that the relationship between the state and the citizen rarely follows the evolution charted by Marshall – from political to civil to social rights – and is more likely be messy and haphazard.

> Citizens are often the 'target populations' and subjects of state-driven development and welfare programmes and policies as well as the active agents of clientalistic political relations.

This literature aims to unsettle some of the normative ideas embedded in the concept of citizenship, in particular those that are unable to account for the overlap or crossover between people who are clients of powerful political patrons while simultaneously also being rights-based citizens. Rather than seeing one framework as supplanting the other, according to a 'progressive and linear narrative' that leads to the realisation of liberal citizenship (not very unlike the evolution in European societies mapped out earlier), Robins, Cornwall and von Lieres argue that apparently contradictory discourses, of clientalism and rights-based citizenship, are deployed by the same actors depending on the contexts within which they operate. Patronage regimes are not able to 'obliterate individual agency' and people shift between exercising clientship, and, in a large number of cases, rights-based claims on citizenship. In much the same way, politicians also move 'seamlessly' between being powerful patrons and democratic representatives of functioning states. In the context of Africa as the 'postcolony' these authors emphasise that beyond seeing the people as 'tribal subjects of illiberal and irrational rulers', the continent as 'a place of undemocratic and illiberal politics and "failed," "weak," "partial," "criminal," and "shadow" states', it is necessary to recognise and study the 'thoroughly hybridised character of African political cultures (something that) can apply just as easily to other parts of the Global South'.

What scholars of post-colonial citizenship (see Cornwall 2000, Dagnino 2007, Chandhoke 2003, Lazar 2004, Taylor 2004) argue is not that the citizenship project, as it evolved and emerged in Europe, is wholly irrelevant in explaining the relationship between the state and its citizens in the Global

South. Rather, they emphasize that different historical and political contexts shaped the way citizenship was defined in different Western societies, and that it is equally necessary to engage with 'more grounded forms of enquiry' that can provide a more substantive basis for understanding the framework for state–citizen interaction in the post-colonial world. This conception of citizenship is 'a far cry from the binary established' between rights-based citizens and the 'obligation performing functionary of the patron-state' (Robins, Cornwall and von Lieres 2008, 1075–85). It is more likely to straddle the neat divide often drawn between social relationships and the impersonal character of the state–citizen relationship into which citizenship must evolve.

Citizenship in Europe developed within a political and social context that pushed either its development from 'above' or from 'below'. This notion also required an interaction with a certain kind of state institution that was struggling to accommodate political freedoms and property rights within the ambit of a capitalist economy. Despite these advances in state–citizen relations taking place in Europe over three centuries, Mann (1987) rather cynically argues that war, especially the destructive nature of the two World Wars, resulted in a certain formation of citizenship that emerged rather as a necessity than an ideal. He argues that by 1950 'a cross between Marshallian citizenship and American liberalism dominated the West, less through its internal evolution than the fortunes of war. It still dominates today' (1987, 351). Political events, particularly those as destructive as wars, are known to be 'game changers' when it comes to the question of rights of citizenship, so that what is deemed acceptable before the event is transformed in the aftermath.[1] Similar arguments have also been advanced in the aftermath of calamitous disasters, particularly famines in the twentieth century that resulted in the avoidable deaths of millions of people, altering to some extent what rights were considered inalienable in the wake of such suffering.

Rights, Entitlements and Famines

The debate on rights and entitlements around the study of contemporary famines owes its emergence to the work of Nobel laureate Amartya Sen. His monograph, *Poverty and Famines*, published in 1981 was the first to present,

[1] As Turner (1993) suggests, this has been particularly true for 'subordinate classes', for example African Americans in the USA, women in Europe, and so on.

at the time, the radical idea that famines are not the result of food availability declines (FAD) but that, in fact, they have often occurred in years when food production has increased, in boom rather than slump conditions. He argues instead that famines are the result of 'entitlements failures', when some people are unable to 'establish command over food, using the entitlement relations operating in that society depending on its legal, economic, political and social characteristics' (Sen 1981, 162). Without presenting a lengthy discussion of Sen's entitlement approach, it is worth highlighting a few key features. Rooted in economic theory, this approach suggests that each person has a commodity bundle that he is able to acquire through endowment (which is what he owns/produces) and exchange (which is what he is able to get by selling his produced goods and services from his endowment). The exchange entitlement mapping, which includes all alternative commodity bundles that the person can command for each endowment bundle, is additionally also dependent on legal, political, economic and social characteristics of the society in question. A person can collapse into starvation as a consequence of either producing less food which is called a 'direct entitlement failure' or he is able to obtain less food through exchange which is called an 'exchange entitlement failure'. It is sometimes also possible for groups to suffer both, especially if they produce food for subsistence (Sen 1981).

An 'exchange entitlement failure', in Sen's work, is clearly a failure of 'rights within the given legal structure within that society' (1981, 248). As an economist, Sen sees food insecurity as a demand-side issue of access to food regardless of its availability, and notes that famines occur even if there is adequate supply of food and markets are functioning well. 'This is a crucial insight. As Sen emphasised, there is no technical reason for markets to meet subsistence needs – and no moral or legal reason why they should' (Devereux 2001, 246). This is also where Sen reveals himself to be coming from the Keynesian school of thought, by bringing in state intervention on the issue of rights and legality. Sen acknowledges, at the end of his book, that his 'entitlement approach' emphasises legal rights, particularly 'freedom from famine' (de Waal 1996), and concludes that 'starvation deaths can reflect legality with a vengeance' (Sen 1981, 166).

Subsequently, over the next few decades, this concept of rights and 'freedom from famine' as an entitlement of citizenship has been developed significantly. In particular, the works of Sen (1990) and Dreze and Sen (1991) argue that famines are unlikely to occur in countries with a free and independent media and democratic institutions, emphasising the role of 'effective programme(s) of public action for famine prevention' (Dreze and Sen 1991, 75). This has equally been criticized by de Waal (1996, 1997) who has argued that it is not so much that 'freedom from famine' became a right in all democratic states; rather it clearly demonstrates the case of Indian exceptionalism. This right was used by the Indian National Congress as part of the same discourse on national independence and freedom from imperialism; in fact, de Waal calls it a 'conceptual sibling' of the very notion of political rights in India. He states 'that freedom from famine arises within a specific form of social contract, developed through political struggle. This is the crux of the Indian experience' (de Waal 1996, 199). Before going on to illustrate that, in comparison, there has been little to no opportunity for 'freedom from famine' to emerge as a right in Africa, de Waal and also Devereux and others identify one shortcoming in Sen's work – its limited engagement with the political context of the empirical cases studied, concluding that the entitlement approach privileges the economic over the social and political (Devereux 2001).

Leach, Mearns and Scoones (1999) have therefore argued that it is very restrictive to see entitlements (in the context of famines and other environmental disasters) as legal rights only. They propose instead a set of 'environmental entitlements' which extends the idea of entitlements to include not just the formal–legal but also the socially sanctioned mechanisms for access and control of resources. These authors argue that an extended entitlement approach which includes the socially determined is more fluid and dynamic. It also sees entitlements as the 'outcome of negotiations among social actors, involving power relationships and debates over meaning, rather than as simply the result of fixed, moral rules encoded in law' (Leach, Mearns and Scoones 1999, 23). This is particularly true in the case of famines and natural disasters when death and destruction beyond a certain scale, or for a prolonged period of time, might be considered societally unacceptable regardless of legality.

To further elaborate this idea of the 'socially sanctioned' as entitlements, I take a closer look at the situation in India after the Famine Codes were instituted by the British government in 1880. De Waal states that while on paper the codes were a drastic break from the past, key factors remained the same. First, the Famine Commissioners were determined that famine relief should be seen as an administrative duty rather than a political right; second, things carried on much like before and the Indian famine of 1896–97 was as severe as any before it. The state response was only marginally improved in the famine of 1899–1901 which resulted in the deaths of over a million people. In addition to the large number of starvation related deaths, tens of millions others were also affected. The resulting public outcry in India also became a political scandal in the UK and gave impetus to the Indian National Congress's anti-imperial struggle. Suddenly, things changed quite quickly and de Waal notes that while 'the post-1901 Famine Codes were superficially similar to their predecessors, as actually implemented they were far more comprehensive' (1996, 196). In fact, he goes so far as to say that the famine relief system in India went on to become the most sophisticated the world has ever seen. Despite this, 'a right to food' was never actually instituted, and the British state continued to view famine relief as an obligation rather than a right. Eventually, famine prevention did come to be seen as a political right (de Waal 1996), one that was an integral part of the social and political contract between the state and its citizens in India. Regardless of whether the 'right to food' or the right of 'freedom from famine' was legally ratified or not, at some point in the wider socio-political struggle to prevent deaths from starvation, it became a socially sanctioned entitlement or a substantive element of citizenship.

As a final note on this literature on entitlements and calamitous famine-like disasters it is important to highlight that while the authors cited here question aspects of the entitlement approach and more broadly Amartya Sen's perspective, in all of their works the importance of state intervention is clear. Indeed, one of the critiques to Dreze and Sen's work on famines is from economists, particularly in the contemporary neo-liberal tradition, who disagree with 'the importance they attach to the *public* provision of the goods needed' (Ravallion 1992, 75). In fact, Dreze and Sen are emphatic in their support for large-scale public works programmes and other forms of direct state interventions like the ones that, they suggest, prevented famines in Bihar in 1967, Maharashtra in 1973, West Bengal in 1979 and Gujarat in 1987. They insist that, regardless of how strong they are, social or informal networks are not an adequate response to the crippling challenge presented by a famine. It is, therefore, especially important to design 'famine prevention systems that do not leave the rural community to its own fragile devices' (Dreze and Sen 1991, 75).

The theoretical discussion thus far has made a few key points worth re-emphasising. First, even within the liberal Western tradition of citizens being tied together to the notion of the state through a relationship defined by the social contract, citizenship is neither unified nor monolithic, and different typologies of citizenship exist. The social and political context, in particular, came to define the extent to which citizenship in a particular society was driven from 'above' or from 'below', signifying whether it was active or passive. These neat categories, defined in sociological terms as the divide between the citizen as 'a subject of an absolute authority' and the citizen as 'an active political agent', were blurred as the concept of citizenship came to include more and more of the post-colonial world. Authors studying citizenship in the 'post-colony' argue that it is entirely possible – in fact, even likely – that citizens in the developing world would be a mix of three types: the target population of state-driven development, active political agents, and passive clients of powerful patrons. Understanding how the citizenship framework operates with a local and more grounded context is, therefore, critical.

Beyond the question of whether this citizenship is supply-driven by the state (from above) or demand-led by the citizens (from below), what is equally crucial in its development and evolution are social and political events, such as wars and famines, that resulted in the reordering of society. Literature on the latter in particular has effectively illustrated that deaths relating to starvation are more a result of paucity of rights within citizenship rather than the scarcity of food. It is, therefore, possible for a social contract to evolve that protects against such deaths by instituting 'freedom from famine' as a right, regardless of whether it is institutionalised by law. The level and scale of public provision that is necessary to ensure this can only be done by the state and not by informal or social networks. If, along with actions taken by the state and citizens, social and political events such as wars and famine have been instrumental in the establishment of the citizenship framework, it is worth looking at what is known about disasters and the social contract.

Disasters and the Social Contract

If one accepts that the motivating force driving leaders in incumbent regimes, whether democratic or not, is the desire to remain in power, then disasters are politically very problematic indeed. Natural hazard-based disasters are able to bring political instability and threaten the basis of that political power, making them problematic for ruling governments (Drury and Ohlson 1998). For Cuny, this challenge to power is presented through a civil society that often activates after a disaster and produces new leaders, who are motivated to enact change in an attempt to replace ineffective leaders (Pelling and Dill 2008). In extreme situations and against the background of a troubled political history, 'disasters can throw into question the defence value and even the very legitimacy of the authoritative allocation process itself – the regime' (Olson 2000, 271).

Albala-Bertrand has gone as far as to say that in developing countries even vulnerability to disasters 'is primarily a socio-political issue rather than a question of disaster-proof technology' (1993, 5). This would also help to explain why natural disasters hit 'politically peripheral regions' the hardest (Pelling and Dill 2008), and have lasting impacts on the vulnerability of politically marginalised groups. This, in turn, results in heightened political tensions, as the disaster shores up regional/class/ethnic inequalities prevalent in the area and feeds into existing political struggles. Disasters, therefore, deepen existing fault lines and inequalities in society (Le Billon and Waizenegger 2007). The resulting grievances among the affected population, according to Shefner, then need to be constructed and presented as political issues with the help of 'contentious supporters' for political mobilisation and change to take place (Shefner 1999). Disasters make it possible for citizens to 'talk back' to those in power.

Literature on the politics of disasters also points out that natural hazard-based disasters will not always lead to positive socio-political change. In examining the 2001 earthquake in the Kachchh region of Gujarat (India), Simpson and Corbridge demonstrate that the Hindu right was able to successfully capture the post-disaster political space and further their political agenda, in particular, through their use of reconstruction initiatives that utilised various symbolisms and manufactured collective memories that were deeply connected to their politics of Hindu nationalism. The incumbent right wing Bharatiya Janta Party (BJP) was able to utilise the post-disaster space to perpetuate its vision of the 'Hindu' nation, resulting in a Kachchh that was more exclusionary in favour of caste Hindus than before 2001 (Simpson and Corbridge 2006).

In a similar fashion, the Chinese government used the Sichuan earthquake as a 'vehicle for nationalist sentiment' and managed to reinforce their grip over the country and strengthened existing power structures, at least in the short term (Pelling and Dill 2008). The ruling communist party gained 'international recognition' for what was globally seen to be a swift, coordinated and sensitive government response to the seismic disaster. Beijing's leaders 'came across as transparent, accountable and responsible managers of a serious natural disaster' (Ayson and Taylor 2008, 5). Pelling and Dill note that the fear of political change also led the Chinese government to turn to suppression of rights to ensure an acceleration of the status quo, consolidating and entrenching the power of the pre-disaster elites even further. The suppression, along with efficient disaster management, was an effective policy for the incumbent regime to follow. Had the Chinese government failed altogether in delivering upon its perceived responsibilities, or failed in actual service delivery in the aftermath of the earthquake, a very different political turn might have occurred.

Much of this work reiterates the findings on famines and entitlements in suggesting that, first, disasters are highly political and must be analysed as existing not only in the physical geography of the affected area but also within a social and political context. Second, a disaster impacts the state–citizen relationship usually negatively, because the state is seen as unable to provide basic human security to its citizens, thus challenging the very basis of the contract. Pelling and Dill's work, in particular, examines disasters opening political space for contestation of a social contract and catalysing moments for change (2010). Their framework (explained further by Pelling 2011) examining the socio-political consequences and 'critical junctures' of change after a disaster has considerable intuitive appeal. For these authors, disasters represent a failure in a social contract and open political/civil space for a renegotiation in structures and processes between citizens and the state, or even between different non-state actors. They point out that 'temporary breaks in dominant political and social systems post-disaster open space for alternative social and political organisation to emerge' (Pelling and Dill 2010, 25).

The instability that sets in when the dominant actor (duty-bearer) is unable to meet its responsibilities leads to an opening in political space that can be occupied by new or existing groups. Redistribution of power will also be dependent upon the manner and rate at which dominant actors respond to what Habermas refers to as a crisis of legitimacy and, thus, an exposed vulnerability in a social contract. If these changes in governable spaces and renegotiation of rights for human security have a long-term affect in revising or changing the very nature of a social contract – for instance in a way that makes disaster prevention a fundamental feature of the contract – it is possible to conclude that a 'critical juncture' has been reached. This is the point that signifies an irreversible political change or composition in the structure of the incumbent regime. It is also just as possible for the 'tipping point' in a social contract to be closed through repression or even co-option of the change-seekers by the dominant actors. This would result in transitional change that might well be visible, but would fail at creating transformative socio-political change that could seriously disturb the established status quo (Pelling and Dill 2010).

In this discussion of disasters, then, they are seen to delegitimise the social contract and open space for alternative political ideologies such as the resurgence of the Hindu right in Kachchh, or result in authoritarian state suppression such as in the aftermath of the Chinese earthquake. The disaster, while clearly seen to have political consequences, is rarely, if ever, known to push certain progressive elements of the social contract along. The argument in this book will illustrate just that. Broadly, it will demonstrate not only that a framework for citizenship exists in Pakistan but also how rights-based citizenship and active political agency were pushed further along in the aftermath of the disaster.

The floods in 2010 and 2011 clarified a number of the concepts discussed so far in this chapter. It illustrated that people in lower Sindh have an understanding of a wider social entity of the state as an entity meant to provide certain basic rights and entitlements. Equally, the large-scale flooding disaster, affecting over 20 million people in 2010 and over 5 million people in 2011, did not trigger famine-like conditions because of large-scale public provisions and a basic quantum of citizenship rights that would have been impossible for social networks to provide. Finally, because large-scale entitlement failures did not occur and the social contract was not evidently broken between the state and its citizens in the aftermath of the disaster, alternative ideologies and politics were not able to capture any serious political space. The idea of a larger social entity, the state, remained resolute in lower Sindh.

Empirical Research in Three Districts

The empirical evidence gathered for this work uses an anthropological mode of inquiry and uses intensive rather than extensive research techniques.

Relatively recent research, such as that done by Healy and Malhotra (2009), has examined the effect of disaster damage and effective government response (through the variable of federal government spending on relief) on political preferences (measured through voting behaviour), across 3,141 counties in the USA, from 1988 to 2004. Their results concluded that voters reward leaders for effective disaster relief, though not for disaster preparedness (Healy and Malhotra 2009). A similar study was done by Gasper and Reeves (2011) to specifically examine the impact of rain, hence the disasters of floods and droughts, on voting behaviour. They used quantitative data from across all but two states of the USA, over the three-decade period between 1970 and 2006 (Gasper and Reeves 2011). Cole, Healy and Werker (2012) also ran regression analysis on voting data and climatic disasters such as floods and droughts in 28 states in India in the period between 1977 and 1999, and concluded that governments are punished for climatic disasters unless they are seen to be dealing effectively with relief.

The significance of such research is that it is able to make a causal link between climatic disasters and political preferences. It is not, however, able to explain this link or why it exists. I was interested in telling the political story about the floods and I was not sure what my data would say. The story I eventually came back with from the field was about more than the flooding disaster; it was about the state at a local level and citizens in lower Sindh and how they interact with each other. Such a method of inquiry, however, does not naturally lend itself to quantitative research and needs to be based on a more qualitative methodology so that the researcher is able to 'embark(s) on a voyage of discovery rather than one of verification' (Bryman 1984, 84). This research is based on seven months of ethnographic fieldwork that I conducted in three districts of lower Sindh – Thatta, Badin and Tharparkar – in two phases; between May and September 2012, and between December 2012 and April 2013. I let my informants frame the story, and their narrative was one which outlined their expectations from the state.

My methodological choices also began to make sense once I began fieldwork, because I could tell, quite early on, that there was more to people's interaction with the state in lower Sindh than often meets the eye. The view that the state does 'nothing at all' (*kuch bhee nahin*) and is 'absent' only seemed to me to be one piece in a much bigger picture. It became equally clear that many of the popular perceptions of oppressive, even violent, 'feudal' relations in Sindh, and the 'takeover' of Islamist groups in flood-affected areas of Pakistan, were narratives that did not quite conform to what I could observe in the field, and I was keen to unpack that complexity.

Wedeen states that 'ethnography adds value to political analyses in part by providing insights into actors' lived experiences' (2010, 261). In particular, this allows the researcher access to the verbal and non-verbal 'off-stage' where hidden transcripts circulate. Since I was dealing with sensitive issues of political support, access to the 'off-stage' was the only way for me to address a number of queries central to my research project. For instance, when asked about the kind of state support received after the flooding disaster, a common response from interviewees belonging to these flood-affected communities was that the state did nothing and was nowhere to be seen either during or after the disaster. It is important to understand that it was my repeated interactions, and the significant amount of time spent with my informants, that allowed me to be able to see beyond what was being actively presented to me.

The discussion till this point makes it fairly evident that this research will not be following the positivist philosophical tradition within social sciences.

Positivists, who believe that scientific enquiry has to be observable and measurable, focus on 'objectivity' and 'measurement', employing quantitative data and moving from general principles to specific instances. This research is instead based on the interpretive philosophy. Interpretivists see the social world as being inhabited by human beings; therefore, their interest is in the way in which people attach meaning to and experience their material world. As interpretivists 'believe that the social world is constructed by people' (Williamson 2006), it is not objective reality but the subjective meanings that they seek to access and interpret. To that end, my research will be following a constructivist epistemology and will avoid 'invent(ing) the viewpoint of the actor' (Becker 1996). Methodologically, the aim of the ethnography is to be able to see objects from 'the perspective of the participants' (Crotty 1998). This research pieces together a narrative of the state–citizen relationship beyond the obvious and interprets the meanings and complexities hidden within the stories I heard.

Research design

I used an inductive approach to my field research. I first developed basic interview protocols for three groups of informants and interviewees – members of the flood-affected community, incumbent representatives of the state (including elected MPAs and district-level bureaucrats), and the alternative political agents who provided people with rescue and relief services from a non-state platform. Then, I began my first round of fieldwork in May 2012. The chapters and content of this book are structured around the themes and narratives that emerged from this research.

My field research started through a grassroots civil society organisation based in Badin city who introduced me to communities affected by the flooding disaster there, and then also in other towns and villages outside the capital where they worked. While extremely grateful for their support, I was keen to be seen as 'independent' of this local NGO and, therefore, wanted to use as limited support from them as possible. This was made possible because of the very welcoming and hospitable culture in Sindhi communities which meant that I only had to be introduced to about four or five individuals through the NGO before I was able to work on my own. Soon these initial informants were able to introduce me to others, who led me to their contacts, and a 'snowball' effect had been initiated. In fact the non-urban community set-up of the region, even in fairly large villages with hundreds of households, often resulted in people talking to their friends and neighbours about me. Consequently, by the second month of the field research, many of my newly met informants would mention how they had known everything about me even before our first meeting.

I used a similar approach in Thatta, where the local staff of an international NGO agreed to act as my 'entry point' into communities. Because Tharparkar was the last district I spent time in, I already had such an extensive pool of informants who were able to connect me to various community members, activists and politicians in the district that no organisation was needed to act as an 'entry point' into the district. Approaching the Islamists was a more complicated situation.

My first informant from the Jamaat-ud-Dawa (JuD) was the Director of their Sindh chapter whom I met within days of arriving in Badin. After shadowing him for a few days, and building a good relationship with him and his family, it became clear to me that he had a high-level position within the organisational hierarchy of JuD. His role included a significant amount of public interfacing – managing press and media relations for the organisation, speaking to foreign journalists and NGO employees, and being very active on social media sites. It was, therefore, evident that I would not be able to move beyond the rehearsed 'party-line' when speaking to him about JuD and their flood relief activities. It was much harder to use my local level contacts to meet with the JuD cadre, the young men who were physically part of the rescue and relief activities, because they were most often also the ones who had returned from *jihad*.

Eventually, however, I was able to build good relationships with people who had worked with the JuD or the Sipa-e-Sahaba (SeS) during the floods and they would accompany me to meetings with members of these groups. The heightened sense of insecurity at this time, particularly as I started fieldwork only about a year after the Raymond Davis incident[2] had captured

[2] On 27 January 2011, an American citizen, Raymond Davis, shot and killed two men on a motorcycle in a central location in Lahore city. Soon after the shooting, the American Consulate car that came to get Davis out of this situation ran over a passer-by, who was also killed in the process. The news that an American citizen had killed two people and caused the death of a third resulted in anger on the streets of Pakistan, stoked by the religious right in the country who make the most anti-America noise and have a considerable amount of street power. Though Davis was arrested and placed in custody by the Pakistani Police, his trial was never completed as a settlement was reached under which Davis gave blood money to the victims' families and disappeared from Pakistan overnight. The whole incident remains shrouded in

the imagination of Pakistanis all over the country, meant that often it would require a few meetings with the JuD cadre before they were convinced that I was not a '*Birtania ki agent*'[3] and could speak freely in my presence.

I conducted a total of 118 interviews across 96 *goth*s (hamlets), 15 of which were also with informants who had not been affected (or only very marginally affected) by the floods. These were primarily semi-structured or open-ended conversations in my areas of interest. After a few interviews, I was able to steer the conversation to more general areas without needing to stick to a strict question–answer format with my interviewees. There were of course variations in interviews as well – while some interviewees stuck quite closely to the question–answer format, more often others would call for tea and want to engage in long and detailed conversations. I welcomed any and all opportunities to understand the people's point of view better, so 'interviews' often ended up taking entire afternoons.

I was able to gain valuable insight into communities and political agents through more ethnographic engagements with people, and the JuD's cadre in particular. As a general rule, I had chosen not to say 'no' to any invitation or suggestion, either by local contacts, who eventually became friends, or the people I was meeting to interview. For instance, when a family asked me to stay for lunch and wanted to show me how badly the local school and barn had been affected by the floods, I accepted. In the same way, when I was invited to a JuD *markaz* (centre) or into the homes of JuD cadre for dinner, I always agreed. While it is certainly not common for women to be given such access, something I was repeatedly told, the fact that I was not local or Sindhi, and the fact that I always approached people through a reference or contact, made most situations easier. Additionally, I was accompanied by a male, native Sindhi-speaking chaperone and a native Balochi (the second most common language

---

mystery and it captured the media and public's attention for months. Some reports suggested that Davis was a contractor for the CIA working on tracing militants in Pakistan, while the British press even reported that he was actually the acting head of the CIA in Pakistan. Not just in Pakistan but also the world over, few were willing to believe that Davis was a technical staff member at the American Consulate in Lahore as claimed by the American government; the British newspaper *The Telegraph* asked in an article 'What sort of a "diplomat" carries a weapon?' The incident led to a general feeling of insecurity and suspicion in local communities that anyone they did not know or recognise could turn out to be an 'agent' sent by powerful authorities to spy on them and their neighbours.

[3] 'Agent sent by Britain,' implying that I was a secret agent sent to spy on local activities.

spoken in 'rural' Sindh) driver. They both usually acted as my chaperones and were always referred to in all conversations as *bhai* (brother). My chaperones ended up being very valuable in my interactions with people. Their presence not only ensured that I was following social custom and etiquette, and because they were seen to be culturally and linguistically one of the people, I was also, by extension, considered to be less of an 'outsider' than if I had been on my own.

It is important to point out that though I was able to speak conversational Sindhi half-way into my time in Sindh, and dressed and behaved in a manner that I thought was most socially and culturally acceptable, I am not Sindhi. No one knew my father nor had ever heard of the Punjabi *biraderi* my family belongs to. It was therefore inevitable that some people were hesitant to talk about political allegiances in my presence, or ended up saying things they thought were agreeable and non-controversial. Also, because I introduced myself as a resident from Karachi studying in the UK, people often believed that my privileged position meant that I could help them access aid or find employment; hence, their answers to certain questions were inevitably biased by these assumptions. In most cases, however, it was quite easy to tell when people were uncomfortable talking about a certain subject, which I would then avoid. Equally, I was aware when they were saying something because they believed I could help them. Wherever possible, I will try to be reflective of its implications on my data.

CHAPTER 2

The State as a Complex Web of Social Relations

In studying state–citizen relations at a local level, particularly the 'absent' nature of the state and 'fragmented' citizenship, the province of Sindh, outside of the two urban centres of Karachi and Hyderabad, is an ideal place to start. A dearth of contemporary research on this region, the widespread prevalence of historical stereotypes (see Titus 1998 for a better understanding of ethnic stereotypes in Pakistan), and popular perceptions that reinforce those narratives have resulted in a social and political construction of 'interior' Sindh that epitomises the situation of a missing social contract between the state and its citizens in Pakistan. In this chapter, I use my empirical evidence from lower Sindh to argue that while certain forms of political patronage exist, there are other important factors that also determine political processes and an understanding of the state on the ground.

Before moving to the social and political geography of the region of Sindh, where this study is based, I will briefly define the physical geography.

Table 2.1 Fast facts on Thatta, Badin and Tharparkar

	Thatta	*Badin*	*Tharparkar*
Area	17, 355 sq km	6,726 sq km	19,635 sq km
Population	1,778,043	1,448,870	1,175,722
Number of *talukas*	9	5	4
Affected by flooding in	2010	2011	2011
No. of people affected	874,030	1,021,301	907,179
No. of *talukas* affected	9	5	4

Source: Data obtained from UNDP and OHCHR websites.

Figure 2.1 Map of Pakistan highlighting Sindh

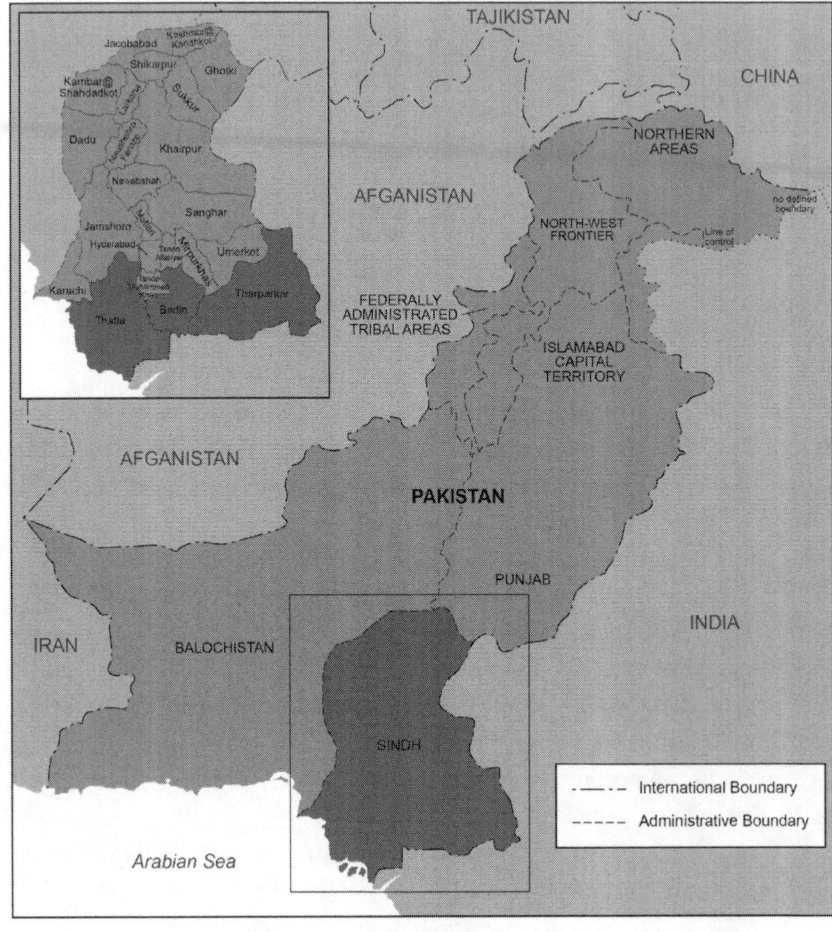

Note: Map not to scale and does not represent authentic international boundaries.

The Indus River basin covers an area of about 1,140,000 square kilometres stretching from Afghanistan through China, India and Pakistan (Lashari 2011). Approximately 56 per cent of the basin area lies in Pakistan, and the entire delta area of 41,440 kilometres lies in the province of Sindh (Akhtar 2013). Additionally, the entire area of the Indus River that is hydrologically and morphologically defined as the 'downstream segment' is located in Sindh, and flows from the province's northernmost Guddu Barrage into the Arabian Sea (Akhtar 2013). This segment is made up of a floodplain with a flat topography and meandering channel patterns and deltas. These features make

Figure 2.2 Indus Basin highlighting the area in Sindh

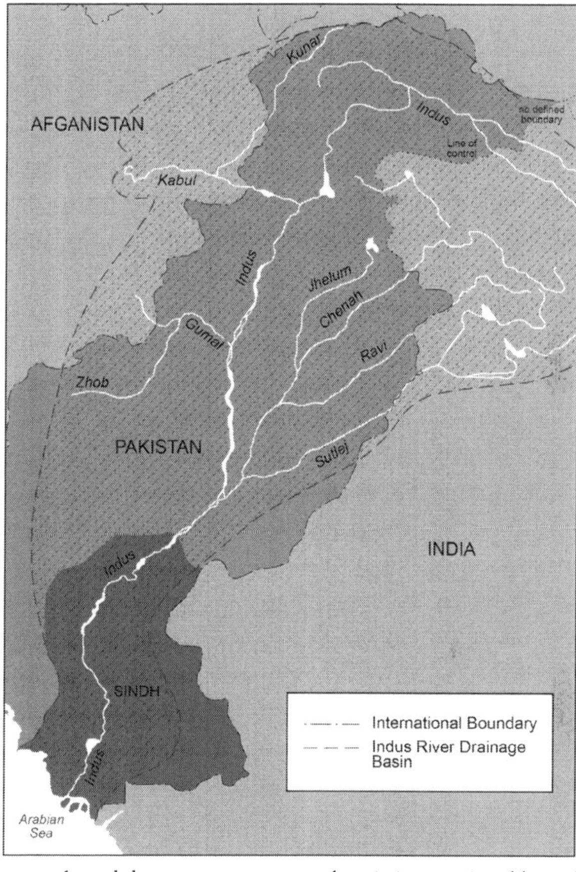

Note: Map not to scale and does not represent authentic international boundaries.

the area particularly prone to frequent floods that breach the flood-protection infrastructure, causing damage and loss of life.

Additionally, the dependence on a single river system makes Pakistan's economy and society very vulnerable to the slightest changes in river flow. These physical challenges (single river system, arid conditions) (GOIRP 2003), compounded by socially constructed problems (wasteful and damaging use of the water that is available) (Kamal 2009) and a faulty water resource development paradigm (very technocratic with little regard for the social considerations) (Mustafa 2007), are further complicated by high population densities in the agricultural plains (Briscoe and Qamar 2005). These challenges, however, are also made worse by governance deficit that turns

Figure 2.3 Flood-affected areas in Sindh

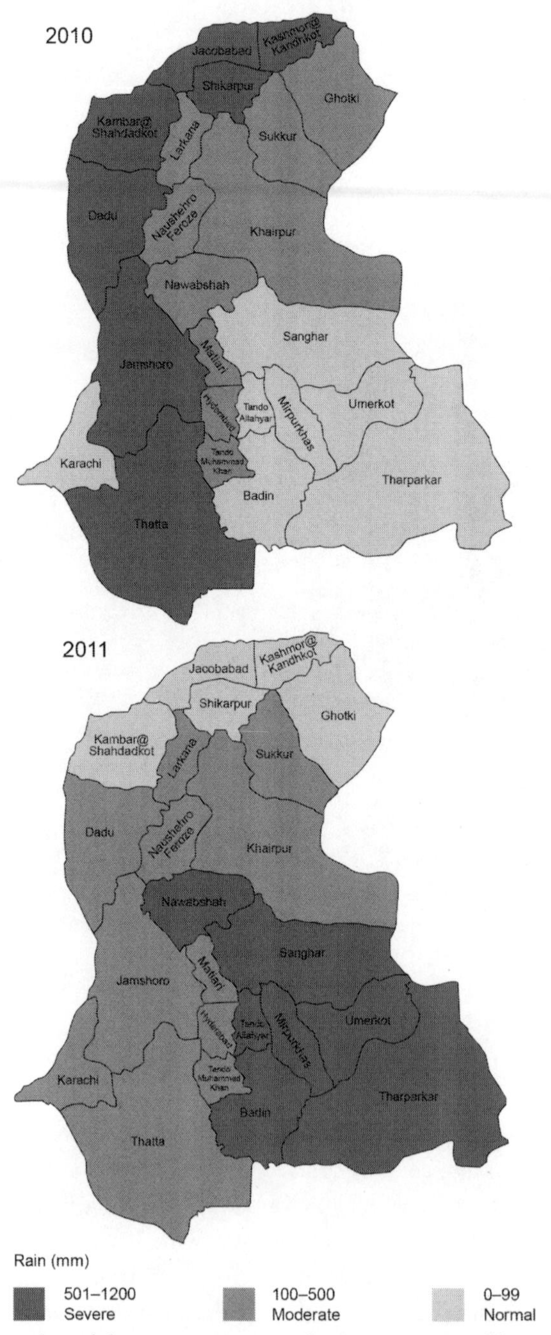

Note: Map not to scale and does not represent authentic international boundaries.

irregular or extreme weather events into calamitous disasters in Pakistan, with particularly serious consequences for Sindh. Khan directly supports this by clearly stating that Pakistan has 'suffered from bad policies, bad governance and corruption in its water administration'. One problem of course is the class of powerful landowners who are part of the country's political elite, and are generally able to threaten, intimidate or bribe irrigation officials (Khan 2009). As Briscoe and Qamar (2005) point out, Pakistan has, so far, fallen considerably short of being able to maintain and build its water infrastructure at all levels – physical, human and institutional – with dire consequences for its economy and people (2005).

The flooding disaster that affected most of Pakistan in 2010 (and exclusively the province of Sindh in 2011) was a consequence of decades of mismanagement and poor understanding of the country's water-related troubles (Mustafa and Wrathall 2011). In July 2010, Pakistan received record levels of rainfall, causing flash floods in the northern part of the country that overwhelmed its water management capacity. By August, the flood waters reached the lower part of the river basin and soon 84 out of the 121 districts of the country were inundated, and one-fifth of Pakistan's landmass was under water (Mustafa and Wrathall 2011). The southern part of the province of Sindh, lower Sindh, was badly affected, with 1 million internally displaced people (IDP) in the region leaving submerged villages for higher ground. Additionally, in places such as Thatta city, levee surfaces, saturated by floodwaters, deteriorated and burst, thus exacerbating the human dimension of the disaster and resulting in the displacement of 95 per cent of the residents of the city (Tran 2010). The floods of 2010 had devastating consequences in the district of Thatta, one of the three districts where I did fieldwork.

The following summer, in 2011, the floods were back, and this time they wreaked havoc in a different part of the province. By August 2011, 8 million people in Sindh had been affected by large-scale floods resulting from higher than average amounts of rainfall. According to one report, at the height of the flooding in late August, lower Sindh received 22 inches of rainfall in just one week (Lashari 2011). It was widely reported that the floods in 2011 had more to do with a faulty, World Bank–funded, drainage management system called the Left Bank Outfall Drain (LBOD).

The LBOD is a 1,950 kilometres long surface drainage project that cost US$636 million to build, of which 60 per cent was provided by various multilateral development banks (MBDs) such as the Asian Development Bank and the World Bank, and the remaining 40 per cent came from the Government of Pakistan (GoP) (Qureshi et al. 2008). Construction on the project started in 1985 and was completed in 2002. It was built to provide surface water drainage to districts in upper and central Sindh. Running independently of the Indus River, it is designed to carry highly saline subsurface drainage water from an area of about 577,000 hectares (Ritzema 2009) in Nawabshah, Sanghar, Mirpurkhas and Hyderabad,[1] into the Arabian Sea via Badin.

This drainage project epitomises the supply-side, large-irrigation-project-focused mindset of bureaucrats in Pakistan. Simultaneously, it illustrates the opposition to such projects by communities on the ground. In the aftermath of the large-scale floods in 2011, article after article was published in local media outlets against the LBOD project (*Dawn* 2012, 2011; *The Express Tribune* 2012, 2011; Lashari 2011). Politicians whose main constituencies were in flooded areas, as well as community and social movement leaders, accused the LBOD project for the destruction that was caused by its breached levees and dykes. The districts of Badin and Tharparkar were among the worst affected by this flooding.

Locating Sindh in Southern Pakistan

Within the physical boundary of this province of Sindh, there are in fact two Sindhs. The largest city of Pakistan and its commercial hub, Karachi is the capital of the province of Sindh. In the last official census that took place in Pakistan in 1998, the population of Karachi was reported as being 9.3 million residents. Unofficial estimates for 2013 suggest that the number of people living in Karachi is close to around 23.5 million (Amer 2013). A more recent ethnic break-up of population is harder to come by since it is a politically explosive issue, but historically the largest ethnic group[2] in the city are the Urdu-speaking migrants from north India known as *muhajirs*.[3] Karachi also has a large migrant population of Pushtuns that has been steadily increasing since the Afghan War in the 1970s and the city is now considered the largest Pushtun city in the

[1] Districts in upper and central Sindh.

[2] Urdu speaking 48.2 per cent, Punjabi 13.94 per cent, Pushtun 11.42 per cent, Sindhi 7.22 per cent and Balochi 4.34 per cent, according to the 1998 census.

[3] The Muslims who migrated from north India to the area that became Pakistan in 1947 saw their migration akin to the journey Prophet Mohammed made from Mecca to Madina in the face of growing persecution from non-believers. The Prophet's journey is called *hijrat* and the Meccan refugees were called *muhajirs*.

world. For various reasons, some of which include the ethnic composition of the city, the ensuing multiculturalism, the commercial and business activity that centres in and around the city, Karachi does not 'feel' like a Sindhi city in the way that perhaps Lahore, the capital of Punjab, still feels like a Punjabi city.[4] Sindh's second most urbanized, though much smaller, city is Hyderabad. Since Pakistan's independence in 1947, demographically, there have been more *muhajirs* than ethnically Sindhi residents in Hyderabad as well.

The rest of Sindh has traditionally been seen as the rural part of the province and has colloquially (and somewhat pejoratively) been referred to as 'interior' Sindh. It is ethnically overwhelmingly Sindhi-dominated, and the economic mainstay in many of these areas is largely agriculture. At the same time, recent studies have shown that the population in these traditionally 'rural' districts in Sindh has increased by as much as 81.5 per cent between 1998 and 2011. In the district of Jacobabad in the northern part of Sindh, known as upper Sindh, for instance, the population increased by a whopping 111.4 per cent from about 0.75 million to a little over 1.5 million (Khan 2012), and the capital city of Jacobabad is a bustling small (by South Asian standards) city with small businesses, traders and numerous other commercial activities taking place. The same is also true of other cities in upper Sindh, such as Sukkur or Khairpur, or those in lower Sindh, such as Jamshoro or Thatta (Khan 2012). While the unfortunate label prevails, 'interior' Sindh can no longer accurately be described as overwhelmingly 'rural'.

Additionally, most geographers now also recognise that the rural–urban divide is more complex than this rigid binary, and that such neat divisions can sometimes even be misleading. Talking about Southeast Asia, Rigg, for instance, states that 'to write of discrete rural and urban worlds, whether they are articulated in terms of space, sector or class, is increasingly difficult' (1998). While Preston's work (1992) on Bolivia has further emphasised that these categories are far more fluid than is often recognised, people change their roles often, making it difficult to identify people as 'rural' or 'urban'.

[4] The majority of the population in Lahore is Punjabi-speaking. According to the 1941 population census, the Municipality of Lahore had a total population of 671,659. Muslims constituted the majority with 64.5 per cent, and there was a small population of Christian, Parsi and other minority groups, but the remaining 36 per cent of the population was Hindu and Sikh. Communal riots started in March 1947 and by mid-August Lahore had been emptied of all Hindus and Sikhs, leaving the city essentially an exclusively Muslim, Punjabi city (Ahmad 2004).

Despite this, the common image that is constructed of 'interior' Sindh in most parts of Pakistan outside 'interior' Sindh is one where social and economic relations are almost entirely dependent on the traditional landlord–tenant agricultural relationship. The views encompass the following assumptions: the landlord's economic and social power enables him to be a political force in the area, regularly contesting and winning elections from his constituency; the landlord's traditional economic and political power is tied to his social and religious position in 'rural' Sindhi society as well. There is an established body of historical work on which this understanding is based. In particular, Cheeseman's study (1997) on economic relations between the peasants and landlords in colonial Sindh and Ansari's work (1992) on Sufi saints and their social and political power, both of which were published in the 1990s.

These are influential works in the field of 'Sindhology' but they illuminate the key aspects of social and political life in the province about a century ago. Despite work by authors such as Arif Hasan (2009), Akbar Zaidi (1999) and Haris Gazdar (2008) arguing that things are changing on the ground, and that if the modes of production are no longer 'feudal' then political relationships between different classes of the agricultural sector cannot be defined as such either (Mohmand 2011), few studies have dealt with processes other than social relations and structures. Ansari suggests that Sufi saints have remained powerful in post-colonial Sindh not because socio-political processes have not changed but because '*pirs* themselves have displayed a continuing readiness to be flexible when confronted with changing political circumstances' (Mohmand 2011). Yet the general narrative on 'interior' Sindh is still one where political society in the region is understood to operate within the confines of these very rigid and unchanging social structures; relations that also regularly encompass people's only form of interaction with a distant and often absent state.

Some relatively recent works on the relationship of the state with its citizens also seem to extend the same analysis. Kabeer, Mumtaz and Sayeed's work (2010) drawing on qualitative data from 'interior' Sindh (and south Punjab) finds that a universal foundation for citizenship does not exist and the very concept of being a citizen is entirely unclear to people in this part of Pakistan. Their study suggests that social fragmentation around caste and kin groups has been a significant factor in the failure to build a common bond of citizenship in the country. This has been made worse by a state that has not attempted to reach out to its citizens either. The entire framework for citizenship in Pakistan, particularly in rural parts like 'interior' Sindh, is seen to be wholly absent (Kabeer, Mumtaz and Sayeed 2010). Lieven's thesis

(2011) on Pakistan is also built around the primacy of kinship networks in most aspects of political, social and economic life in rural Pakistan, and is generally supportive of such analysis.

The failure of citizenship has therefore been theorised (particularly by those I refer to earlier as the social structuralists) as an obvious result of hierarchical social structures and an indifferent, largely absent state. In 'interior' Sindh, social relations are 'organised' (Kabeer et al. 2012) around the *biraderi,* which is the most 'significant' (Khan 2007) social unit, or even the 'primary unit of identity' (Mohmand and Gazdar 2007). Even beyond social relations, however, some literature suggests that a family's income and livelihood possibilities, prestige and honour, political expression and dependence are directly connected to their relationship with their social group or *biraderi*, and the rank of that social group in relation to other groups in that society (Kabeer, Mumtaz and Sayeed 2010).

Along with the socially restrictive and hierarchical structure of the *biraderi*, another common feature of 'interior' Sindh that defines its political society is the people's economic dependence on the head of the *biraderi*, who is normally the landlord. Each social group, whether at the *biraderi* level (Mohmand and Gazdar 2007) or at the *jaati (*sub-caste) level, has a traditional hereditary leadership, passed on from the father to the eldest son, known as the *wadera, mir, sardar, or khan* depending on the ethnic origin of the social group (Khan 2007). The head of the *biraderi* is normally a landowner with significant landholdings and many members of the *biraderi* and other tenants dependent on him for their livelihoods. The *wadera* is also able to interact with larger landowners and state functionaries on behalf of his *biraderi.* He is, thereby, able to maintain his position of power if he is able to move his *biraderi* forward economically. In such a way the *wadera* is seen to be a key social, economic and political player in 'interior' Sindh, often at the heart of oppressive social structures that do not allow people and communities to move forward in order to maintain his position of dominance.[5] This may also easily extend to social structures in non-agrarian Pakistan as well. As one study notes, even if landowning families move away from their ancestral lands their 'domestic workers' are still likely to come from that village and maintain boundaries in their interactions with their employers (Gazdar and Khan 2004).

[5] Over time and in an effort to adapt to changing conditions, the role of the *wadera* has also in recent times included more market-driven changes, such as facilitating access to markets or bypassing bureaucratic procedures, thereby allowing him to remain relevant in contemporary society.

Another important aspect of social relations in 'interior' Sindh has emerged from the syncretic tradition of Islam practised by its people. One of the practices prevalent within this tradition of 'folk' Islam is reverence of Sufi saints and their descendants known as *sajjadah nashin*s. In South Asia, the saints are known by the Arabic term *sheikh* and their descendants are known by the Persian term *pir* (Lieven 2011). Followers worship at their shrines, which are found all over Pakistan, but traditionally these practices have been thought to have a stronger base outside urban centres, particularly in Sindh and Punjab.

The political significance of *pir*s has been highlighted by Maqsood (2012) in her doctoral work on Lahore, where she emphasises that politicians, particularly in the Pakistan People's Party (PPP),[6] continue to use their hereditary position for purposes of electoral success. At the same time, however, such religious practices are also seen to be 'irrational,' 'superstitious,' and 'backward' among urban middle-class Pakistanis. Sindh, outside of Karachi and Hyderabad, is often seen as epitomising this *piri–muridi* culture.[7] In such discourse, '*Pīrs* are usually seen as cunning and corrupt men who take advantage of the hapless, uneducated and superstitious masses' (Maqsood 2012, 26), thereby providing another raison d'etre for 'interior' Sindh's label.

'Pakistanis hold many identities and the concept of citizenship as such is not widely understood' (Lall 2012a, 73). This is particularly believed to be true in areas such as 'interior' Sindh. Here, the primacy of social structures, the organisation of social relations around the *biraderi* or kinship group, and the *wadera* using social and economic power over his *biraderi* to be elected to political office limit people's ability to exercise any kind of citizenship or to develop an understanding of the state. The *wadera,* on the other hand, is able to dispense patronage – through his political position – to those who elected him, thereby continuing the cycle of patron–client relationships that have come to define people's relationship with the state. A state–citizen social contract is, therefore, seen to be one-dimensional and entirely mediated through personal relationships.

Additionally, the reverence for Sufi saints also allows heads of *pir* families to establish similar clientalistic relationships with their followers and use

[6] The incumbent party when I was doing fieldwork and which has its biggest vote bank in the province of Sindh.

[7] *Piri-muridi*' as the term is usually used, rather pejoratively in Pakistan today, means blind devotion of the lay follower (*murid*) to a *pir*, whom he expects to act as a spiritual mediator.

those to be elected to political office. This fragmented and hierarchical nature of society in 'interior' Sindh has created an enabling environment for successful patron–client relations to function and flourish. Such socio-political complexities have made it difficult for a universal foundation for citizenship to be created in 'interior' Sindh. The state, too, has not made any serious efforts to reach out to people as citizens rather than as clients of powerful patrons, members of a caste or kin group, and so on (Kabeer, Mumtaz and Sayeed 2010). This mix of factors has resulted in rural citizens of Pakistan being 'described as dependent and coerced, as over-socialised members of kin groups and as vote-selling clients of political patrons all at the same time' (Mohmand 2011, 7).

Local Politics in Thatta, Badin and Tharparkar

In the three districts of Thatta, Badin and Tharparkar, political families exist who have utilised some degree of traditional kinship networks and patronage politics in varying ways to be elected to political office. Set against a background of prevalent social structures in 'interior' Sindh it is tempting to conclude that these socially dependent and hierarchical relationships have made it difficult for people in lower Sindh to politically construct themselves as citizens of a functional state or to exercise their right to citizenship. My findings from the field, however, reveal that the story is more complex than what meets the eye. The political families in these districts are politically important and influential. They do not, however, fit into these traditional social structures; rather they seem to derive and hold on to their power through a range of different sources, including as manifestations of wider political processes such as the bigger entity of the *sarkar*, or even political parties. *Biraderi*s, *wadera*s and Sufi saints are important social institutions but they do not capture the myriad ways in which people in lower Sindh understand the state and their own position as citizens of this state.

Political families in each of the three districts reveal different characteristics of the state beyond simply patronage and kinship ties with *wadera*s and *pir*s. They help to tell a bigger political story, one that includes political ideologies and political parties and people's desire to see an individual as a manifestation of an approachable state, which together explains why Sheerazis of Thatta, Mirzas of Badin and Arbabs of Tharparkar exercise the kind of influence they do.

The Sheerazis of Thatta and the 'shaadi-ghami' phenomena

The Sheerazi family has been politically important in Thatta district since the 1990s and during my time in the field, members of the family were elected representatives in the National and Provincial Assemblies despite being in opposition to the incumbent party at the time, the PPP. Fresh elections were held in Pakistan after I had completed my fieldwork in May 2013 and despite some opposition, the Sheerazis still managed to hold on to most of their seats in Thatta. One out of the two National Assembly seats for Thatta and three out of the five seats in the Sindh Provincial Assembly went to various members of the Sheerazi family (see Table 2.2).

At a glance it might be possible to see the Sheerazis' rise to political power and importance as confirmation of the popular narratives on the primacy of social structures and patronage politics in 'interior' Sindh. In my interview with Syed Shafqat Shah Sheerazi, the sixty-something-year-old head of this family emphasised his family's noble lineage, explaining that they are Syeds (descendants of the Prophet Mohammad) who had migrated to Sindh relatively late, compared to the Arab invasions in the eighth century. Sheerazi informed me that his family traced their roots to the city of Shiraz, in southwest Iran. His forefathers had migrated to Sindh about 600 years ago. Various informants also confirmed that, in popular narrative, people in Thatta also believe Shafqat Shah's forefathers to be 'religious people' because of their Syed title.

The Sheerazis had successfully established their position of religious importance even before Thatta had been colonised (along with the rest of Sindh) by the British in 1843. Though published in 1855, a selection from the records of the Bombay government titled *Memoirs on Sind* reveals that the last Talpur ruler, Mir Noor Mohammad Khan Talpur, was giving a grant of Rs 12,000 a year to twelve 'tribes' in Thatta, 'for keeping the tombs, masjids etc in repair, and affording charity'. While it does not seem that they were all 'tribes', as some of the names in this list include 'Sooffee', 'Moolvee' and 'Mooftee', terms of respect used to refer to religious people, it does include the name 'Shirazee' as well (Thomas 1979).

After the British annexation of Sindh, these religious men, each with a large following of *murid*s (followers or disciples), were patronised by the imperial rulers, allocated large land grants and given access to various government officials in Sindh in order to keep the Sindhi countryside acquiescent.[8] It is

[8] The exact dynamics of this politico-religious power of the *pir*s is discussed in Sarah Ansari's works (see Ansari 1992).

believed that Shafqat Shah's forefathers were also among the numerous *pirs* in Sindh who gained power and prestige during the years of imperial rule, and, while they no longer associate themselves with their religious past or with a specific saint or shrine, it was how they rose to prominence. This wealth and influence led to increased landholdings and, by the 1990s, the Sheerazis were a dominant force in the political landscape of Thatta.

The city of Thatta is also considered a hotbed of Sindhi nationalist politics, something that is supported by visual evidence in and around the city. I saw many flags and campaign slogans of Sindhi nationalist parties all over on the buildings and walls in the city and also along the highway leading into the city. I attended two different nationalist political rallies, one organised by the leader of Jeay Sindh Quomi Mahaz (JSQM), Dr Niaz Kilyani, in Sajawal city, and another one organised by Ayaz Paleejo and his Awami Party in Thatta city; yet it is the Sheerazi family that manages to mobilise enough people and support to control the seats for Thatta in the National and Provincial Assemblies.

The socio-political role of Sufi saints and *pir* families within the wider social structures of Sindh can explain their rise to power. It would not, however, provide any clarity into how or why the Sheerazis have been consistently able to maintain this position of political importance. Especially when, as one of my informants suggested and as recent reports have indicated, this was a 'PPP era (PPP *kay daur main*)' and a number of 'feudal' families had been unsuccessful at holding onto power (*The Economist* 2013). One estimate suggests that after the 2008 elections, 'the number of national lawmakers from feudal families shrank to 25 percent from 42 percent in 1970' in the Punjab Assembly (Tavernise 2010). In a political environment that has been getting less and less favourable for 'feudal' landlords (Hasan 2009) to hold on to absolute power, what then explains the Sheerazi families' continued political prominence and ability to win votes in a politically challenging area such as Thatta?

It became clear to me early on in my time in Thatta that the Sheerazis are clued in on the needs of their constituents, who increasingly see themselves as part of the political process. The Sheerazis' method of delivery, instead of being based on kinship groups or simply clientalistic relationships, engages with people's construction of a state and its political process.

During my time in Thatta, the Sheerazis' grassroots style of politics was often emphasised by a number of my informants and cited as the main reason why they choose to vote for this family. One of my key informants, whom I spoke to on a number of occasions during my time in Thatta, was Khwaja *sahab*, a journalist in his sixties. He had been working for *Dawn*, Pakistan's most widely circulated English language daily, for 35 years, reporting primarily in the district of Thatta and the surrounding areas. Khwaja *sahab* admitted that he had never once voted for the Sheerazis. He considered them to be '*ghundas* (thugs, criminals)' and had a personal dislike towards them. Yet in one of our conversations he said:

> If the Sheerazis ever join a (political) party they enforce their perspective on it and insist that they will follow their own objectives (*wajood*). They are strange people; you might not have met them; their great 'tycoon' is Shafqat Shah Shirazi. If you get time in the evening you should go to Syedpur; it's a small village near Sujawal. If you ever end up there in the evening you will find Shafqat Shah playing football with the local residents of the surrounding villages, 'without rest he plays daily'. Until sunset he plays football and among the football players you will find barbers, waiters and people from all (socio-economic) backgrounds. You will find him every evening in his 'play costume' on that field. He spends his time from morning to evening with people to such an extent that even on that field people gather around, so that as soon as he is free he listens to their problems, sometimes making phone calls, sometimes writing request letters to help them out. He spends 24 hours of the day with his people, they never leave him. If you meet him today and then see him after 10 years, he will call you by your name. He is barely literate but even if you converse with him in (a foreign language such as) English, he will reply to you. It is an astonishing (*mayer-ul-uqol*) thing that a person who has no formal education has learnt so much from the school of life, so much in fact that he is able to use that to 'dominate' people. One person is able to 'dominate' everyone. He has a whole group, his brother and his nephews. In this time when People's Party swept the elections in Sindh, the Sheerazis won the seats here. Out of nine seats they have got four, from Jhatti and Sujawal. His son is MNA, another is MPA.[9]

This very approachable and people-friendly style of politics was reaffirmed when I went to meet Shafqat Shah Sheerazi a few weeks later at his *autaaq* (meeting place primarily for men) in his village of Syedpur. It was an unimpressive cement and concrete shed with a few sofas but there was no security or restricted entry of any kind. Anyone who wanted to come in was welcomed and, in fact, as I was leaving, an old man of obviously meagre means did come in to see Shafqat Shah and went straight up to him and shook his

[9] As is common amongst Urdu speakers, educated in the English language, Khwaja *sahab* and I had this conversation in a mixture of Urdu and English. All the single quotes represent the parts of the conversation that were in English.

hand. In Sindhi culture, where social hierarchy dictates the protocols to be followed during such meetings, I was surprised that this old man neither touched Shafqat Shah's feet nor looked down in subservience, but rather looked him in the eye as he shook his hand, before starting a conversation.

Even before I had begun my interview with Shafqat Shah, he informed me very politely that he would have to excuse himself and leave in two hours and that while he is sorry to do so,[10] he has to be at the football field where he plays football every evening, with the local boys, at six o' clock. His very personable and down-to-earth character, and his extreme informality with the driver and male chaperone who were accompanying me was surprising, even though Khwaja *sahab* had told me about this aspect of his politics. It was, therefore, far less surprising that this was the main reason most of my informants in Thatta gave for voting for them. Despite some opposition to the Sheerazis, primarily from the PPP loyalists,[11] a large number of my informants agreed with the sentiment conveyed by one interviewee's words: 'They lend their support in *shaadi–ghami* (weddings, denoting happiness and funerals, times of sadness).' Another middle-aged male informant in Jhatti district said: '... he had come to eat *biryani*[12] with us when I married off my daughter, and sent his son to pay respects and help carry the body of my brother to his grave.'

It is especially important here to briefly emphasise this *shaadi–ghami* phenomena and its role in local politics in Sindh. I interviewed the chairman of a Thatta-based social movement and a well-known activist, Shah *sahab,* in Karachi in May 2012. In our conversation, he emphasised the fact that despite the Pakistani state's well-known failures in delivering developmental services 'people's expectations of this state are still alive.' He then went on to explain the *shaadi–ghami* phenomena as an example. Stating that the physical presence of the MNA (or other well-known political representatives of the state) during a particularly joyous occasion such as a wedding (*shaadi*) of a family member or in the funeral procession after the death (*ghami)* of a family member is

[10] This was a break from traditional rules of Sindhi hospitality which dictate that the host is almost never allowed to determine when the meeting with the guest will end. It is the guest who must indicate when he would like to leave.

[11] Zulfiqar Ali Bhutto, the founder of the PPP, himself filed nomination papers from Thatta in the election in 1970. Older residents of Thatta who remembered that time were more likely to be PPP supporters.

[12] On happy social occasions such as weddings, the Pakistani food that is served is normally a rice and meat dish known as *biryani*. It is a source of pride for the host to invite a guest to eat *biryani* at his house, and an honour for the guest to be invited.

of paramount importance for local communities, who vote such individuals into office. Meeting an individual who is seen as a manifestation of the state remains important to people in lower Sindh.

The desire to engage with an individual as the manifestation of the state is distinct and different from a clientalistic relationship with a political patron that results in economic or social benefit. It can be referred to, as Fuller and Harris (2009) do, as part of the 'indigenisation' of the democratic political process in South Asia and 'the masses' having bought into this process. The importance that local communities in southern Sindh assign to participation of their elected representative in *shaadi–ghami* is high and also very real. This was epitomised in a conversation I had with a young man in a village in Tharparkar district who had lost all six of his buffaloes in the floods. When speaking about elected representatives in parliament there, whose style of rule was remarkably different to that of the Sheerazis, he said, '*baishak* (even if), they had given us nothing it would have been fine, never mind, but they should have at least come to ask (*poochnay toh aatay*). Are you alive? How are you? Or are you all dead?' Such sentiments were expressed by a number of people in different villages in Tharparkar district. People wanted to encounter a state that cared and, while being responsive, was also sympathetic towards their loss and displayed empathy. Clearly, for this man in Tharparkar, empathy was more important than the economic response.

Besides providing a partial explanation for why the Sheerazis of Thatta have continued to hold on to the reins of power in their districts while the political family in Tharparkar has had less success and less street level popularity in comparison, this also illustrates one further point. If clientalism was the primary or only relationship the Sheerazis had with people in Thatta and 'political clientalism describes the distribution of selective benefits to individuals or clearly defined groups in exchange for political support' (Hopkin 2006, 2), people's demands should include economic 'benefit' and not just a desire for a sighting of a political individual in their *shaadi–ghami*. In my time in Thatta I did not come across any village, community or individual who had a relationship of economic dependence with the Sheerazis and saw them only as powerful patrons. The Sheerazis' position as large landowners, or as *pir*s who belong to a traditional Sufi saint family, is undoubtedly an important factor in their interactions with people in Thatta. However, it is equally important to state that the Sheerazis are able to hold on to this political power, in no small part, because of their grassroots-style of politics and their ability to provide people with what they need. Often that is just a need to encounter a human, caring manifestation of the state, actually indicating that the state is an important political actor in spite of the Sheerazis' hereditary social power.

In another interesting conversation I had with my informant Khwaja *sahab*, he presented Shafqat Shah as the epitome of non-'feudal' politics. He said:

> Once I was in Syedpur, there were many people sitting there at his annexe and his assistant said, '*Sahab* is in a bit of a rush, he is going to Karachi to meet the Chief Minister. Please be quick in your conversation with him so that he is able to leave on time.' When Shafqat Shah arrived, everyone was having tea; an old man beside me was also having tea. As Shafqat Shah came closer, the old man got flustered and 'in haste', he stood up and his boiling hot tea fell on Shafqat Shah. I thought that he would slap the old man, because by now hot tea was burning his body and clothes, but his reaction was astonishing. He asked the old man, '*Chacha* (uncle), what happened? Are you ok? Did the tea burn you?' Instead of blaming the old man, he asked if he was all right. He told him, 'You should have waited, I was coming towards you, the Chief Minister is not as important as you!' He impressed all the people; this is 'patience'. He is a politician par excellence; I am so impressed by him that, yes, he is not educated, but he knows politics. These people will go and vote for him tomorrow not because he holds a whip in his hand but because he knows what behaviour people want from him and he delivers. I would call that 'service delivery', wouldn't you?

Shafqat Shah likely came into power, and established his political dynasty, on the basis of his forefathers' success as *pirs*, yet he is described here as the antithesis to the traditional *wadera*. Furthermore, it seems improbable that he would have been able to maintain this power without the tireless work and effort that he seems to have put into his political career. This is especially true in a place such as Thatta, where every vote in every election is hotly contested. Shafqat Shah has to provide people not material wealth, which is relatively simpler to do when dispensing patronage, but rather stay clued in on the needs of his constituents. One of the most common demands of the latter is a physical manifestation of the state, the service of presence, and participation in their *shaadi–ghami* is a service he is astute at providing.

The Mirzas of Badin and PPP politics

The Mirzas are a political family who have gained prominence in Badin in the last 15–20 years, despite having no historical or traditional roots in the district. The story of the Mirzas' rise to power is particularly interesting. Not only is it starkly different to the Sheerazis' rise to power in Thatta or of the Arbabs in Tharparkar, but it also fits none of the narratives of traditional social structures helping political patrons into power. The Mirzas do not belong to a family native to Badin, and their extended family is not rooted in the political landscape of the district. It is essentially just one household – Dr Zulfiqar Mirza, his wife, and son – who have all held political office and are now influential figures in the politics of Badin; but residents know very little about their extended family: fathers, uncles, brothers, etc.

Second, unlike the Arbabs and the Sheerazis, the Mirzas rose to power and significance neither as leaders of a *quom* (tribe) nor through religious connections to *pir*s, and neither had the state given them large land grants in colonial or post-colonial Sindh. Rather, Dr Zulfiqar Mirza's father was a high court judge in Sukkhur in upper Sindh, and Mirza himself had regularly acknowledged his quintessentially middle-class origins. If the traditional social structures of *wadera*s or *pir*s do not explain their rise to power then what does?

Much like the Sheerazis of Thatta catering to the needs of the people in lower Sindh, which requires the participation of an individual manifesting the state in their *shaadi–ghaami*, the relationship of the Mirzas to local politics in Badin tells us much about the role of the PPP in lower Sindh. The Mirzas have been able to rise to political power in Badin because of Dr Zulfiqar Mirza's relationship with the Chairman of the PPP and the former President of the country, Asif Ali Zardari. While acknowledging his family's humble background, Dr Mirza famously stated on national television, when announcing his resignation from the MPA seat for Badin in 2012:

> It is my good fortune (and not personal achievement) that I was born in Justice Zafarulla Hussain Mirza's home, went to Petaro (for schooling), where I met my dearly beloved friend, dearer to me than life itself, *mohtarum* Asif Ali Zardari *sahab*. That meeting slowly 'develop(ed)' into a friendship, and today I sit here, son of Justice Zafarullah Hussain Mirza but 'product', to such an extent that even the clothes on my back, my cars, houses, sugar mills and lands – everything I own have all been given to me by Allah, but the channel through which I received them was *shaheed* (martyr) *mohtarma* Benazir Bhutto *sahaba* and Asif Ali Zardari. I am product of these two people.

Mirza credits the patronage and support his family received from the Bhutto–Zardaris for his own family's position in Badin. Thus, the case of the Mirzas of Badin illustrates quite successfully that, among other things, political parties can also play an influential role in making or breaking political families in lower Sindh.

When I was doing fieldwork in 2012 and 2013, the PPP dominated the political landscape in the district; the party won all seven seats from Badin in the Provincial and National Assemblies. In the 2008 elections, Dr Zulfiqar Mirza won the Provincial Assembly seat PS 57, and was made Home Minister of Sindh by the PPP government. His wife, Dr Fehmida Mirza, won the National Assembly seat NA 225, and served as Pakistan's first woman Speaker of the Lower House, from 2008 to 2013. Dr Zulfiqar Mirza, however, resigned from his seat in the Sindh Provincial Assembly in August 2011, after publicly expressing outrage and staging a dramatic press conference at the Karachi Press Club. He cited his differences with the ruling party in Karachi, the Mutahida Quomi Movement (MQM), as the reason behind his resignation.[13] After his resignation, by-elections were held in Badin for the PS 57 seat and Zulfiqar Mirza's son, 29 -year-old Hasnain Ali Mirza, won this election and became MPA, effectively taking charge from where his father left off.

It became clear during my time doing fieldwork that the Mirzas are able to maintain their dominant position in Badin even though they hold only two seats (one in the Provincial and one in the National Assembly) because of the strong PPP presence at the grassroots level in this district. In the 2008 election, Dr Zulfiqar Mirza won his seat with 33,111 votes; the runner-up candidate from PML-Q had 13,853, almost 20,000 votes fewer than Mirza. The same favourable mandate is true of most PPP candidates in Badin, and there is seen to be little serious opposition to the party in the district. This was also the only district where I regularly interacted with PPP party workers (comrades); I met various informants at a PPP public office, in the town of Shadi Large in Badin, that was regularly visited by residents from neighbouring villages. When I asked people why they chose to vote for the PPP in this area, I received answers that were often a variation of the answer I received from an elderly man in his seventies who lived by the LBOD in Shadi Large:

> Because when I need any help I call the comrade and he comes.

I met the comrade this old man was talking about and, over the course of my time in Badin, I interacted with this PPP political worker frequently. He was a charismatic man in his late thirties who had spent his whole life in and around

[13] A party dominated by the ethnic Urdu-speaking *muhajirs*.

Shadi Large and had good relations with the local communities. He had also spent the last two decades working as a 'comrade' for the PPP, using his social relations with the people to encourage them to go to the polls during election time. This informant, Shahid, provided me with the best demonstration of local-level party politics that I had seen in any of the districts or towns where I undertook fieldwork. Shahid spent many hours a day riding his Yamaha motorcycle around the district, be it the blistering heat of the summer or the cold of winter, maintaining his contacts and networks with people and making sure that he was available to them. While the Mirzas did not play football with their constituents like the Sheerazis, they had a network of comrades maintaining community-level relations for them.

The comrade was a trusted member of the Mirzas' political support network and admitted that until Dr Zulfiqar Mirza bought his first sugar mill in 1993 in Badin, few people, if any at all, had heard of him. I asked Shahid how much agricultural land and other wealth the Mirzas had managed to acquire in Badin in the last 20 years. He replied,

> Madam *jee*, a few years ago when they were supposed to 'file papers' with the Election Commission (declaring their assets)[14] there was serious panic. *Sahab* called me and said he needed my help and I went in a rush to his farm house. After that madam (Fehmida), *sahib* (Zulfiqar), two lawyers and two other comrades spent four days running around trying to find all the property papers and calculate their net worth but it was all to no avail. We were unable to come to any reliable conclusion and just had to fill in a random number. Now you tell me, when the owners are themselves not sure of their total property how can I tell you their net worth?

While an estimation of the total assets acquired by the Mirzas since their move to Badin may be difficult, it is very clear that the family's economic and political influence is not linked to any significant hereditary landholding. After setting up Mirza Sugar Mills in 1989 and winning the MPA seat from Badin in 1993, Dr Mirza then went on to invest in land in Badin. However, unlike in Thatta or Tharparkar, where I was occasionally given some indication of the many thousands of acres of land owned by the Sheerazis or the Arbabs, or where it

[14] Constitutionally, according to the provisions of Section 42A of the Representation of the People Act 1976 and Section 25A of the Senate (Election) Act 1975, all elected representatives must submit detailed accounts of their assets and liabilities to the Election Commission at the end of each financial year.

might be located, the lands that may or may not be owned by Zulfiqar Mirza and his wife in Badin played no role at all in the public narrative.

When it comes to the story of the Mirzas and their influence in Badin, it is essentially the central role played by PPP patronage that explains their rise to power. It is especially significant that it is Zulfiqar Mirza and Asif Ali Zardari's friendship that resulted in the Mirzas wielding such power and being embedded in the political party structure. Unlike kinship and dynastic networks that are often emphasised when theorising politics in Sindh, the case of the Mirzas reveals that positions of power can be acquired not only through hereditary relationships but also through individuals exercising their own agency and exploiting opportunities to create social privilege for themselves. The PPP connection helped to establish the Mirzas as the 'first' family of Badin despite not being native to the area. What seems to have made it possible for them to stay in this position of influence is a very effective system of local politics that ensures that even if the Mirzas are unable to participate in the lives of their constituents in any direct way, they have representatives in the form of comrades and a network of *jiyala*s (Paracha 2011) who make sure that people are continuously reminded of them.

To further illustrate this point about the centrality of the PPP to the Mirzas' rise to power in Badin, two or three different informants told me on different occasions that the Mirzas are in this important and enviable position in Badin only because they are representatives of the PPP in this district. To emphasise the fact that the Mirza name does not, and could not, on its own win seats in parliament from Badin, these informants narrated the story of how Fehmida Mirza politically backed her brother Kazi Asad Abid in the election for a Provincial Assembly seat in the 1990s. Kazi Asad Abid stood for elections as an independent candidate against the PPP candidate from that constituency in Badin. Despite the Mirza family throwing their full political support behind Abid's campaign the MPA seat from this constituency was won by the veteran PPP politician, Dr Mandhro, who practises medicine in Badin city and is not a big landowner.[15] This goes to demonstrate the importance of the political party and not just social relations in the construction of state in this region.

It is also important to point out that the same network of PPP comrades mentioned earlier was also seen to be hard at work during the aftermath of the floods in Badin in 2011. While some of my informants expressed

[15] I asked Dr Mandhro in an interview how much land he owns and he said: 'I have 100–200 acres of land in a coastal *taluka* of Badin where cultivation is not possible.'

disappointment at the way the comrades had 'done corruption' in the distribution of relief goods, an equal or larger number had informed me that they used the help of the comrades to either find a safe place during the rescue efforts or asked them for relief goods during the relief and rehabilitation phase after the floods of 2011. Residents of Badin who had been in relief camps visited by Dr Fehmida Mirza were especially moved that the Speaker of the National Assembly herself came to ask about their circumstances. Instead of a relationship based on kinship or clientalistic networks, it seems that the Mirzas of Badin represent the way in which political party structures and mobilisation also play a role in relations between people and their state in lower Sindh.

Earlier in this chapter I presented discussions of fragmented citizenship in Pakistan resulting from prevailing social structures such as kinship groups, *waderas* and Sufi *pirs*, and compounded by an absent state that was making no effort to reach out to people as citizens, not just as members of a caste or kin group. Such work does not engage seriously with the role of political parties, seeing them essentially as a way for political patrons to dispense targeted patronage rather than universal service delivery (Hasnain 2008). The limited work that has been done on political parties in Pakistan has primarily focused on their general 'weakness' or irrelevance as a mobilising force in rural Pakistan (Mohmand 2011). The case of the Mirzas of Badin, however, clearly illustrates that this relationship between a political party and its local followers can also be more complex and cannot be explained only through existing social structures. A closer look at the state–citizen relationship beyond just the dominant social relations that exist in lower Sindh might provide more insight into this local phenomenon. I will explore the ethnographic constructions of the state and its citizens in lower Sindh in the next chapter.

The Arbabs of Tharparkar and their changing constituency

The political family that has been significant in Tharparkar for over two generations is the Arbab family. It was interesting that though the incumbent party at the centre – and in Sindh – after the 2008 elections was the PPP, both the Sheerazis of Thatta and the Arbabs of Tharparkar managed to win the majority of the seats in their districts despite in the opposition to the PPP. Hence, I was often confronted with a confusing narrative in both these districts, from members of the Sheerazi and Arbab families, that seemed to be quite anti-government, despite them being in government. It soon became clear to me, however, that beyond the anti-PPP and anti-government rhetoric, these political families shared little else in their styles of politics.

There is a narrative around the PPP and '*azaadi* (freedom)' which I encountered while doing fieldwork in Sindh but also in the work of scholars such as Arif Hasan (2009). Yet it was interesting that I heard it most often in Tharparkar, a district where PPP opposition was in fact in power. One of the earliest people I spoke to about the Arbabs in Tharparkar had voted for the Arbabs in a previous election but in 2008 had voted for the PPP. This interviewee, Ghafoor *chacha*, was a 72 year-old resident of Kaloee town in Tharparkar district. I was introduced to Ghafoor *chacha* by my local contact, as he was walking down the main road in Kaloee. I was keen to speak to Ghafoor *chacha* in depth, so I asked my local contact if there was anywhere suitable for us to have a chat with this informant. Ghafoor *chacha* immediately replied 'follow me' and led me to the house of a PPP ticket-holder, an ex-MPA and local activist, whom I will call '*saeen*'[16]. Ghafoor *chacha* was an old, simply dressed man, who clearly seemed to be from a humble background. With considerable confidence, he opened the gate of the most modern-looking, and reasonable-sized, house in the town, shook hands with the guards and invited me in.

Once I had made myself comfortable in the general *autaaq* area where *saeen* used to meet with local residents seeking his help, I was informed by my local contact that *saeen* was actually out of town but that anyone who needed a place to sit, or needed to wait for *saeen*, was welcome in his *autaaq* at all times. In the course of my conversation with Ghafoor *chacha*, I asked him why he had decided to vote for the PPP instead of the Arbabs. He replied, because this government (by which he meant the PPP) has 'given us *azaadi* (freedom)'. He was sitting with his feet on the chair; he pressed his heels against the chair harder to make a point and said:

> See how I am sitting, with my feet on this chair when Saeen is not even at home, drinking his tea? When we go to see the Arbabs they will not even let us sit on a chair; they will expect us to sit on the floor, at their feet so that we are reminded of our social position. So that we know at all times that they are important and we are poor.

I was only able to record 21 minutes of our conversation on an audio recorder after which we had lunch and took a walk to a new hospital that Ghafoor

[16] *Saeen* is a Sindhi term of respect to address people in Sindhi-speaking culture.

chacha insisted was made on the orders of the PPP government. In those 21 minutes, Ghafoor *chacha* used the word *azaadi* four times. He was adamant that this was because there was a Federal and Provincial PPP government. Before the PPP government came into power in 2008, Arbab Ghulam Rahim had been the Chief Minister of Sindh under the rule of General Pervez Musharraf. The Arbabs are seen to be close to the military establishment in the country and even contested the 2008 elections on PML-Q (the political party put together by General Pervez Musharraf) tickets.[17] Hence, every time Ghafoor *chacha* talked about *azaadi*, it was as if it was a new concept, emphasising that whereas 'earlier' it was not possible for 'a poor man like me' to order even an ordinary '*sipahee* (policeman) to do my work, now I can put my feet on the table and order even the DC[18] to do my work'. While Ghafoor *chacha* might have exaggerated his new-found empowerment to make a point; he insisted that even animals have a different *chaal* (stride/attitude) since the PPP government has come into power, pointing out that since the shepherd is *azaad* his sheep now have a different stride. At the same time, however, the importance of his narrative cannot be overemphasised. For this interviewee, something that was confirmed by various others in Tharparkar, the dominance of the Arbab family has little to do with people's politics and more to do with coercion and autocratic control.[19]

Tharparkar was the most polarised district, in terms of political support, of the three I did fieldwork in. While there is a general belief that non-Muslim minorities, and even minority Muslim sects, are more likely to vote for the PPP due to its largely secular ideology, this was far less visible in the other two districts. After spending a few months doing fieldwork in Tharparkar it began to become more and more evident that all my informants who belonged to a

[17] What people refer to as '*Arbabon kay daur main*' (during the era of the Arbabs) is the period 2002–2008, even though the Arbabs were still holding onto most of their positions in the post-2008 era as well.

[18] District Commissioner.

[19] Arbab Zakaullah, one of the Arbabs who was the MPA of Tharparkar (NA 229), was the most well-armed National Assembly member in 2009. In his declaration of assets to the Election Commission, he declared owning licences for 14 'prohibited and non-prohibited' weapons. While it is not uncommon for parliamentarians in Pakistan to own weapons, some of which may even be unlicensed, the large quantity of expensive weapons owned by Arbab Zakaullah was surprising enough to make it to the news.

religious minority or were economically marginalised landless tenants had voted for the PPP in the 2008 elections. At the same time, almost all individuals who looked religiously devout, and more likely were Ahl-e-Hadis, had voted for the Arbabs. I was able to infer that a certain kind of Islamist religious support was available to the Arbabs. The three interviewees who were most supportive of the Arbabs were:

- Rehmat, who was the cleric of a *goth*, and three or four other residents who were part of this conversation, where the primary population was that of Naurias. This cleric clearly identified himself as belonging to the Ahl-e-Hadis *fiqh* and believed that teaching boys about their duties towards *difa* (defence) of Pakistan and *jihad* for Islam was necessary.
- Zahid, a member of the Sindh leadership of the Karachi-based Jamiat-e-Ahl-e-Hadis, lived in a particularly remote area in Deeplo, and was very suspicious of me and my research. He said repeatedly that he is ideologically opposed to '*jamhooriyat* (democracy)' because he thinks that there is no concept of such a political system in Islam. Regarding the Arbabs, however, he said 'they are always available to serve (*khidmat*) us; they protect us and they make whatever we need available to us. Hence we fully support (*wabastagi*) them'.
- Saleem, was a middle-aged man in a mid-sized *goth* in Deeplo *taluka* of Tharparkar. This interviewee, and three or four of his neighbours, all said that they would continue to vote for Arbab who they see as their 'national hero'. They described their broad kinship group, Nauria, as a *quom* (tribe), and called Arbab their '*quomi* hero' (in English). Later in the interview, it also became clear that, though they identified themselves personally as Ahl-e-Sunnat, their *goth* had strong connections to an Ahl-e-Hadis *madrassa*, Dar-ul-Uloom (literally translates as 'centre of education', which is a generic name for many *madrassas*) in Karachi, which they said was one of the biggest religious seminaries in the city and is spread over seventy acres of land.

This is not to say that only three of my interviewees supported the Arbabs politically but to illustrate the point that, more often than not, interviewees who did vote for this political family were either Ahl-e-Hadis or seemed to have social ties with the Arbabs. Related to the religious polarisation between the PPP and Arbab voters was a polarisation along socio-economic lines as well. That is perhaps more a result of social processes that limit economic opportunities for particular groups of minorities in certain contexts rather than independent from it.

The relationship that the Arbab family had with the people of Tharparkar was also very different to the one that the Mirzas had with their constituents in Badin. For instance, the Arbab patriarch and ex-Chief Minister of Sindh, Arbab Ghulam Raheem, went into self-imposed exile in Dubai when the PPP came to power in the 2008 elections. Yet he did not give up the National Assembly seat that he had won on a PML-Q ticket and remained an absentee MNA. By the time I went into the field, many ordinary residents in villages were asking, 'If he is so concerned about us, where is he? Why has he not bothered to come to Thar in five years?' The grassroots-level connections that the Mirzas maintained with their constituents through their network of comrades, further supported by their own physical presence during trying times, was clearly absent in Tharparkar.

Of the two groups of polarised voters one group included the religious (almost all the *maulvi*s and *mufti*s I met), the commercial (the owner of a chalk mine and a few small traders) and the agricultural (a landlord with about 350 acres of land), all of whom supported Arbab Ghulam Raheem and his sons and nephews. They talked of the improved services that the Arbabs had provided the people of Tharparkar (especially during Arbab Ghulam Raheem's tenure as Chief Minister from 2002 to 2008), such as more irrigation water, and highways and roads that have now made the vast majority of this 'desert district' accessible to large cities. Zahid said, 'Now with the network of roads and electricity connections, etc., I do not feel like I live in the desert; I feel like I live in Karachi.'

The second group included the large number of landless tenants, many amongst them lower-caste Hindus; the Muslim residents of the town and villages of Tharparkar who continued to follow its syncretic religious tradition of saying Muslim prayers in Hindu temples; and livestock owners who have little or no land ownership. These were the classes of people whose socio-economic vulnerability either resulted in their feeling pressured into voting for the Arbabs or admitted to voting for the PPP. Some of these informants also said that they had been unable to cast their vote because every time they had been to vote on an election day, they had been shooed away by local, Arbab hired muscle. One interviewee, a middle-aged man who has spent his whole life in Tharparkar, said that when he went to cast his vote in 2008, he was told, '*Tumhara ho gaya, ab tum jao* (your work is done, now you go).' While unable to verify the truth of such claims about the violation of rights in Tharparkar, these claims remain critical to people's lived experience of the Arbab regime in the towns and villages of this district.

The former group of people whom I will refer to as part of the 'pro-Arbab' narrative present a different picture with regard to the rise of the Arbabs to political influence, as compared to the latter group of people who are part of the 'anti-Arbab' narrative. The pro-Arbabs I met during fieldwork emphasised that the Arbab family is the leader of the Nauria *quom* (people).[20] It was this position of social power that resulted in the colonial state allocating Crown lands to them and patronising the elders to keep the peace. Through these lands the Arbabs were able to acquire additional wealth and political clout. This narrative assumes that the Arbabs were already important and influential before Pakistan was created and while Sindh was under imperial rule.

The anti-Arbab narrative in the towns and villages that I visited was summed up for me by some teachers of a government primary school in Mithi, the capital of Tharparkar district. They said that the Arbabs acquired their lands through a system of fraud locally called *koka-kari*. This, they explained to me, was a late nineteenth century phenomena when the capital of Thurr and Parkar districts was based in Bhuj. Farmers from Tharparkar were required to deposit their taxes to the Crown in the city of Bhuj in Gujarat (present-day India). As this was both an expensive and time-consuming journey, the anti-Arbabs say that because the Arbabs were financially somewhat better off and also leaders of their *quom*, they were normally entrusted with the responsibility to take people's money or agricultural produce, travel to Bhuj and pay off their taxes while also settling their own. The Arbabs used this as a way to have this land transferred to their own name, so that gradually they became the largest landowners in Tharparkar.

---

[20] Raikes (1977), writing in the latter part of the nineteenth century, mentions that little is known about when or why the Naurias came to the desert of Tharparkar though it is likely to have been around the sixteenth century. They were based primarily around the western end of the district 'bordering on Sind proper' and the tribal heads owned some land in that area though how much is unclear. The majority of the Nauria people were pastoralists, something Ibrahim's (2011) work mentions as still true in Kutch today. Partition, the creation of Pakistan and subsequent migrations have, however, changed the socio-economic composition of Naurias in Tharparkar, and today they are more likely to own land than to lead a nomadic life in the desert.

In terms of historical evidence, I spent some time looking at material in the Sindh archives in Karachi between January and April 2013 but was not able to prove or disprove either of these narratives. The only fact that the records prove is that when magistrate Captain Stanley Napier Raikes' *Memoir of the Thurr and Parkur, Districts of Sind* was published in 1856 (Raikes 1977 [1856]), the Naurias were less important as Thurr and Parkur were majority Hindu districts and dominated by Rajput and Sooda *biraderi*s. In addition, the geographical location of Thurr and Parkur, between the Rann of Kutch and the plains of Sindh, presented an administrative challenge to the imperial state. The main theme running through most of the earlier records on the region is whether Thurr and Parkar should continue to be ruled by a deployment of British officers in Kutch (1843–1856) or integrated into Sindh (Ibrahim 2011). Umerkot (a separate district since 1991), a historically important part of Tharparkar, was governed by a Hindu, the Rana of Umerkot, until the creation of Pakistan in 1947. Some Sindhi intellectuals, such as a professor from the Jamshoro University whom I interviewed in Badin, said that it is more likely that a significant amount of Nauria migration into Tharparkar took place after Partition in 1947. This large influx of 'their people' is believed to have resulted in their rise to political power.

Though there is some evidence to suggest that Arbab Ghulam Raheem is the leader of the Nauria *quom*, it would still be very difficult to define his political interaction as the traditional *biraderi–wadera* relationship. Not only does his physical absence make it impossible for him to fulfil some of the traditional roles of a *wadera*, it also seems that he has actively pursued and developed a new constituency of voters that includes the religious right, particularly from the Ahl-e-Hadis *fiqh*. This could partly be explained by his close association with the military, and the special status of Tharparkar as a 'border' district. An evident voter-split along religious and economic lines between the Arbabs and the PPP cannot be adequately explained by any of the social structures discussed earlier. Tharparkar, therefore, clearly demonstrates that apart from voting for political representatives who manifest the state in a personable and approachable manner, and the relationship of the political family to a political party, the wider political agenda or message followed by those being voted into office is also important to the people in lower Sindh.

This obvious political polarisation that I found in Tharparkar can further be supported by the fact that it was the only one of the three districts where the elections of 2013 resulted in a significant shift, in contrast to Thatta and Badin where both political families were able to hold on to power.

Tharparkar has four seats in the Provincial Assembly and two in the National Assembly. The party of the Arbabs, the PML-Q, won five out of these six seats in the 2008 elections,[21] with three out of these five going to Arbab Ghulam Raheem and his son and nephew, while PPP only won a single seat. In the elections of May 2013, only Ghulam Raheem was able to hold on to his seat in the Provincial Assembly; the other five seats went to the PPP.[22] By 2018, they did not remain among the largest landowners in Tharparkar. At the same time, however, this election result also illustrates that beyond being just over-socialised members of kinship groups and *biraderi*s the people in lower Sindh also exercise some agency as voters and citizens.

This chapter demonstrates that despite a dominant narrative that sees people in 'interior' Sindh as entirely dependent on rigid and oppressive social structures, people do engage with the state beyond socially determined hereditary relations. My ethnography across three districts illustrates that while there is some element of patronage politics operating along hereditary *pir* or kinship lines, this does not capture the full picture. There were other forces that allowed political families to rise to power and then stay in those positions of influence. Social structures and hereditary relations were only one part of a wider story of political power and expression that included other aspects of state and party politics. It was something that people recognised and addressed not simply as clients of these patrons but as residents and citizens. It is, therefore, important to recognise that there is a more complex relationship between the state and its citizens, beyond social relations, in the districts that I studied. It is equally possible to extend this analysis to assume that should important political individuals/families be ethnographically studied, a similar mix of traditional power with other aspects of state representation and political party power is likely to reveal itself in other parts of Pakistan considered to be 'rural'. In the following chapter, I illustrate some of these features of the ethnographic state and show how this state–citizen relationship is constructed in lower Sindh.

---

[21] Election results for the 2008 and the 2013 elections have been listed in Table 2.2.

[22] In 2008, it is believed, the Arbabs benefited from the patronage of the Musharraf regime, still in power.

Table 2.2 MNAs and MPAs from Thatta, Badin and Tharparkar districts in 2008 and 2013

Constituency	2008	2013
THATTA		
PROVINCIAL ASSEMBLY		
PS 84 (Thatta I)	Sadiq Ali Memon (PPP)	Aijaz Ali Shah Sheerazi (PML-N)
PS 85 (Thatta II)	Sassui Palijo (PPP)	Amir Haider Shah Sheerazi (PML-N)
PS 86 (Thatta III)	Shah Hussain Shah Sheerazi (PML-Q)	Shah Hussain Shah Sheerazi (PML-N)
PS 87 (Thatta IV)	Mohd Ali Malkani (PML-Q)	Mohd Ali Malkani (PPP)
PS 88 (Thatta V)	Mohd Usman Jalbani (PPP)	Owais Muzzafar (PPP)
NATIONAL ASSEMBLY		
NA 237 (Thatta I)	Abdul Wahid Soomro (PPP)	Mrs Sham-ul-Nisa (PPP)
NA 238 (Thatta II)	Ayaz Ali Shah Sheerazi (PML-Q)	Ayaz Ali Shah Sheerazi (PML-N)
BADIN		
PROVINCIAL ASSEMBLY		
PS 55 (Old Badin I)	Mohd Hasan Khan Talpur (PPP)	Bashir Ahmed Haleepoto (PPP)
PS 56 (Old Badin II)	Bashir Ahmed Khan Leghari (PPP)	Allah Bux Talpur (PPP)
PS 57 (Old Badin III)	Zulfiqar/Husnain Mirza (PPP)	Husnain Mirza (PPP)
PS 58 (Old Badin IV)	Dr Sikander Mandhro (PPP)	Dr Sikander Mandhro (PPP)
PS 59 (Old Badin V)	Mohd Nawaz Chandio (PPP)	Mohd Nawaz Chandio (PPP)
NATIONAL ASSEMBLY		
NA 224 (Old Badin I)	Ghulam Ali Nizamani (PPP)	Sardar Kamal Khan Chang (PPP)
NA 225 (Old Badin II)	Dr Fehmida Mirza (PPP)	Dr Fehmida Mirza (PPP)

Contd.

Contd.

THARPARKAR		
PROVINCIAL ASSEMBLY		
PS 60 (Thar I)	Arbab Ghulam Rahim (PML-Q)	Arbab Ghulam Rahim (PML-N)
PS 61 (Thar II)	Arbab Zulfiqar Ali (PML-Q)	Dr Mahesh Kumar Malani (PPP)
PS 62 (Thar III)	Sharjeel Inam Memon (PPP)	Makhdoom Khaliluzaman alias Naimatullah (PPP)
PS 63 (Thar IV)	Abdul Razzaque Rahimoon (PML-Q)	Dost Mohammad Rahimoon (PPP)
NATIONAL ASSEMBLY		
NA 229 (Thar I)	Arbab Zakaullah (PML-Q)	Fakir Sher Mohammad Bilaiani (PPP)
NA 230 (Thar II)	Ghulam Hyder Samejo (PML-Q)	Pir Noor Mohammad Shah Jeelani (PPP)

Source: Data obtained from website of the Provincial Assembly of Sindh: http://www.pas.gov.pk/index.php/home/en.

CHAPTER 3

The Ethnographic Social Contract

Evidence from my fieldwork in three districts in lower Sindh, presented in the previous chapter, suggests that people exercise more agency than structuralist accounts of the state in Pakistan have given them credit for. If kinship networks and clientalistic relations with a political patron, such as a powerful *wadera*, defined people's only interaction or understanding of the state, Dr Zulfiqar Mirza would not have been able to gain political prominence in Badin district. Similarly, if it was just the Sheerazi family's *pir* background that resulted in their rise to power in Thatta, they could potentially also have been voted out of office like other 'quintessential "feudal lord(s)"', such as Mustafa Khar or Nawabzada Iftikhar Ahmed, who have lost elections in recent years (Akhtar 2012). It is evident that there is more to people's relationship and understanding of the state beyond *pir*s and *biraderi*s in Pakistan. If not through hierarchical social relations or, to quote Mohmand, as 'patrons, brothers and landlords' (2011), how then do people construct the state, citizenship and the relationship between them?

This chapter answers these questions by using anthropological tools to interrogate what the state means 'from below'. This is then complemented by an interrogation of citizenship 'from below' in order to understand the wider state–citizen relations in Pakistan. Does a citizenship framework hold any meaning for people and how do they see their rights and responsibilities as citizens of this state? Studies on citizenship in Pakistan have concluded that the concept does not exist in the political imagination of people. An explanation that is often provided for this shortcoming is that the state has failed to provide a framework or foundation on which citizenship can be built (Kabeer et al. 2012). Instead, the focus of the state has been an exclusionary religious foundation that 'seeks to create practicing Muslims rather than democratic citizens' (Ahmad 2004, 39; also see Lall 2012b, Dean 2005, Leirvik 2008). This work generally builds upon definitions and understanding of 'universal' citizenship often problematised for being context-specific. Yet much of the work emphasising the failure of the Pakistani state to build a framework for citizenship, or participatory democratic citizens, has been developed using European liberal ideals considered 'universal' that have very little flexibility built into them (Delanty 1997).

On the other hand, most studies on citizenship in Pakistan which fall into the social structuralist camp argue that there is no concrete construction of citizenship because of the oppressive dominance of kinship, caste and other social relations that fragment society. Those that do look at local context overemphasize social relations and see state–citizen interactions as entirely part of wider social structures in towns and villages in Pakistan. In the words of one scholar, 'Most landlords, however, have no alternative but to aid villagers in the way that would be done by the state in the West' (Lyon 2002, 187). Lyon's study on patronage in Punjab sees the 'landlord' as taking on the role of the state because he studies power and asymmetrical relations at a social level, and then extends that same model and analysis to include state functions and functionaries as well; again, the interpretation of the social contract is that of it being entirely mediated by these 'feudal' landlords. Serious analysis that situates the state and its citizens within the local cultural context of Pakistan, but at the same time refuses to explain away the state as subsumed within social structures such as *biraderi*s or *wadera*s, has never been undertaken. We, therefore, have a very limited understanding of how people in small towns and villages of Pakistan, such as those in lower Sindh, construct the state, citizenship and state–citizen interactions.

I, therefore, turn to anthropological methods of inquiry to understand how people in this part of Pakistan construct the state. In particular, to examine the ways in which they interpret their own interaction with this state and explain what this means for an ethnographic social contract in this region.

There is a general consensus among anthropologists that, as a discipline, anthropology did not engage with the study of politics or the state for much of its development (Spencer 1997). It was an oversight that had particularly serious consequences for non-Western states. 'That neglect has contributed to the tendency in scholarship on the state to reproduce the Weberian argument that formal legal rationality eclipses substantive cultural factors, so that all modern states are fundamentally the same' (Fuller and Harriss 2009, 2). Anthropologists, on the other hand, move away from defining states as one standard type and argue that 'the state', like 'the economy', is not a universal category. In fact, in their edited book *The Anthropology of the State*, Sharma and Gupta (2006) are critical of classifications such as 'weak', 'strong' or 'failed' states. They argue that these terms look at modern liberal democracies as the ideal against which all other states are judged, stripping 'the unit of analysis – the state – from its cultural moorings' (Sharma and Gupta 2006, 10). They emphasise that culture plays an important role in informing and forming states, so that states are not only instrumental in producing and reinforcing culture but also are effects of cultural processes. This explains their use of the term 'state effects'[1] that I utilise in this analysis as well. Gupta has skillfully explained the need for an ethnographic understanding of the state; he writes:

> Focusing on the discursive construction of states and social groups allows one to see that the legacy of Western scholarship on the state has been to universalise a particular cultural construction of 'state–society relations' in which specific notions of 'statehood' and 'civil society' are conjoined. Instead of building on these notions, this article asks if one can demonstrate their provincialism in the face of incommensurable cultural and historical context. (1995, 378)

In the next section, I follow in the tradition of this work, and undertake an ethnography of the state and citizenship in lower Sindh, thereby illuminating key features of the state in this part of Pakistan. I then move on to undertake the same for citizenship in the region and conclude by explaining that these local constructions of the state and citizenship enable a tangible social contract to exist in lower Sindh.

The Everyday State: *Sarkar*, *Hakumat*, *Riyasat* or *Gornment*?[2]

Relying on the anthropological tradition of the 'everyday' state, I draw on my ethnographic engagement in southern Sindh to examine how people see the state, and the terms on which they understand their own interaction with it as citizens or something else. My analysis is based on the discursive construction of 'the state' and 'social groups' that have emerged more recently through ethnographies of the post-colonial state (Gupta 1995). In addition to problematising terms such as 'the state', I emphasise that 'the state' cannot be

[1] Taken from Mitchel's (1991) seminal work.

[2] While acknowledging that in political theory there is a distinction between 'state' and 'government', see for instance a discussion of this in Rose and Miller (1992). Due to the nature of my empirical enquiry, however, I intend to use the terms synonymously.

objectively described; the state means different things to different people in different locales at different times.[3]

I specifically engage with this literature on the 'everyday' state that points to 'blurred boundaries' between definitive and contained categories such as 'state' and 'society'. Particularly, as Gupta's work (1995) illustrates, in the case of India, where the 'state-system' is profoundly shaped and influenced by social forces making the boundary between state and society blurry, porous and unclear. The same was evident in the districts of lower Sindh where I did fieldwork. In my study districts, political families derived some of their power and influence from social forces but they did not 'become' the state. In recent years, research efforts have been made by anthropologists (but also historians and others) (Gould, Sherman and Ansari 2013) to understand what, besides social forces, constitute the 'everyday state' in India.

This scholarship sees the 'everyday state' as being constructed through the mundane and ordinary practices negotiated between government employees and citizens (Gupta 1995). Examination of the state in this way is also supported by anthropologists who have argued that '(1) State power has no institutional fixity on either theoretical or historical grounds. (2) Thus, state effects never obtain solely through national institutions or in governmental sites' (Trouillot 2001, 126). Given that the state is not an 'institutional fixity' and identifying effects of this state is often a complex task, it is necessary to understand the state beyond the 'empirically obvious', and through these practices of interaction and exchange (Trouillot 2001, 126). It, therefore, makes sense to interpret the state ethnographically in a way that takes its fluidity and multiple layers into consideration. Rather than following in the footsteps of some socio-cultural anthropologists who see the state as an 'unanalyzable given', I take the approach followed by scholars in the field who turn this 'unanalyzable given' into a study of the effects of the state through the subjects they help produce (Trouillot 2001, 126). In particular, theorising the state through the 'everyday' interactions of people in lower Sindh with what they interpret as the state.

In this literature the state is often a site of competition or dispute among various interest groups (Fuller and Harriss 2009) where those who have understood the ways in which the state operates and the principles on which

[3] In this chapter I use the state (without the quotes) when I am making a point about the state as the main power broker or duty-bearer in southern Sindh or even providing some analysis. Everywhere else when I am talking about interviewees and their testimonies and how they see 'the state', I will be referring to 'the state' in quotes.

it is based are able to use them to mediate everyday transactions (Gould, Sherman and Ansari 2013). These transactions then begin to frame people's interpretation of the state and the effects that it produces, allowing the analysis to move beyond that of a social contract mediated entirely through 'feudal' power brokers. While work on civil service employees, by historians examining the everyday state, looks at the case of both Pakistan and India, for the most part anthropological examinations into the state examine ethnographic data primarily from India (see Fuller and Benei 2009, Gupta 1995 and Hansen 2005). My own argument follows in the course of this established body of work because Pakistan and India emerged from the same colonial empire and retain common state characteristics, but also because, as Fuller and Harriss note, 'the modern Indian state plays an important part in popular consciousness and understanding, as well as in people's daily lives, and it does have some distinctively Indian characteristics' (2009, 2). This is a fact that holds just as true for most parts of Pakistan as well.

Gupta's local encounters

Gupta's ethnography of the state (1995) looks at people's interaction with the 'everyday state' to interpret the discourse around corruption in a village in north India. For him, much like in my own experience, 'the state' is constructed through cultural practices and local encounters that are symbolically represented through government actors and local citizens. Two characteristics of Gupta's 'everyday state' are particularly salient for the purposes of this research. First, he deconstructs the idea of the state as a cohesive monolith entity[4] that stands away and apart from people and society. In fact, in his research, the unitary entity called the *sarkar* (the state) was never invoked; rather it was specific departments, often specific individuals within these departments, that were identified. He concludes that 'at the local level it becomes difficult to experience the state as an ontically coherent entity: what one confronts instead is much more discrete and fragmentary – land records officials, village development workers, the Electricity Board, headmen, the police and the Block Development Office' (Gupta 1995, 384). While people might be aware of the existence of the 'state' as a wider philosophical construct, in their regular interactions they are unlikely to see themselves as engaging

[4] Corbridge et al. call this the 'Weberian aggregate' (2005, 20) and agree that most people would not see the state in this way.

with this abstract entity. Rather, in these interactions the 'the state' takes on a very functional and tangible role (in fields such as irrigation, police protection, cooking gas connection, and the like).

My field research illustrated very similar ways in which people encounter 'the state' in southern Sindh. The *encounter* with 'the state' that was most commonly cited by my informants was a visit to the office of the District Coordination Officer (DCO).[5] This office building is where most of the district government functionaries are housed. When the DCO himself is not present, or when he is 'busy', it is usually possible to meet with his deputy, the Deputy District Officer (DDO); if not him, then someone else, such as an Executive District Officer (EDO); and if not him, then an assistant or a clerk. I stopped by the DCO office in Thatta, without an appointment, at 4 p.m. on a very warm summer day in June 2012, and was told that the DCO *sahib* himself had left, but that the DDO was seeing people until offices closed at 5 p.m. I had to wait in queue in the waiting area, filled with local residents, but eventually the DDO did see me for a short chat. This was not an uncommon *encounter* with 'the state'.

For most of my informants in southern Sindh, their interaction with 'the state' consisted of these encounters with district officials such as DDOs or clerks, postmen who brought their Benazir Income Support Programme pay orders,[6] or irrigation department officials, even if they did not honour their commitment to repair and maintain breached canals. In some cases, this handful of individuals encompassed the sum total of people's interactions with the government; in other cases, people had more points of reference through which to interpret the state. In most of these instances, however, people were familiar with these officers' names and could have readily supplied me with information about their homes and often families. These encounters make 'the state' far more personal and familiar to residents in lower Sindh than to residents of big cities in Pakistan. This familiarity also helps explain why

---

[5] The DCO is the administrative head of the district administration, and has wide-ranging powers and responsibilities. While in office, the DCO is among the most important and influential individuals in the district.

[6] The Benazir Income Support Programme (BISP) is a social protection programme initiated by the PPP government in October 2008. It provides an unconditional cash transfer to the poorest women-headed households across the four provinces but has the widest reach in Sindh. Further details of this programme will be discussed later in the chapter.

people in my study districts in lower Sindh, but particularly in Thatta (where as my findings show this familiarity has been prioritised as a voting issue), had an expectation that an individual who represents the state (MNA, MPA or even a Union Councillor) would participate in their *shaadi* and *ghaami*. The construction of 'the state' in lower Sindh is based on a number of disjointed encounters and it is a more intimate relationship than is often recognised;[7] a relationship that regularly needs individuals as manifestations of 'the state' for that relationship to sustain itself.

This does demonstrate that, in lower Sindh, the nature of 'the state' is familiar and personal, and is built on various different encounters people have with those who they see as aspects or effects of 'the state'. It does not, however, mean that all my informants had a uniform understanding of this state but, rather, 'the state' means different things to different people at different times. To some extent, individual interpretations of 'the state' are also relative, based on people's own position within it, so that citizens less able to acquire economic or socio-political capital feel a greater need for 'sightings of the state' (Corbridge et al. 2005) than citizens more able to do so for themselves.

The second characteristic of Gupta's 'everyday state', which also resonates with my experience of lower Sindh, is that 'obviously' not everyone imagines the state in exactly the same way. He notes that people's constructions of 'the state' are not uniform; they differ substantially and are based on a range of varying factors, such as previous interactions with state officials, or even their own specific set of circumstances that frames their experience of 'the state'. In fact, most people provided me with very different and individualised understandings of 'the state'. My discussion with an elderly couple, residents of a small, relatively remote village in Badin who were no longer working due to various health problems, revealed that they had voted for the incumbent PPP government in the previous election. Despite some disappointments, they said they would continue to do so in the future. It was because, the husband said:

> This government has given us roads, it has given us jobs, and it has even undertaken developmental projects (*tarakiyaafta kaam*). What else do we need? This is what we need.

[7] This finding broadly supports Alpa Shah's work on the state in eastern India. She argues that the Indian state's inability to build a more personalised and intimate relationship with the Adivasis in India has been a significant factor in the Maoists' success in recruiting from these marginalised groups (Shah 2013a, 2013b).

For this interviewee 'the state' was doing its job when it was being an interventionist and developmental state, quite opposite to the contemporary shift taking place in most parts of the world to the neo-liberal state. While this 'vernacular understanding' of 'the state' is not unique to Pakistan, it must be highlighted that to expect (certain effects) of 'the state' to intervene, not only in service provision but in livelihoods and lives, is a far more South Asian construction of the state than a liberal European one (Corbridge et al. 2005). His wife added further details of '*mansubay* (development projects)' the state had implemented in the four-or-so years of PPP rule. It was also clear in the way they spoke of the PPP that they believed that while it was in power it had come close to providing many of the tangible services that they saw as requisites 'the state' must fulfil.[8] This also supports my findings on the Mirzas' rise to power in Badin district, because here the PPP is often recognised as a party that delivers on service provision. While this makes it tempting to conclude that people living in villages in Sindh, at a considerable distance from the 'technologies of development' (Corbridge et al. 2005), fundamentally construct 'the state' as a service provider, that would be too simple.

This, of course, illustrates that service provision is seen to be an integral part of the 'state effect'. That said, however, it is not the only or often even the primary expectation people in lower Sindh had of the state. Corbridge et al. (2005) cite the work of post-colonial scholars on India to make the point that the reality of the English-speaking elite is a stark contrast to the lived world of their 'subaltern or vernacular counterparts'. Hence, it would follow that their constructions of 'the state' are unlikely to coincide (Corbridge et al. 2005, 5). The elite either interact with a state that is a partial provider of services or they are able to utilise their own resources to acquire those services, reducing the utility of state services to some extent. For the vast majority of people in South Asia that is, however, not an option. The state is the *only* provider of public services and often even non-public services, such as jobs in the rural economy. This makes the terms on which the elites interact with the state differ significantly from the ways that a villager or small-town dweller does.

It is, therefore, very improbable that a resident of one of the expensive neighbourhoods in Karachi will see 'the state' in the same way as a landless tenant in the town of Nagarparkar in Tharparkar. It has been suggested that

[8] During my time doing fieldwork, the PPP was in power so it was common for my informants to refer to the state in terms of the PPP state.

only the elites imagine 'the state' in terms of more lofty ideals, like political freedom and justice, while the vernacular masses are only able to understand 'the state' in terms of routine services. The idea that the vast majority of Pakistanis only see 'the state' as a means of providing access to '*roti* (bread), *kapra* (clothing) and *makan* (shelter)'[9] is reductionist at best. Corbridge and his co-authors, in fact, emphasise that even if 'vernacular understandings of government' have little space for ideals of fairness or morality, poor people do have rule-based understandings of their own, and they do exercise agency to achieve such ideals (2005, 20–21). While the elderly couple demanded a state that delivered tangible services and public works projects, this was not, however, a universal construction of 'the state' amongst the residents of this region.

Close to the town of Jhatti in Thatta district, I met Akhtar *bhai*, a middle-aged male rickshaw driver, whose construction of the state was completely different to that of the elderly couple, and based almost entirely on ideals of political freedom and expression. He mentioned that politically he supported the PPP and insisted, '*Vote uss hee ko dain gay* (vote will always be given to PPP)' a few times in our conversation. He went on to explain his reason for this:

> It is simple: we might be poor, we might not be able to afford *atta* (flour) or *ghee* (cooking oil),[10] but at least if we want to block a road (in protest), or if we want to have a *dharna* (sit-in), if we want to raise our voice (in defiance) no one will stop us. The police will not touch us, sister, *guarantee* (in English).

In Akhtar *bhai*'s construction of 'the state' it became clear that he saw the fundamental role of the state as providing political empowerment and allowing a certain degree of political expression and activism. For this interviewee, the PPP government fulfilled his idea of a state's role, which was less about service provision – or indeed economic safeguards – but far more about creating spaces to voice dissent.

It is of course possible that the reason for Akhtar *bhai*'s protest is service delivery but the point he is making here is larger and more significant than the reasons for public protest. He is emphasising that, for him, his experience of

[9] Popular slogan used by Pakistan's populist leader Z. A. Bhutto during his political campaign.

[10] This is in reference to the massive food inflation that occurred during this government's time in power. People regularly told me how much less per kilo they used to pay for flour or sugar during the previous political regime.

'the state' was about having freedom of political expression and the ability to physically manifest that freedom through 'road blocks', which was ultimately most important. This desire for greater democratic expression and citizen engagement came up repeatedly in my research and will be explored later as well.

The perceived difference between elite and vernacular constructions of 'the state', and the different understandings of 'the state' by Akhtar *bhai* and the elderly couple need one further explanation. Gupta states that 'all constructions of the state have to be situated with respect to the speaker' (1995, 102) and emphasises that the positionality of the individual obviously influences his understanding of the state. The two interviewees' financial conditions and area of residence could explain partly why they saw 'the state' in such different ways. The elderly couple were older and less well off now than they had been a decade or two ago. They also mentioned the difficulty associated with living at a distance from any urban settlement, making access to services such as a hospital more difficult. It is, therefore, understandable that they see 'the state' as the primary delivery mechanism for infrastructure and social programmes that would make their lives easier. Akhtar *bhai*, despite his reference to being 'poor', was a relatively well-off resident of his village and owned one of the bigger brick (*pucco*) houses and had a steady stream of income. He was also based minutes away from the town of Jhatti itself which was a good-sized urban settlement. Economic assistance and better infrastructure were perhaps not an immediate concern for him because he already had access to some of these services.

Having established some features of the 'everyday state', it is now important to highlight an important inconsistency, something quite common in ethnographic constructions. The local-level *encounter* with the state in lower Sindh is usually with government employees who, as Gupta states, are as likely to be found at roadside tea-stalls or at their homes as in their offices. These individual people or the encounters with them, however (much like the point I have made on social relations and political families), do not represent people's complete understanding or interpretation of the state. The *construction* of 'the state' and the way that it is *imagined* by the elderly couple and Akhtar *bhai* is not entirely in these local terms but also as a larger and far more significant entity. This makes my findings consistent with Gupta's, that '(it is this seemingly contradictory fact that we must always keep in mind) it is precisely through the practices of such local institutions that a translocal institution such as the state comes to be imagined' (1995, 384).

The larger entity, 'the state'

It is precisely because this larger entity of the state exists, and is an important part of the political imagination in lower Sindh, that it is common to see people making demands on and having expectations of 'the state'. My data from the field consistently revealed that it was seen to be the job of this larger entity of 'the state' to keep people safe and provide a basic level of human security. During times of crises or disaster it is not these local encounters, or even relations based on kin or caste, that people called upon to deliver a basic minimum but the larger entity of 'the state'.

In my conversations with my informants in the *goth*s (hamlets) in Thatta, Badin and Tharparkar, the question that I inevitably asked, in some form or the other, was:

> Whose responsibility is it to keep you, your family, and your property safe in times of natural disaster?

It is also the only question that, across the three districts and across income differentials, religiosity and political affiliation, almost universally elicited the same answer; in all but two interviews and conversations, the answer was always different versions of 'the state'. The overwhelming majority of responses were *hakumat* or *gornment* (colloquial pronunciation of the English word 'government', with *hakumat* being its Urdu/Sindhi translation). The second most common response, used by some of my informants, was *sarkar* – the same word that Gupta points out is never invoked, and never mentioned in my own field research experience, when discussing the *encounter* with 'the state' at a local level. A third answer, that I received only once or twice, was *riyasat*.[11] In all of these instances people replied to the question using these terms without really thinking about it and in a most matter-of-fact way, or these words were preceded by versions of 'obviously' or 'definitely'. For the residents I spoke to in southern Sindh, it was obvious that it is the 'responsibility' of 'the state' to ensure the safety and security of its citizens in times of disasters. In fact, when I asked one interviewee from a particularly impoverished village in Thatta why

[11] The word *riyasat* shares a root with the word *raees*. While in Urdu, *raees* means a rich person, in Sindhi (and Arabic) it means the head of a clan. A *riyasat*, etymologically at least, brings in the personal/paternalistic element of an individual as a head of the state but also suggests that the *riyasat* has a relationship with its people known as *riaya*.

he thought it was 'obviously' the government's responsibility, he looked at me incredulously and said in an irritated tone:

> This is Pakistan, right? So obviously, it is the government of Pakistan that is responsible, not Indians or Americans.[12]

Villagers from a Leghari[13] *goth* in Badin identified themselves as belonging to the Ahl-e-Hadis *fiqh*[14] in Sunni Islam. They used a significant amount of religious terminology[15] in their conversation and seemed to be religiously devout and close to the Ahl-e-Hadis militant group, the Jamaat-ud-Dawa (JuD). They were of the view that the floods responsible for the misery and hardship in their lives were a calamitous disaster signifying God's wrath upon people who have become careless about their duties towards God and man.

At the same time, however, they also believed that it was the *hakumat*'s responsibility to keep them safe during the floods and they felt let down by a government that had failed them. The villagers explicitly stated that the floods were 'a punishment for our acts; you reap what you sow' and explained that it was indeed the questionable acts of people that resulted in the '*Allah ka azaab* (calamitous disaster from God)'. At the same time, however, in different parts of the conversation, they would return to the '*hakumat*' and that it is 'responsible for running the state system', and in failing to protect them, 'the state' had failed in fulfilling one of its primary duties. This conversation demonstrates just how compelling the *idea* of 'the state' is for people in southern Sindh.

---

[12] In an article published in the *New York Times* magazine, Harvard University Professor Michael Ignatieff writes on 'The Broken Contract' (2005) between the state and the citizens of Louisiana in the aftermath of Hurricane Katrina. It is striking just how comparable the words of this interviewee are to those of a woman stranded at the New Orleans Morial Convention Centre after her house had been destroyed by the hurricane in 2005. 'We are American', she told the news anchor reporting from the convention centre. Ignatieff states, '"We are American": that single sentence was a lesson in political obligation.'

[13] *Goths* in Sindh as in other parts of Pakistan are commonly named after individuals. This *goth* is among many in Sindh named after an individual belonging to the Baloch–Sindhi kinship group Leghari.

[14] In Arabic, the word means 'deep understanding' or 'full comprehension'. Here it refers to the principles of Islamic jurisprudence.

[15] Arabic words referring to the gracious qualities of God, such as *Alhamdulillah* and *Mashallah*, and more generally mentioning Allah and his will frequently.

While no one would have articulated it in this manner, people in this village clearly expected the *hakumat* to protect them from what they believed was the punishment and wrath of Allah, the divine master and creator of life and the universe. This is not an entirely unprecedented or far-fetched inference to make. Gupta's ethnography in north Indian cites one villager as saying, 'not even God looks after us, only the Congress', words that clearly indicate that for such villagers where divine power fails, state power begins. In lower Sindh, too, people seemed to have similar expectations, that 'the state' should have protected people from a disaster sent by divine will. This indicates just how powerful and prevalent 'the state' in southern Sindh is constructed to be.

In a different context, in a *goth* in Tharparkar, the majority of the individuals belonged to the Nauria *quom* (people).[16] As I explained in the previous chapter the landowning political family of Tharparkar, the Arbabs, belong to this kinship group. This was the only *goth* amongst all the villages and towns I did fieldwork in where I was clearly informed by the local cleric and a few community members that they had voted for the Arbabs because of this kinship connection. Evidence presented earlier also illustrated how local-level politics seemed more polarised across religious and socio-economic divides between the PPP and the Arbab family in Tharparkar. On a few occasions, those who politically aligned themselves with the Arbabs also emphasised the need for voting for 'one of our own'; this was something that did not seem to be a real concern in Badin or Thatta. This could partly be explained by the geography of Tharparkar; it is primarily a desert area on the border with India. This has resulted in successive governments, both before and after the creation of Pakistan, treating it as a marginal region in favour of more 'mainstream' parts of the country.[17] Hence, people are keen to vote for those who they are tied to by blood, marriage or other social relations, in an effort to not be ignored or forgotten by 'the state'.

In this particular conversation, too, the cleric and community members from this *goth* mentioned that they belonged to the Nauria *quom* three different

---

[16] While Urdu words such as *awaam* or *log* would be a more direct translation of the English word 'people', in this context this informant is speaking specifically of the Nauria people as a *quom*.

[17] I base this conclusion on Tharparkar's human development indicators, such as health and education, that are considerably lower than the average in Sindh, among the lowest in the country and comparable to countries like Somalia and South Sudan. See Reliefweb.org (available at https://reliefweb.int/disaster/dr-2014-000035-pak) for figures.

times and had to follow the wishes of 'our elders (*humary baray*)',[18] who were looking out for the best interests of the community, especially when it came to political issues. It was evident that, in this village, a number of people understood 'the state' to be something they needed to infiltrate with 'one of our own'. Yet their responses made it clear that the nature of this entity, 'the state', was more than just their social relations with the Arbabs. It was the duty of 'the state', and not of 'our elders', to keep them safe during a disaster. The cleric who seemed to emphasise the role of the 'elders' the most added that after 'the state', 'the second responsibility is of our elders, who must tell us what to do' during a disaster. In this context as well, regardless of the power of local elders and the strong association with the kinship group, the *idea* of 'the state' as a strong pervasive agent that is supposed to be the provider of safety to citizens at all times holds sway.

These ethnographies also make it possible to see that 'the state' in lower Sindh as a significant and omnipresent entity can in some situations be constitutive of social relations, along with other 'state effects' such as providing human security and other service provisions. The reverse, which is the perspective presented by the social structuralists, was not one that I encountered at any time during my seven months of fieldwork. The kinship connection or other social structures were never called upon to deliver those 'state effects' that people had already identified as the job of 'the state', such as delivering basic services.

This all-pervading construction of 'the state' by people in lower Sindh is based on ethnographic evidence but it is also etymologically consistent. The word *hakumat* derives from the root word *hukum*, which literally means 'to order'. It is also a word that is used when the relationship of the persons is not an equal one. *Hukum* is the word used to describe decrees passed by kings, commandments sent by God for people to follow, or even, in an unkind manner, the order given to servants or paid employees. A *hukum* is not questioned or challenged, just followed. The power and reach of the *hakumat* passing these *hukum*s is therefore awesome and awe-inspiring. The word *sarkar* has similar roots, where *sar* means 'chief' and *kar* is 'agent' or 'doer'. In this context, 'the state' is not just the 'chief doer'; *sarkar* was also widely used in both Urdu and Hindi to refer to the British colonial state.

[18] These are likely to be among the eldest people in the community. But it is not just age; they would also need to have some influence and powers of persuasion within their families and neighbourhoods.

Historically, given the wide reach and immense power exerted by the *Angraiz sarkar* (British colonial state), particularly during times of crises (see de Waal 1997, Davis 2001, Whitcombe 1993, Hall-Matthews 2005), the *idea* of an all-encompassing state able to do almost anything it wills itself to do is contextually understandable. In the post-colonial Indian context as well, 'the state' is often *imagined* in similar fashion. People were told, 'Place all your prayers at the feet of the *sarkaar*, the omnipotent and supremely enlightened state' (Fuller and Harriss 2009, 8).

My evidence from lower Sindh also revealed that 'the state' in popular *imagination* is still all-powerful and omnipresent, even supposed to prevent the 'wrath of God' because that is 'its job'. Within this context then it is possible to see that this construction of an all-pervasive state held on to by most people in southern Sindh also explains some of its inadequacies for regular people. In fact, Corbridge et al. support and extend this claim when they say, 'The weakness of the private sector in India propelled the country's new citizens towards *sarkar* for all manner of benefits and safeguards that the state could not meet in full or even in large part, and *which perhaps no state could ever meet,* (2005, 37; emphasis added). While doing fieldwork in lower Sindh, I regularly came across people's unfulfilled expectations from 'the state'; these remained unfulfilled not only because of the inadequacies in the 'state effects' but also because of the enormous scale and nature of such expectations.[19]

Demand-based expectations

It is now important to emphasise the representation aspect of this large and extensive entity 'the state'. Fuller and Harriss (2009, 4) explain the 'domination and extensiveness' of the Indian state, in Khilnani's words, 'towering over (Indian) society today is the state. This state is far from supremely effective … Yet it is today at the very centre of political imagination'. These authors emphasise, in fact perhaps even overemphasise, the democratic tradition in India as being responsible for this extensive state. They point out that all types of citizens see themselves as being able to exert influence on this ever-expanding state. In the words of another author, this has resulted in a 'demand overload' on 'the state' because of the assertive and energetic way 'the masses' have taken to the democratic process. Bureaucratic processes that were mysterious and distant

[19] This finding is consistent with the work of other ethnographers on the state in Pakistan as well. See Soekefeld (2012) and Verkaaik (2001).

are now a part of everyday structures and routines (Fuller and Harriss 2009, 24–25). I would argue that despite Pakistan's chequered democratic history, progressive politics and anti-military movements have played an important role in political society in Sindh (Paracha 2012). To a large extent, the demands on the state discussed by Fuller and Harriss (2009) in the Indian context capture the essence of the demands made on the state in this region of Pakistan as well.

In the Leghari village, when I asked people why they believed it was the government's responsibility to keep them safe during times of disaster, one middle-aged man who was a small landowner cultivating six acres of land replied:

> The government takes tax from us, prepares and announces a 'budget' (in English), it is (therefore) its responsibility to run the (state) system. Of course, some work (to ensure safety) should be undertaken by oneself, and we should not completely depend on government, but still, it is their job.

The fact that this individual had himself never been in a taxable income bracket to pay direct taxes[20] does not make his views invalid; they are still significant. This interviewee is not expressing angst at a government that takes his money and gives him nothing in return;[21] rather he is clearly articulating the demands he has on 'the state' and why he believes these are reasonable demands to make. For this interviewee, and numerous others I met in the field, the *sarkar* was omnipresent and expected to have God-like powers, or, as in the case of the Leghari *goth*, have powers perhaps beyond those of the divine in reaching people, but at the same time it was not revered and feared like God. The state's main role was to serve them and provide them with the services they needed. This demonstrates that regardless of a long tradition of electoral democracy (comparable to India), the people in lower Sindh expect to interact with a state that is responsive to their demands because that is what it is meant to do.

In trying to understand why the vast majority of the people thought it was government (*hakumat*) or state (*sarkar*) responsibility to keep them safe during times of natural disasters, I directly asked people, or tried to understand through conversation, why they believed the state was responsible. In this case, the answers I received most frequently were variations of 'because we

---

[20] Only 0.6 per cent of Pakistan's population pays income tax; the state, therefore, relies on indirect taxation for revenues, the burden of which falls disproportionately on lower-income citizens such as this informant (Khan 2012).

[21] A common complaint of the middle-classes in urban Pakistan.

voted for them and put them in office', or 'it is therefore their "*farz*" (duty)'. There were some versions of this answer that specifically included references to the incumbent PPP election promises and party ideology, highlighting the importance of these factors in producing the 'state effect'. It was also noticeable that amongst many of my informants, the lines between the democratic state and the PPP state in Sindh were blurred; hence, they often made references to the PPP state and 'the state' interchangeably.

Since 1972, the PPP has managed to form the government in Sindh in all years, except during the two military regimes (1977–1988 and 1999–2007) and briefly during Nawaz Sharif's (PML–N) second term in office (1997–1999). Given that, for almost a generation now, the people in lower Sindh have either experienced a state run by the PPP after an election or an army-run state after a military coup, it is unsurprising that they distinguish between the martial-law state and the democratic state but not between PPP and 'the state' during civilian rule. Informants often saw the PPP as synonymous with 'the state' because I was doing fieldwork during a democratic time in Pakistan with the PPP in power both at the centre and in the province of Sindh. They also saw this 'state' as being responsible for providing them basic security and safety even during normal times.

Shakeel *bhai*, a Baloch Sindhi belonging to the Lund kinship group, was one of my closest contacts and one I met with frequently over many months. This citizen of Badin district, who owned a small shop in the town of Shadi Large, believed it was the PPP state's responsibility to provide basic human security. In one of our conversations, he said:

> It is their 'duty' [in English] (to provide human security[22]). We voted for PPP because we were told 'dictatorship' [in English] will end. People will get '*roti* (bread), *kapra* (clothing), *makan* (shelter)'[23] and means of employment.[24] But this democracy is worse than dictatorship.

Despite being disheartened by the PPP state and its failure to deliver economic development, in one of our last conversations he finally states:

---

[22] He was not referring to 'security' as a military-led or state-centred venture. His understanding of security seemed to relate quite closely to the concept of human security and wider basic needs.

[23] The popular slogan and populist ideology used by Zulfikar Ali Bhutto (the founder of the party) to win the election in 1973.

[24] Together these features can guarantee a certain level of human security.

> I have thought about not voting for the PPP in the next election, but the problem is if I don't vote for them, then who do I vote for? What is the alternative?

My conversations with Shakeel *bhai*, in which he often talked of how demoralised he was by the PPP government, revealed something more significant than just disappointment. He was this unhappy about the system because he had high expectations of the democratic state as being responsive to him and his needs. He told me a detailed story of how he had led a group of people in his village 'all the way up to the high court' in an attempt to get drinking water to his village, which was a few miles away from the city where his shop was located. This story began three years before I met Shakeel *bhai*, in the DCO office where a 'clerk' to one of the 'big officers' told him their village could not get drinking water till a pipeline was laid. Shakeel *bhai* explained how he, with the help of his small group of village supporters, went about writing *darkhuasts* (applications) to various public officials and meeting with a number of government employees. Despite receiving official letters and arranging several meetings with them, once he realised no action was being taken, he filed a case with the district court, believing that a 'court order' would force the district government into action. At the time of my last meeting with Shakeel *bhai*, his case was awaiting summary judgment at the Sindh High Court; he said sadly, 'Now our file is so heavy, it weighs five kilos because we have been collecting all correspondence and letters from the government from day one and yet nothing has happened.'

This interviewee was understandably disheartened with 'the state's'[25] response to his demand for drinking water, something he considers a *bunyaadi haq* (fundamental right) and, therefore, is meant to be provided by the 'the state'. Far from illustrating that the state was 'absent', however, the experience of this informant shows that 'the state' was recognising and engaging with its citizen. This small shop owner from the obscure town of Shadi Large knew how to engage with 'the state' and he utilised various channels to do so. In the words of Gupta, 'He understands its composition as an entity with multiple layers and diverse locales and centres' (Gupta 1995, 391).

Shakeel *bhai* also had an expectation that 'the state' would respond to him at these different levels. In fact, Matthew Hull's (2012) work shows

[25] In his case, it was not only at a local level but up to a much higher provincial body: the high court.

that these practices of writing through the governmentality of paper are the means through which people participate in government in Pakistan. Equally important is the fact that the state did fulfil that request and responded through letters, orders and judgments, albeit not at the speed Shakeel *bhai* was expecting. Returning to what Fuller and Harriss said, about 'the masses' having bought into democracy in India leading to the 'routinisation of state authority', Shakeel *bhai*'s interactions with 'the state' 'nonetheless, (illustrate) in all those "everyday structures", bureaucratic procedures have now become extremely familiar, so that demotic discourse about government is at least as much modernist as traditionalist' (2009, 19). Both the *dharna* (protest sit-in) and the *darkhuast* (application) are indigenised instruments regularly used to demand rights and get responses, even if they are ineffective, from 'the state' in lower Sindh.

While it is not possible to present all the evidence from the field in support of this fact, my research in lower Sindh consistently showed that the *construction* of the omnipresent, all-encompassing *sarkar* was almost always one that was responsible for and (meant to be) responsive to the citizens it was thought to serve. As this section has illustrated, the idea of the state is ontologically fragmented, means different things to different people relative to people's own position within it, and is even conflated with the political party in power. Yet the state is at the very centre of political imagination in lower Sindh. When it comes to delivering services such as *tarakiyaafta kaam* (developmental projects) or *bunyaadi haq* (fundamental rights) such as drinking water, or even security and safety such as during times of disaster, there is no question that, in lower Sindh, it is seen to be the state's 'job' and 'duty' to provide these.

Seen another way, this also effectively highlights the limits of 'state effects' in areas such as lower Sindh. The state is invoked to provide rights, human security and large-scale projects, things that cannot be addressed at an individual or community level. Soekefeld (2012), in his work on the politics after a landslide in the northern areas of Pakistan, points out that practically speaking the state did not matter too much in the everyday lives of people. Once the landslide occurred, however, expectations that the state would be everywhere and do everything – in terms of disaster response – were extremely high. People in the area of Gilgit–Baltistan believed that the state would be able to reach out and help every single individual and community affected. Hence, Soekefeld's work also supports my earlier findings that the state in Pakistan is often 'burdened with high and mostly unaccomplishable expectations' (2012, 203). Furthermore, it also reveals to some extent that it is not from the 'everyday state' in Pakistan, be it lower Sindh or Gilgit–Baltistan, that people have high expectations and a surety that it will respond, but from the 'exceptional state'; in exceptionally trying times, the state is expected to respond to them as demanding citizens.

Hence, the citizen enters this debate as the intended beneficiary of the interaction with 'the state'. As the section that follows illustrates, constructing a narrative of 'citizenship' in lower Sindh was more complicated than that of 'the state'. This was partly a result of my own short-sightedness and partly a consequence of contextual political processes. My understanding and vocabulary of 'rights', 'entitlements' and 'citizenship' were almost entirely a product of my Western education and ideals, and talking about this in the context of lower Sindh required me to listen more carefully and learn to read between the lines as well.

Citizenship: 'What do you mean?'

It is not possible to speak of the nature of 'the state' and its construction at a local level in lower Sindh without discussing what this says about the framework for citizenship and how that is exercised (or not) in my field site. I follow in the tradition of scholars such as Trouillot (2001) who argue that it is not possible to first theorise the state and then examine society or even vice versa. 'Rather, state and society are bound by the historical bloc which takes the form of the specific social contract of and, thus, the hegemony deployed in a particular social formation' (2001, 127). To understand this social contract and its social formation I do not see the state and citizenship as two unique and separate wholes that must be explained in distinct and different ways. Instead, I build on the argument made earlier, about the pervasive and omnipresent state that encompasses much more than social relations, and illustrate that my informants in lower Sindh have a lived understanding of citizenship that has not been adequately addressed in existing literature on this subject.

While popular literature has often been valuable in understanding the shortcomings of the state in the area of 'citizenship building' there is more beyond these frameworks that is worthy of academic attention. It is partly an issue of vantage point and partly of how citizenship has been examined so far. If the concept and categories of citizenship are exogenously imposed 'from above', but proof of its existence is sought in textbooks and in local language in the field, there is no doubt that there is limited evidence that Pakistanis in areas such as lower Sindh have any universally constructed ideal of 'citizenship'.

If, however, one looks beyond such frameworks, it is quite evident that people have a lived understanding of what it means to be citizen, which is worth examining in greater detail.

Some of the answers I received from my interviewees early in my fieldwork also seemed to support this master narrative that there is no understanding of citizenship in Pakistan. This seemed particularly apparent when I interviewed people who ascribed to different political ideologies and struggled with the idea of a citizen of Pakistan. Dr Niaz Kilyani, the Chairman of the Jeay Sindh Quami Mahaz (JSQM), an ethnic nationalist political party with a poor electoral record but founded on the idea of getting Sindh independence from Pakistan, said there is no such thing as a citizen of Pakistan because:

> The state of Pakistan is unrealistically based and a mythical fiction. There is no such thing as a Muslim nation; Punjabis are a different nation, Baluchi are different, Pathans are different and we Sindhis have our own nation... (Today) Sindh is not independent – it is a slave of Pakistan.

It was only after some time that I was able to look back at his words and see that it was not that Dr Kilyani does not have an understanding of what it means to be a citizen. In fact, he has a very certain understanding of the concept that includes ideals of social and political equality, but that he is very deliberately and cleverly 'mixing up' ideas of citizenship with those of nationality and religion in order to make citizenship in Pakistan seem meaningless. Dr Kilyani's inability to construct citizenship is not a result of failure of understanding but predicated on his political ideology and that of his party. His deliberate construction of citizenship in a manner that suited his political ideals was also replicated by other political agents as well.

It was equally problematic to discuss the idea of a citizen of the state of Pakistan when I spoke with an active JuD militant who had participated in *jihad* in Afghanistan and Kashmir. He said a citizen of Pakistan was:

> Any person who loves this country of Pakistan and is willing to make sacrifices for its *difa* (defence). It doesn't matter if they are Baloch, Sindhi or Punjabi – all are brothers.

For this interviewee, what seems to serve as a foundation for building citizenship across national and ethno-linguist divides was people in Pakistan subscribing to *jihadi* ideologies of the JuD or other such groups. While this interpretation of citizenship clearly seems to be 'mixing up' issues of religion and nationhood with citizenship, it is once again evident that, much like with Dr Kilyani, this was a deliberate effort on his part. Instead of illustrating a 'failure' in understanding citizenship, these political agents have demonstrated a clear and cogent understanding of this concept and participate in this idea of citizenship. In fact, they even take ownership of it in creative and clever ways.

Other than political agents who were deliberately confusing the concept of citizenship to meet certain political purposes, I also found it difficult to have a conversation about citizenship because of vernacular language barriers. I will highlight why having a conversation about a *shehri* of Pakistan is a difficult exercise in contexts such as lower Sindh. For now, however, it is critical to point out that in spite of political agents and leaders deliberately confusing the concept of citizenship to suit their agenda, and the limited vocabulary in discussing citizenship, people were aware of their rights and roles within the state–citizen interaction and were able to intellectually construct for themselves what this means.

It is significant that 'the state' as a concept is well-developed or, as some scholars have argued, 'over-developed' (Alavi 1972) in the case of Pakistan, which could explain why there are many words to refer to it in conversation. Even while it means different things to different people, there is a common thread of an omnipresent *hakumat* responsible for its people[26] running through all such constructions of 'the state'. The construction of 'citizenship' in lower Sindh is more complicated.

Citizenship is a difficult concept to engage with ethnographically in lower Sindh when the language and the context for the concept's development have been Western, liberal and democratic. Bachmann and Staerkle (2003) trace the evolution of 'citizenship' from its Latin origins (*civitas*) taken from the Greek term *polites*. The Greeks, though founders of this concept, were in favour of citizenship by exclusion. Those who did not belong to Athens, along with women, children and slaves, were all unable to 'participate in the citizenship' of ancient Greece. Citizenship then clearly began as a privilege. The evolution of this concept through the Roman empire, and the anti-monarchical eighteenth-century republics in France and the USA to 'modern citizenship in the Nation-

---

[26] This finding is broadly supported by Khan's (2007) ethnographic study of a village in upper Sindh as well, where she notes that services such as irrigation, water tanks, and the like are all seen to be the responsibility of this *hakumat*.

State' has resulted in the concept changing from 'privilege' to '"social process" through which individuals and social groups engage in claiming, expanding or losing rights' (Bachmann and Staerkle 2003, 22). Hence, there is a history of social and political struggle that came to define what 'citizenship' means in Western thought.

Unsurprisingly, then, there is no exact translation of the word 'citizenship' in Urdu or Sindhi.[27] The people of Pakistan (and thereby Sindh), until only seventy years ago, were 'subjects' of the British Crown, and this transition from 'subject to citizen' has been discussed in many recent works on citizenship (see Jayal 2013 and Sherman, Gould and Ansari 2011). The word commonly used in both Urdu and Sindhi for citizen is *shehri*. It comes from the word *shehr*, which means city. Literally translated then, a *shehri* is a resident of the *shehr*;[28] it fails to capture much of the implicit understanding around rights and entitlements that are automatically associated with the English word 'citizenship' as it stands today. In conversations with informants in lower Sindh who had experienced the flooding disaster and had been directly affected by it, 'the state' and often its failings came up quite quickly and almost organically. Once 'the state' had been mentioned by one or more of the interviewees, and I began to ask more questions about its role, the responsibilities of 'the state' and what it ought to do, or not do, also came about in a natural way. At the same time, the (Western) construction of the self as a citizen – for people to feel that it is the responsibility of the state to provide protection and security because they are citizens of the state and entitled to it – was not immediately obvious in the context of lower Sindh. People saw themselves in relation to the omnipresent entity of 'the state', but did not speak of this as a relationship of 'citizenship'. I demonstrate that this is more a limitation of such language and vocabulary and less a failure of understanding.

When Shakeel *bhai* talked of his struggle to get drinking water to his village, he said '(access to) water is our fundamental right (*bunyaadi haq*)'. In a conversation with two young Kohli (schedule caste) Hindu men they said that for the state 'we are lesser than them (Muslims), they have higher status (*darja*)'; however they felt that 'equal rights should be given to all'. Also, as

[27] Interestingly this is not true of Hindi; Gupta (1995) translates citizen as *nagarik* in Hindi.

[28] It is ironical that city-dwellers compared to their rural counterparts have a less personal relationship with state institutions, and yet the word for the membership of the state is a synonym of city-dweller.

stated earlier, a number of interviewees mentioned that they had 'voted' for the government and hence the government should provide safety and security in the aftermath of a disaster. In the Leghari village, the interviewee said that people give tax to the government and that is why they should be provided protection by the state. It was, therefore, evident on a number of occasions that people are aware of their rights as citizens,[29] and even recognise that they have a relationship with the state based on provision of certain rights and services. Yet they are still unable to speak of this in terms of 'citizenship', a problem of vocabulary that researchers like me, trained in the Western tradition, have been slow to recognise. The inability to articulate this idea partly explains why scholars have found it difficult to find empirical evidence of 'citizenship' in Pakistan. Hence, as stated earlier, it is necessary that the ethnography is employed to move beyond the 'empirically obvious', and understand that lack of vernacular vocabulary does not make the ideals around citizenship 'absent' in non-urban Pakistan (Trouillot 2001).

My attempts to ask people in the villages, towns and cities of lower Sindh directly, during conversations or in more formal interviews, what makes someone a *shehri* of Pakistan, or how they would define a *shehri*, proved to be fairly unsuccessful. The responses I heard most often were: 'I don't understand your question' or 'Huh? What do you mean (*kya matlab*)?'

In questioning this issue of being a *shehri*, I expected my informants to respond by telling me about 'citizenship' in the way that they spoke about the *sarkar* or the *hakumat*, which was always in a manner where I was immediately able to understand that they were talking about the 'state' or the 'government'. The parallel with citizenship, however, was not as evident. In fact, Sharma's work (2011) on subaltern notions of rights and justice has laid some of the groundwork for this exploration into local understandings of citizenship. Based on her research in a village in north India she states, 'Their (subaltern) citizenship claims draw upon multiple discourses, extending well beyond the law, mixing morality and materiality, ethics and politics, and traditional and bureaucratic languages of power, and thereby muddy the very distinctions on which modern citizenship rests' (Sharma 2011, 965). It was evident to me that people in lower Sindh were keenly aware of their rights and able to articulate them. They were also able to list services that should be provided by 'the state'; this did not, however, mean that they immediately associated the word *shehri* in terms of a modern citizenship discourse applied to Pakistan.

---

[29] This is supported by Lall's (2012) research as well.

At the same time, it is also important to reflect on my own positionality as a researcher. Admittedly unconsciously, I was expecting the word *shehri* to represent and contain all the implicit ideals for the people of lower Sindh that the word 'citizenship' represents for me as a Pakistani educated in the Western tradition, and that I would find it easier to identify a construction of citizenship that included the 'normative burden' of participation, inclusion, or universality in a recognizable way. It was not until many months after my conversations with Dr Kilyani and the JuD informant that I was able to see the extent of their participation and ownership in their construction of citizenship in a way that made it their own. For a long time, I only understood it to mean that they were unable to answer my questions on citizenship, using *shehri* as a framework. I encountered similar delays in my own understanding of how my informants were constructing citizenship in lower Sindh. Eventually it was evident to me that, even if they were not able to articulate it in a way that was familiar to me, my informants had a lived experience of citizenship.

While speaking to Ali, a small shop owner in Tharparkar, I received a confused look and a shrug when I tried to talk to him about being a *shehri*. The moment, however, someone else in the shop mentioned the Pakistani National Identity Card (NIC), commonly known as the 'NADRA (National Database and Registration Authority) card' in Pakistan, the conversation took a very interesting turn. He said:

> A Pakistani citizen can be identified with this card. This doesn't mean that we know what his intentions are or how he feels about Pakistan, whether he is interested in living here or not, but the card tells us that he is *pukko* (proper) Pakistani ... Whoever has an NIC is Pakistani ... In my area now, over 90 per cent of people have had NICs made. Earlier it was not this common, but now, after becoming a computerised system, teams came to every home.

Ali was not able to talk about the amorphous *idea* of citizenship earlier in the conversation but he was able to instantly make the connection between the NIC and being a citizen of Pakistan. What Ali states then is essentially 'one core aspect(s)[30] of the citizenship question, viz. citizenship as legal status' (Jayal 2013, 13). Anyone who has a NADRA-issued NIC is legally a citizen of Pakistan, entitled to all the rights and services of the state. This ID card service has existed since the 1970s but the push towards getting everyone

---

[30] The other two being citizenship as rights and entitlements and citizenship as a form of identity and belonging.

registered, and computerising the database, emerged out of the post-9/11 security imperatives in the country (Khan 2012). Regardless of the motives behind the registration drive, this was a supply-driven intervention pushed by the state to include all citizens within a legal–institutional framework. There is significant evidence that, today, on the ground, it is being interpreted as a legal right of citizenship, something I will elaborate in the next chapter.

In a conversation some months earlier, while engaging with questions of being a *shehri*, I asked a group of middle-aged men, in the town of Keti Bandar in Thatta district, who they would consider a *shehri* of Pakistan. One of them, Javed, suggested that a *shehri* 'must have a (NIC) card'; his friend quickly added, 'But the card is not enough,' and went on to explain:

> A citizen is one who abides by the laws in Pakistan, who thinks about (the well-being of) Pakistan and loves Pakistan, has sympathy towards the country. He must do something or the other (positive) for Pakistan. He cannot be carrying out bomb blasts and other (terrorist) activities and also be a Pakistani citizen, (in that case) even if he has a card and is also born here but still for *us* he will not be a Pakistani. These are things that people with ID cards are doing.

This interviewee makes an important point, and one that supports Ali's construction of citizenship as legal status. In emphasising that even if an individual has an NIC card but engages in activities they find reprehensible, for *them* – in their *construction* – he is not a citizen of Pakistan, despite being considered as such by the state. Clearly, then, for this group of people in Thatta hundreds of miles away from the village in Tharparkar, the idea that anyone with 'a card' is legally considered a citizen of the state is also beginning to take root. While both interviewees might not yet be talking about the 'normative burden' of citizenship in terms of rights and entitlements that I would easily have understood, they are still confident about who 'the state' sees as a legal citizen. This legal construction of the citizen has been supply-driven and emerged from the services of the state, rather than being based in the demands of people.[31] It was on receiving services, such as the NIC card and often times, as Ali points out, while staying at home that made them realise that this omnipresent state was able to reach out to them. Their citizenship had now taken a tangible and physical form. This citizenship emerged not only

[31] Sarwar (forthcoming) also makes this wider point, that the Pakistani welfare state is entirely supply-driven.

through grassroots struggles but as an effect of the state widening its reach and acknowledging people as such.

Kabeer, Mumtaz and Sayeed (2010) in their work on citizenship in Pakistan emphasise the fragmented nature of Pakistani society and point to the failure of the citizenship project in binding the various ethnicities, castes and religions into citizens of the state.[32] They specifically recommend that the state should reach out to its citizens using social protection interventions, especially social transfer programmes, to create a foundation for citizenship in Pakistan.[33] These authors make two suggestions regarding the design of such a programme. First, they state that it should be universal; 'ideally, this would be a transfer programme that provided a universal minimum social floor, that transcended parochial identities and affiliations, that was financed by a "citizenship" tax with exemptions based on "means" rather than identity and that, in principle, should be available to all citizens' (Kabeer, Mumtaz and Sayeed 2010, 16). Second, they also suggest that one way of establishing this 'universe of eligible beneficiaries' (Kabeer, Mumtaz and Sayeed 2010, 15) is through the NADRA ID cards. The same year that their paper was published, the Pakistan government initiated the Benazir Income Support Programme (BISP) along very similar lines as suggested by Kabeer, Mumtaz and Sayeed (2010) in their work. The BISP is a relatively successful social transfer programme, and in all villages and towns that I undertook fieldwork, there was some presence of this programme and people admitted to receiving regular payments. Even though it was not immediately obvious to people in the same way, given that the programme was only a few years old and one that had a number of teething problems in the beginning, the BISP was another example of the state trying to reach out to its citizens in an attempt to build universal citizenship.

Other than this supply-driven, legal citizenship that Ali and Javed were able to recognise, there were other ideas of citizenship that were present. I had a conversation with Mohammad Mallah, a fisherman in his late thirties, in a fishing village in Thatta, who had a very clear and cogent idea of citizenship. When I asked him who he thinks is a Pakistani *shehri*, he articulated his response in the following words, without any pauses or breaks:

---

[32] Lieven (2011) refers to this phenomena as 'Weak State, Strong Societies'.

[33] Such policies have been pursued with the explicit goal of building citizenship in countries in the Caribbean and in South Africa. See Ashwill and Norton (2011) and Lund (2009).

(*a*) A Pakistani *shehri* is a person who is able to play a role in the way that the government runs the state and in political representation. For example, after we vote we feel that our 'role' (in English) (in political representation) is over, as if our only purpose as Pakistani citizens is to cast our vote. We are told 'give your vote and then step aside (*vote do aur baith jao*)'. So, a Pakistani citizen is an individual who is able to exercise some kind of role in the *gornment*. Only such an individual can be considered a *shehri* of Pakistan and not anyone who lives here. I mean tomorrow an American person can come and live here and say I am Pakistani too but he will not just become Pakistani. (*b*) And people (*logon*) should have the right to local resources, they should belong to the public (*awam*) but the resources of Pakistan are in the control of the 10 per cent elite classes (*amrah*) on top who are the primary beneficiaries, while ordinary people are getting no benefits from them at all. Take for instance the oil that is extracted from Badin,[34] the petrol that comes from there is taken away by the 'federal government' (in English) and Sindh gets nothing.[35] To such an extent that even the cleric in the mosque there has been brought to the area from elsewhere, from a different province. We are Pakistani, what I am saying is not that no one should be allowed to come from Punjab to earn a living (*rozi*) here, my point is a different one. What I am saying is that the first 'right' (in English) to local resources should belong to the local populace. (*c*) Now, 'fishing' (in English) is common in this area (as a means of livelihood), but we are the ones toiling to catch the fish and others come and take away our catch, until very recently this is what was happening; that system has just ended. Before, local fishermen would go out and catch fish but the local

---

[34] According to the *District Vision Badin* (2006), written by the environmental NGO IUCN, funded by the World Bank and published by the District Government of Badin, oil production in Badin accounts for 44 per cent of oil produced in Pakistan. Available at http://cmsdata.iucn.org/downloads/badin_idv.pdf (accessed on 16 August 2016).

[35] The complaint expressed by the interviewee, of an extractive federal government that takes revenues from the provinces but fails to allocate resources to the provinces equally and effectively, is a common one in the provinces of Sindh and Balochistan. These tensions within Pakistan's federal system are well documented. The state has historically been seen to be top heavy with power dominated by the centre. The 18th Constitution Amendment of 2010 and the National Finance Commission (NFC) Award were steps taken by the PPP government to change that structure, though at the time that I was doing fieldwork it was too soon to be able to see any visible changes on the ground. A detailed analysis on Pakistan's federal challenges can be found in the work of Katherine Adeney (2012, 2009 and 2007).

> strongman (*wadera*)[36] in collusion with the government would take away all his fish, this was called the contract system (*thaikaydaari*). Only after the Pakistan Fisherfolk Forum began struggle against the injustice was it abolished about four or five years ago.[37] This should not be an accepted system and resources should be for the people.[38]

In this remarkably precise monologue, Mohammad Mallah captures the essence of citizenship as (*a*) political participation, (*b*) local ownership and (*c*) entitlements. While the first two are fairly self-evident, I use the term 'entitlements' from Amartya Sen's entitlement approach discussed in Chapter 2. In Sen's words, 'Cases of starvation and famines across the world arise not from people being deprived of things to which they are entitled, but from people not being entitled, in the prevailing legal system of institutional rights, to adequate means for survival' (ODI 2001). Rubin explains this as 'famine prevention must therefore be concerned with the protection of entitlements rather than concerned with food availability per se' (2009, 623). It is true that Mohammad Mallah was not suffering from starvation or famine-like conditions. Yet Sen states an individual's entitlements 'are the totality of things he can have by virtue of his rights' (1981, 72). Clearly then, a system that legally obliged this man to give away his catch, the fruits of his labour, to those who held contracts, forcing him to lead a life of poverty and destitution, was resulting in

[36] Colloquially, the word 'wadera' is used to refer to anyone who is able to exercise power over others; in this case the fisherfolk are referring to individuals who own the licenses to fish as *wadera* though they probably own no land.

[37] The Pakistan Fisherfolk Forum (PFF) is often referred to as a civil society organisation and also as a social movement. It came into being on 5 May 1998 to struggle against what fishermen in Sindh considered an exploitative system of contract fishing in inland waters. In 1980, the Sindh government introduced the Sindh Fisheries Ordinance that stipulated, 'Government may, by general or special order, grant license or lease for fishing in any public waters on such terms and conditions and on payment of such fees as may be prescribed.' This allowed politically influential individuals to attain contracts and use their 'ownership' of these waters to charge fishermen exorbitant licenses or pay them far below market value for their catch. The PFF was the platform that fishermen used to politically campaign against this practice and hold protests, hunger strikes, and so on, until finally the Sindh government relented and in 2007, under the rule of Pervez Musharraf, this system was abolished.

[38] Mohammad Mallah's connection to the PFF and participation in its wider social movement may well be the reason for this precise articulation of demands.

an obvious failure of economic entitlements. The interviewee himself was clear that effective citizenship would not allow such an entitlement failure to occur.

The three aspects of citizenship described by this interviewee resemble the ideas of British sociologist T. H. Marshall mentioned earlier. He highlights three elements of citizenship: 'The civil element (the rights necessary for individual freedom), the political element (the right to participate in the exercise of political power), and the social element', which included a broad range of factors necessary to 'live the life of a civilised being according to the standards prevailing in the society' (Jayal 2013, 5). It seems that some of Mohammad Mallah's political and social ideals were not too different from the European sociologist considered to be the father of modern social citizenship.

It is true that Pakistan's chequered democratic history, with rule by unrepresentative military generals, and powerful hereditary social relations have resulted in people in areas such as lower Sindh rarely demonstrating a universal understanding of citizenship. At the same time, it also seems that people in lower Sindh do not live in a space–time vortex; they are part of and also affected by social and political changes taking place in wider society. Mohammad Mallah's remarkable ideas on citizenship could well have been influenced by his limited involvement with the PFF. This makes it clear that the opening of democratic spaces, such as progressive social movements, are also contributing towards evolving ideas of citizenship. This suggests that, on the ground, these ideals are in flux and are being challenged and renegotiated constantly. Not only did Mohammad Mallah demonstrate a keen awareness of his understanding and rights as a citizen but parts of his conversation, where he refers to the PFF social movement resulting in changing an unjust system, also illustrated, for me, the extent to which he was able to claim and exercise this citizenship.

This interviewee, and some of his friends who also contributed to our discussion, had bought into a narrative their own disenfranchised and disempowered condition. One of them said, 'I am a poor man, what can I do (*hum toh ghareeb aadmi hai, kya kar sakta hai*)', twice in the conversation. He also implied that he felt social pressure, and, though to a lesser extent, even economic pressure (he works part-time as a hired hand on the land of a person close to the Sheerazis), to vote for the Sheerazi family in Thatta. Yet, a little later in the day, when explaining why he preferred a democratic regime over the military government, he said, 'I want democracy because I can go to the *wadera* and even show him attitude (*akar bhee dekha saktay hai*) but who will ever go to the army? If I go and ask the *wadera* for something and he doesn't do my work, I can go and grab his collar; who will go and grab the army by the collar?' Mohammad Mollah also gave me a similar explanation of voters not making their decision entirely independently, and often feeling social pressure to vote for the candidate that their friends and family were voting for, but then later also went on to state, with a considerable amount of excitement, that this time he would not vote for the then-incumbent PPP. He said that he along with his friends had decided to support a relatively obscure new candidate contesting on a 'Sindhi nationalist (*quom parast*)' party, Awami Tehreek, ticket. 'The *wadera* can go to hell,' he said.

The PFF's landmark struggle, referred to by Mohammad Mollah, culminated in the abolition of the contract system on inland fisheries in 2007 (*Dawn News* 2007) and later in the passing of the Fisheries (Amendment) Bill 2011, to this effect, in the Sindh Assembly in 2011 (*The Nation* 2011). These were significant political developments that were made possible because of the 'political participation' of fishermen, such as Mohammad Mollah and his friends, who contributed to this cause. Further evidence of their political empowerment was visible in other ways. They were publicly supporting an unknown candidate from a Sindhi nationalist party over two powerful political forces (the PPP and the Sheerazis) in Thatta. Additionally, the friend had also rather flippantly expressed the importance of *wadera* 'collar grabbing' as the reason why he supported democratic rule. The nearly (but not quite) Marshall-ian articulation of citizenship and, as demonstrated, the various ways in which Mohammad Mallah (and his friends) regularly exercised this citizenship all point to the need to look beyond the dominant scholarship on citizenship in Pakistan. One can no longer continue to discuss the failure of the citizenship project either as a result of people's inability to understand a concept that gets mixed up with religion and nationhood or as a result of oppressive social structures that do not allow a foundation for citizenship to develop.

This ethnography of the state demonstrates that people in lower Sindh have an understanding of the state beyond just social structures and relationships of caste and kin. They see the state as an omnipresent and pervasive entity that may often be disjointed in construction, and may consist of encounters with powerful individuals or families. But when it comes to delivering certain essential services or rights, it is always seen to be the state's job to provide those. Additionally, it is also evident that, despite historical inadequacies, including the building of a democratic framework in Pakistan, there is increasing evidence for a lived understanding of citizenship on the ground. It includes citizenship effects such as political participation and entitlements and has been driven by social and political change. While aspects such as state interventions in granting legal rights of citizenship through a NADRA ID card, or universalising citizenship social transfers, have been supply-driven aspects of citizenship pushed by the state, citizens have also demanded more of the state. Progressive social movements, greater representation, and engaging with the *wadera* not as a traditional leader but someone who is meant to deliver a state service are all signs that, at a local level, a tangible social contract exists between the state and its citizens in lower Sindh. The state is neither as 'absent' nor citizenship as 'failed' as some literature seems to suggest.

What Does This Mean for the Ethnographic Social Contract in Pakistan?

Much of the literature I have cited in the discussion on ethnography of the state and citizenship acknowledges and celebrates a certain degree of fluidity in categories of analysis and understands ideas being in flux or transition. Following in that tradition, it is possible for me to state that the post-colonial social contract, as defined by Keating (2007, 5), seems to be the basis of the relationship between the state and the citizen in lower Sindh. It is explained as 'real' but not 'fixed', and one where the actors, as I have illustrated, are negotiating and rewriting the terms and conditions of democratic governance. The state is defined by local encounters that must be personable and individually tailored but a larger entity, the *sarkar*, must also fulfil more 'lofty ideals' of human security and fundamental rights. At times, the expectations from the state include taking over when divine power, social capital and all other belief systems that can be invoked have failed.

The state, however, is not just a belief system; it is also an 'effect' that is created as a result of the transactions and mediations that people enter into with those who they see as part of this system. This also means that, for the most part, people in lower Sindh, like in all other parts of Pakistan, understand and participate in the state through their engagement with the *dharna* (protest sit-in) and the *darkhuast* (application). The state in Pakistan is also evolving and, as I have illustrated, coming up with ways through which to reach out to citizens on a common and universal platform, often even transcending primordial ties of caste and kinship.

The supply-driven initiatives (regardless where that push came from) have also intersected with people's own construction and experience of citizenship to create a local framework of understanding of this ideal of citizenship. This includes ideas of *wadera*s being politically important, and maybe even bureaucratically necessary for access, but equally also includes constructions of rights and entitlements as citizens of a bigger entity – 'the state'. Citizenship is, in fact, being exercised regularly by people in Pakistan and was extremely evident in the aftermath of the flooding disasters of 2010 and 2011 as the next chapter will illustrate.

CHAPTER 4

Advancing 'Disaster Citizenship'

This chapter continues the story of a social contract in Pakistan, having illustrated so far that there is an ethnographic social contract on the ground and that part of this contract is based on the state providing basic rights and services. This is an understanding that is further complemented by citizenship and citizens who are also demanding more of the state. This chapter demonstrates that contrary to popular accounts and media narratives suggesting that the social contract had 'broken' in the aftermath of the flooding disaster in 2010 and 2011, fracturing the relationship between the state and its citizens. My evidence from three districts in Pakistan illustrates that the state's disaster response interacted with citizenship demands of people, to push along a more progressive social contract and transform citizenship in the region. In using the social contract as an analytical framework, Pelling states that the indicators of such a transformation would be holding political institutions of power and influence to account 'to include the marginalised and future generations' as well (2011, 87).

Pelling and Dill's (2010) work on disasters (2010) describes the 'transformative political space' opened in the aftermath of a disaster. They illustrate how a disaster serves as a 'tipping point', when the state has been unable to provide basic human security to its citizens, resulting in a contestation of rights and entitlements, and creating a political moment for change. These authors emphasize that literature on the direction of this 'change' falls in two camps. One body of work sees disasters as accelerating the pre-disaster processes of change, while another illustrates how 'disasters can catalyze a "critical juncture"' resulting in irreversible political change (Pelling and Dill 2010). While this chapter will illustrate how progressive constructions of citizenship were strengthened in the post-disaster moment, it is important to recognise this moment as a critical juncture. A 'choice point' in the life of a system or regime, when one option is adopted between two or more options, resulting in the system's/regime's ability to embark on a certain path of development (Capoccia and Kelemen 2007). This juncture can be defined as the political moment in the aftermath of a disaster when the very terms of the relationship between the state and its citizens are being renegotiated, resulting in a reimagining of the social contract.

The transformation in this case then is about redefining the notion of a citizen and their rights and entitlements. Such a progression in citizenship could be immensely powerful if it were driven by social and political processes that are then formalised into law and institutional mandates. This would perhaps even make the process comparable to the European Enlightenment that ushered a new era of state–citizen relations in the Western world around the eighteenth century. For the majority of the world's population who live in places such as lower Sindh in Pakistan, however, the *interactions* between social and political *structures* and *actors* can lead to a new, often 'bottom up' understanding of processes of citizenship without it being *institutionalised*. The transformation being discussed here is not a legislative one per se but substantive, evident in the lived experience of citizenship, in the region of southern Pakistan that was affected by a large-scale flooding disaster. The interaction between the state and its citizens was also moved along by internal and external drivers, resulting in transformative outcomes for citizenship and a social contract that was quite different to what was commonly being portrayed as prevalent in the region.

Understanding Disaster Citizenship

Anthropologists working on disasters emphasise the blurred boundaries and complex spaces that emerge in the aftermath of disasters. For instance, Loureiro's ethnography (2012) of a post-earthquake city in 2005 in Azad Kashmir in Pakistan reveals that even dramatic changes, which seemed to be a clear break from the past as a consequence of the disaster, could in fact be located in changes that were part of a longer, more continuous process of change in the region.[1] His thesis, therefore, emphasises the 'continuity of

[1] He begins by mentioning that instead of brown thatched or grey cement roofs, the first thing he noticed upon arriving in Bagh (almost flattened by the earthquake of 2005) was that all the post-earthquake construction had coloured, corrugated, galvanised iron (CGI) roofs. While it would be easy to point out that the earthquake is what resulted in the changed construction and new roofs, Loureiro emphasises that the new construction was also representative of wider societal changes, such as wealth accumulation amongst families whose relatives went to the Gulf countries.

change' rather than that precise moment when change, transformative or incremental, took place (Loureiro 2012).

I follow in the tradition of this work using my data from lower Sindh to illuminate some of the haphazard and unplanned processes, overlapping with the institutional and ordered, to illustrate transformational change in citizenship in this region in the aftermath of a large-scale flooding disaster. I argue that the floods that affected the Sindh province of Pakistan in 2010 and 2011 opened a political space that helped strengthen some of the more progressive elements of the state–citizen relationship in the region. This was also partly made possible by political drivers, including a changed political context in the country, allowing more democratic and civic spaces for citizen activism to emerge. These actors and drivers interacted, along both official and unofficial lines, to create an outcome that was able to push a more progressive form of 'disaster citizenship' along.

Michael Ignatieff, Professor of Government at Harvard University, wrote of the various failings of the government in the aftermath of Hurricane Katrina in an essay titled 'The Broken Contract' (2005). His framing of the disaster explains that 'when the levees broke, the contract of American citizenship failed'. Ignatieff's piece makes it clear that he is angry about the government response to the disaster in New Orleans, and that makes him condemn the state management of the disaster and declare that the state 'had failed the test'. This discursive construction of a weather event as a disaster also creates space to critique power holders in a society, particularly by those 'seeking to break the status-quo' (Warner 2013, 89). In a study of press coverage of five disasters in the UK, Pantti and Wahl-Jorgensen's work (2011) illustrates that, while they appear relatively frequently in news and media reports, 'ordinary people' are usually seen to be passive victims of a political drama that they have no control or influence over. This 'subject position', they argue, changes as the disaster-affected individual exercises his claim on citizenship and expresses his political right. The disaster opens up space for ordinary people to criticise those in power – corporations, governments and institutions that, ordinarily, they are rarely able to hold to account as individuals. This systemic critique of 'complex social processes', Pantti and Wahl-Jorgensen argue, 'makes citizens out of victims even if such empowerment comes at a heavy price' (2011, 118).

Ignatieff (2005) quotes an angry and incredulous woman, stuck at the Convention Centre in New Orleans, as saying, 'We are American'; he then goes on to explain that 'that single sentence was a lesson in political obligation'. He emphasises that citizenship ties are not bound by charity but by a right to claim resources from the government at a time when the citizen simply cannot help him/herself. He sees the hurricane in 2005 almost emphatically as a disaster that was the consequence of, and further resulted in, the state's failure to honour its contract and provide a minimum level of protection and security to its people. His narrative constructs this failure in 'political imagination' as being responsible for a complete breakdown of citizenship, in post-hurricane New Orleans. While this analysis of post-Katrina New Orleans is an illustrative framework that uses the language of rights, citizenship and social contract between state and citizens in the aftermath of a disaster, it is, at the same time, reductive to see the state as having entirely 'failed' or citizenship to have utterly 'collapsed'. Post-disaster political interactions, particularly between citizens and the state, are much more complex. The political space that emerges in the aftermath of the disaster is going to result in 'concentration or contestation of political power' (Pelling and Dill 2010, 22). It is unlikely, however, that this is going to be emphatic political control or complete collapse, but, more reasonably, some combination of the two.

As the ethnography of the state revealed in the previous chapter, employing ideas of citizenship and the social contract that emerged out of social and political processes that took place in Western liberal democracies[2] and then imposing them exogenously onto contexts such as lower Sindh in Pakistan can lead to unhelpful results. To discuss citizenship in the aftermath of a disaster in a post-colonial localised setting requires a more contextualised and nuanced understanding. For example, in an interesting exploration of post-disaster political space, Nielsen concludes that a flooding disaster affecting Maputo (Mozambique) in 2000 created a political moment, realised through urban planning, where 'hitherto illegal squatters were reconfigured as legitimate citizens' (2010, 153) in a resettlement neighbourhood. This moment was not, however, constitutive of either the success or failure of the state in the post-disaster context, but was, rather, made up of complex interactions of different processes. In this moment, the informal parcelling out of land, the corruption of civil servants and local leaders, and the idealism of the municipal government interacted with the creative agency exercised by citizens of the flood-affected

[2] J. Chatterjee, 'South Asian Histories of Citizenship, 1946-1970', *The Historical Journal* 55(4) (2012): 1049–1071.

region in Mozambique to have a transformational impact on post-disaster land titles (Nielsen 2010).

Table 4.1 District-level breakdown of the disaster

District	*Impact of Disaster*
Thatta	Thatta was one of the worst affected districts in Pakistan during the flooding in 2010. Locals called this a *daryaee sailaab* (river flood), when the swollen Indus River submerged one-fifth of Pakistan's landmass under water. While other parts of Pakistan were also affected, lower Sindh was particularly devastated by these floods with six out of nine *tehsil*s in Thatta severely flooded.
Badin	Despite being adjacent to Thatta, Badin was barely affected by the flooding in 2010. The *barsaati sailaab* (rain flood) of 2011, which affected primarily the province of Sindh in Pakistan, was devastating for Badin. All five of Badin's *tehsil*s were badly affected, making it the worst hit area in the context of these floods.
Tharparkar	As Sindh's desert district, the fact that floods would affect Tharparkar is somewhat surprising. Yet the 2011 floods affected some *tehsil*s in the district, and the two *tehsil*s of Deeplo and Kaloi were almost completely submerged by water at the height of the floods in August 2011. Additionally, Tharparkar was host to hundreds of thousands of flood-affected people fleeing disaster from adjacent Badin. It was the only place where I was able to interact with internally displaced persons (IDPs) living in camps one year after the floods.

Source: Author.

The Disaster and a Renegotiated Social Contract

The three districts of Thatta, Badin and Tharparkar, where I undertook fieldwork, were amongst the worst affected by the largest climatic disaster in post-1971[3] Pakistan. Floods devastated towns and ravaged entire communities in 2010 and 2011. The floods of 2010 affected the entire country and, in the August of that year, the UN declared that one-fifth of Pakistan's entire landmass was under water (Masood and Drew 2010). In terms of people

[3] It was in 1971 when the eastern wing of Pakistan, until then called East Pakistan, separated from the country and became Bangladesh. It is debatable whether Cyclone Bhola in 1970 had greater impact and scale of devastation than the flooding in 2010. See Pelling (2011, 143–147).

affected, the UN also estimated that it was the 'greatest humanitarian crisis in recent history'. The number of affected people totalled more than those affected in the Asian tsunami of 2004, the Kashmir earthquake of 2005 and the Haiti earthquake of 2010 put together (Tweedie 2010). The floods the following year were limited in their geographical scope and primarily affected the province of Sindh. The scale of the disaster was still massive and over 5 million people had been affected by these floods. Thatta had been affected by the floods of 2010 known locally as the *daryaee sailaab* (river flood), while Badin and Tharparkar had been affected by the floods of 2011 colloquially called the *barsaati sailaab* (rain floods).[4]

It can be now recognised that the floods in Pakistan in 2010 and the flooding in Sindh province the following year in 2011 were opportunities for political mobilisation. People affected by the floods were able to express a demand for greater rights from the state and hold the administration to account. A report published after the floods of 2010 made this point and argued that people affected by the floods were not simply 'passive recipients of assistance' but rather demonstrated 'active agency' in making demands on a state that oft-times made promises it did not deliver (Semple 2011). In an earlier paper, my research also concludes that in the aftermath of the flooding disaster in Sindh, people wanted an 'interaction with a state that delivers aid and institutes policy solutions. Traditional views on a kinship- or patronage-based social contract were almost drowned out with the rising tide of the Indus River' (Siddiqi 2013, 100). This heightened political environment in the aftermath of the floods of 2010 and 2011 made it possible for citizens in Pakistan to engage with issues of rights and citizenship in a way that, Pantti and Wahl-Jorgensen (2011) have stated, normally lies outside the bounds of acceptable public narrative. This 'critical juncture' revised the terms of the state–citizenship relationship by instituting this change in the social contract (Pelling and Dill 2010).

In the remaining chapter I will explore this critical juncture in the aftermath of the floods in Pakistan that resulted in a transformation in citizenship, especially with regard to vernacular ideals of citizenship in the region. The disaster response implemented by the state, its interaction with not only disaster-affected people but also various non-state actors and existing state

[4] This lived experience and vernacular understanding of the floods in lower Sindh is considerably different from the explanation by meteorologists. See Lau and Kim (2012).

policies created a transformative moment for change in citizenship. The disaster made it possible to observe the ways in which discourse, institutions, individuals, even behaviour, evolved in response to changes prompted by the floods in 2010 and 2011. In this chapter, this transformation through discourse and institutions on citizenship, and its impact on the social contract in Pakistan, will be examined.

Citizenship transformation: State-led initiatives

Until 2007, Pakistan did not have one integrated and overarching framework for disaster management. Different agencies within the government were responsible for a number of overlapping roles and had disjointed chains of command (Ahmed 2013). As a consequence of Pakistan declaring its commitment to the Hyogo Framework for Action (HFA) in 2007 and also because the limitations of its existing approach became apparent during the devastation caused by the Kashmir earthquake of 2005, an integrated disaster management policy was formulated. This National Disaster Risk Management Framework (NDRMF), however, had no legal or institutional standing.[5] It was the floods of 2010 that provided the impetus for the state in Pakistan to review and revise its national framework for disaster risk management. As a result, in December 2010 the National Disaster Management Act (NDMA) was passed as an Act of Parliament, and instituted by law.

This NDMA has been critiqued on a few different counts. It has been referred to as 'reactive' in its approach and 'inadequate' to deal with the scale of disasters experienced by Pakistan in recent years (Mustafa 2013). Perhaps, most importantly, when studying transformation of citizenship in the aftermath of the flooding disaster, it is important that the Act refers to disaster relief as '*ex-gratia* assistance' from the state to affected individuals.[6] Given that the word *ex-gratia* is Latin for 'by favour', Chhotray (2014) in her work on disaster relief and citizenship in India calls such 'gratuitous' relief a 'voluntary act of kindness' that the state indulges the affected citizen in, but is not a right or an entitlement that can be demanded by the citizens from the state. Her work in particular emphasises that disaster relief in such contexts then 'only echoes the injustice of social citizenship' and fails at establishing a binding

[5] National Disaster Management Authority, Government of Pakistan, available at http://www.ndma.gov.pk/new/.

[6] National Disaster Management Act of Pakistan (2010), Chapter II, Article 11 (c).

responsibility on the part of the state (Chhotray 2014, 223). It is interesting, then, that my findings from the field revealed that, regardless of the state's intention, disaster response from the state was increasingly being interpreted as a right by the affected people.

To understand this it is necessary to contextualise the Act rather than judging it against normative values. The NDMA goes some way in declaring 'guidelines for minimum standards for relief' and anyone who 'obstructs' this relief from getting to an affected individual is committing an offence punishable by imprisonment or a fine or both. So, while the Act falls short of declaring disaster relief a 'right', it does go some way in acknowledging that a basic minimum in disaster relief is established, even as it leaves unclear whether this 'minimum' is a duty or responsibility or only a favour. At the same time, it is important to emphasise what I refer to earlier as the 'indigenisation' of the democratic political process in South Asia. Fuller and Harriss (2009) explain that while the institutional functioning of the state apparatus in India might demonstrate its colonial legacy, 'the masses', having bought into the local democratic process, have made it their own. Expecting, therefore, that people or even state functionaries will take their cue from a codified Act is perhaps too simple a way of looking at complex interactions on the ground in the aftermath of the disaster. These interactions shaped an understanding where disaster relief of a 'minimum standard' was seen as a right in Pakistan after the floods of 2010 and 2011.

The state at a federal level implemented a disaster response cash-transfer programme in the disaster-affected areas of Pakistan that was linked to the identity cards of its citizens. After the 2010 floods this programme, called the Citizen Damage Compensation Programme (CDCP), dispersed ATM cards called 'Watan Cards' to all residents who were domiciled in the flood-affected regions. Similarly, after the 2011 floods, cash transfers through ATM cards (this time called 'Pakistan Cards') were distributed to people whose residences were registered as being in the flood-affected region. Pakistan has one of the largest populations in the world registered on its digital database called the National Database and Registration Authority (NADRA); the figure for 2012 indicated that 96 per cent of the total population was registered and had a computerised ID card (Khan 2012). The cash transfers (one per household) made to flood-affected families were made through the Watan and Pakistan Cards, which were linked to the NADRA registration system and made out to the heads of the household's citizenship number or Computerised National

Identity Card (CNIC) number. Additionally, it was also a universal rather than a targeted programme, providing cash transfer to all households in the affected area. While the NADRA in Pakistan was set up in March 2000 to register 150 million citizens in the country,[7] the CDCP was the first time that the NADRA database was used in this manner to identify beneficiaries and triangulate data on citizens.[8] It was, therefore, discursively and in reality extremely difficult to divorce this form of disaster response from what people were beginning to see as legal citizenship in the region.

By people here, I am not only referring to the flood-affected citizens of lower Sindh but also in fact politicians and people in positions of power. I interviewed Dr Sikander Mandhro, Member of Provincial Assembly (MPA) from Badin,[9] in July 2012, who had been on the ground managing disaster response operations in his constituency. I asked him directly why the media and many flood-affected individuals were scathing of the government's response to the disaster. His reply was:

> To do a 'hundred percent' of what people were expecting was not possible, we could not do it, that's true', that 'fact' is there but to whatever extent was possible we tried. We never left out any 'area', any village or any community. We adopted an 'overall approach', it may be possible that some individuals were left out (in the distribution of relief and aid goods), 'quite possible'. After all it is 'humanly impossible' to satisfy a man (who has been the victim of such a disaster), you can help him out but to meet all his 'expectation(s)' (is not possible). (The floods) destroyed his house; his livestock is either dead, drowned or very sick; the fields he had cultivated are now ravaged by floods waters, so 'they are expecting many things' and during such a time it is 'impossible' or 'next to impossible' to fulfil his expectations. So the government made a policy that *every individual, every individual who is a citizen of Pakistan and of this (flood-affected) area, and if he is having a national identity card, he should be provided with ten thousand rupees as a (Pakistan) card*. If you ask all your interviewees, ok you got nothing from the government but did you get a card? They will say, 'Yes, we got a card.'

[7] National Database and Registration Authority, Government of Pakistan, available at https://www.nadra.gov.pk/.

[8] NADRA also provides data management service to other government departments. More recently, it has been working with BISP to populate the database for the nationwide household poverty survey.

[9] From the constituency of Badin II – PS 58.

This MPA's broader message once again refers to what was revealed in the previous chapter, that the state was unable to meet the expectations of its disaster-affected citizens partly because the bar set by people is often quite high. His response also makes two other very important and relevant points with regard to disaster response and citizenship in the region. First, what he calls the 'overall approach' is a direct reference to the universal nature of the cash-transfer programme through the Watan and Pakistan Cards. He is aware of administrative limitations and problems around elite capture that were likely to have plagued state interventions trying to provide relief goods to disaster-affected individuals. This is why he acknowledges that in distribution of such goods, some affected and vulnerable people may have been left out. He emphasises, however, that when it came to the cash-transfer programmes they were universal for 'every individual', and then he takes it a step further and links it to citizenship by stating that it was not only 'every individual' but also 'every individual who is a citizen of Pakistan' and has been conferred this right of legal citizenship by being granted a 'national identity card'. While the NDMA does not refer to disaster relief as a right, it is clear in the MPA's articulation of the disaster response policy and intervention that he interpreted it as a right of every affected citizen (who was the head of the household) in the area.

The transformation in citizenship, one that includes a certain kind of state guaranteed disaster relief as a 'right', lies somewhere between the 'intentional' and 'accidental' spectrum. While the state did implement a disaster response strategy that was universal and inclusive and linked directly to citizenship cards, the fact that most people, even those in positions of political power, would begin to interpret it as a constitutive element in citizenship was not something that was planned or anticipated. It was an understanding and interpretation of the disaster policy that only emerged out of unplanned interactions between actors, institutions, behaviours and discourse in the post-disaster context.

The flooding disasters of 2010 and 2011 took place at a time when a political momentum for strengthening and deepening citizenship had been created in Pakistan. At the same time, it is important to point out that while an enabling environment existed for such a universal disaster response policy through the CDCP to be implemented, the federal state in Islamabad was not entirely aware of the extent to which there was buy-in at the local level. State functionaries and community leaders in Sindh often made it their mission to ensure that their constituents were able to access this cash transfer. While doing fieldwork I began to encounter what became a familiar narrative, generally from someone who had received some kind of a formal education – that he helped a particular group of vulnerable people in relief camps access their 'own' money. The protagonist in this narrative, be it a schoolteacher, an NGO worker or a local community leader, always emphasised that he was helping vulnerable post-disaster people access what was rightfully theirs, by which he meant the Watan or Pakistan Card cash-transfer.

A microcosm of this activism, for what was widely seen as the 'right' of disaster-affected vulnerable people to receive their cash transfers, but from within the state apparatus, played out in front of me as I was sitting in the office of the District Coordination Officer (DCO)[10] of Thatta district in August 2012. A team of young men, dressed in Western office attire, from the NADRA office in the capital, Islamabad, came to speak to the local Sindhi DCO who was wearing a local dress in this office. They explained to the DCO that NADRA had improved the Watan Card money disbursement system, and so the second tranche of payment, that was due to be given out shortly, would be more organised and less complicated with fewer chances of error. Much of what these Western-educated men, dressed in a sharp shirt and trousers, had said implied that the state was trying to make minor changes to the existing disbursement system to enable better inclusiveness and ensure universalism of the programme. The DCO, however, was frustrated by the speed of the programme and the infrastructural limitations of not having sufficient ATM machines in villages, which meant people had to travel long distances and stand in queues for a long time before being able to access what was 'rightfully theirs'.

Once again I heard, this time from a government employee and one who had considerable influence in Thatta, the narrative of giving vulnerable disaster-affected people what the state has 'promised' and 'owes' them. The encounter demonstrated that the state disaster response policy, implemented through NADRA, was attempting to make Watan Cards more empowering, and incorporate lessons learnt in the disbursement of the first tranche of money. The second tranche was going to be implemented in a more effective manner to ensure even greater universality and inclusion, and attempt to resolve some of the difficulties with Phase I of implementation. This is also confirmed by World Bank reports and other literature published on the CDCP (The World

---

[10] The DCO is the highest-level government official at the district level and is able to exercise a considerable level of influence at this local level, even though in terms of powers he is limited in geographical scope and has to take many of his orders from the provincial and federal governments.

Bank 2013a, 2013b). Yet it was the DCO who took the discourse further to include rights of people and responsibility of the state. Given that citizenship is established through a two-way encounter between the state and the citizen, on the supply-side, functionaries of the state, particularly on the ground, were interpreting this disaster response intervention as a right of disaster-affected people, something that is owed to them by the state.

Ethnographic evidence, therefore, illustrates that the interpretation of disaster response interventions, by those in positions of power in lower Sindh, were not necessarily consistent with the way the NDMA and subsequent policies were framed. The state, for its part, instituted a policy that was designed to be universal and inclusive, limiting elite capture and leakages, but did not go so far as to declare such disaster response a 'right' of all affected households. Rather accidentally, then, the lived experience of individuals interacting with these institutions resulted in an outcome that pushed a new and emerging understanding of substantive citizenship along. In doing so, the 'political space' that opened in the aftermath of this flooding disaster in 2010 and 2011 was able to significantly 'transform' informal citizenship in the region.

Chhotray (2014), in her work on disaster relief in India, is critical of the impact of state-led disaster response on just citizenship. She explains that, first, the state frames disaster relief as a 'moral obligation', not a 'legal entitlement'. Second, she emphasises that in the debate on targeted versus universal access to state interventions, it is the latter that helps strengthen just citizenship. In particular, she argues that targeting interventions to the most vulnerable only results in a less cohesive society where 'some citizens resent having to contribute towards this purpose'. Third, but linked to the targeted-versus-universal aspect of disaster relief, is the fact that the state ensures that those worthy of relief are able to demonstrate deservedness. The ideological underpinnings of such state interventions are that 'the "relief state" must not subsidise able-bodied people who can take up physical work provided by the state'. The fact that some citizens are seen as deserving by the state while others are seen to have a 'duty to participate' in government funded infrastructural programmes or such again creates a very fragmented citizenship discourse about disaster-affected individuals. Finally, this work is also critical of the Indian experience of disaster relief because it points out that those who are able to pay bribes and offer incentive payments to government functionaries are able to access what others cannot; the 'experience of disaster relief only echoes the injustice of social citizenship' (Chhotray 2014, 223). It, therefore, sees disaster-affected individuals expressing, and being recognised, as 'victims', not as active agents who are claiming and exercising citizenship (Chhotray 2014).

Theoretically, these are valid critiques and, in principle, the idea of the state seeing itself as a benevolent favour-granting actor in political relations – rather than a state that is bound by a social contract to provide basic minimum level of human security to its citizens – is problematic. Yet, as my ethnographic evidence has revealed, the way that state disaster response policy and subsequent interventions unfolded in lower Sindh was more complex than an 'expressing victimhood–exercising citizenship' dichotomy. It emphasizes that, while the NDMA admittedly mentions relief as *ex-gratia* and the main cash-transfer programmes after the flooding disaster in 2010 and 2011 were governed by such policy discourse, these state interventions were interpreted on the ground as a right of all flood-affected citizens even by those working within or representing state structures.

The cash-transfer intervention through the Watan and Pakistan Cards did face some administrative hurdles. People who were not literate or did not know how to use a bank account found it more challenging to access the money than others who were more aware of these services. Similarly, for people who did not have ID cards or had not registered the death of the head of their households with NADRA – this was especially true in female-headed households – had to first go to NADRA offices to make these changes and could only then access the money. Despite these problems the cash transfers were designed to be a universal intervention which, through an effective delivery system of the cash cards, were successful in reaching almost all affected citizens. The amount of leakage and the number of households that fell through the cracks were also reportedly very small; according to the World Bank impact assessment studies, 95 per cent of registered people received the money (The World Bank 2013b). I interviewed a local president of the incumbent party in power at the time of the floods, the Pakistan People's Party (PPP), in a medium-sized semi-urban town in Badin district in January 2013. He was critical of a number of things the then-incumbent party got wrong in terms of service delivery, but when speaking of the Pakistan Cards his face lit up and he said:

> Hundred per cent of the people who were affected got their cards, hundred per cent. Some people who were well-off enough to not need ten thousand rupees from the government said to me, the losses I have incurred as a result of the floods are in the lakhs (hundred thousands), what am I to do with ten thousand rupees? I then told the 25–30 young boys who used to work in our

> office, make an announcement in all communities in our area if people are hesitant to take this money because they are able to comfortably feed their children, they should still take their card and withdraw their money, but donate the money to us so we can use it to help some orphan or a widow ... Everyone got a card, madam, even if they were living in Islamabad or America, if their domicile was for Badin their 'entry' would be included.

The design and the implementation of these cash-transfer interventions ensured the universal nature of this disaster response. Again, while the state policy did not declare it as such, this interviewee expressed in his own way that he encouraged all citizens who were entitled to a card to access their cash-transfer, which they could elect to pass it along to those who required more assistance. This was an intervention in which landless peasants and wealthy business owners were included and treated as equal citizens by the state.

Even where failures occurred, these were not failures of social citizenship but more shortcomings in planning and oversight. The Watan Card received greater funding because a number of international donors including the World Bank and bilateral agencies such as United States Agency for International Development (USAID) were involved in setting up the fund for its cash disbursement. Under the first phase of the Watan Card, the head of each household received Rs 20,000, which was financed by the federal and provincial governments of Pakistan. Phase II was a reconstruction payment for people whose homes had been damaged or who were deemed to be more vulnerable and were therefore targeted; it was divided into two instalments of Rs 20,000 each (Pasricha and Rezvi 2013). All of my informants in Thatta district had received the money in Phase I but less than half had received the two instalments of Phase II. Similarly, with the Pakistan Card distributed in the following year, the total amount citizens were meant to receive was Rs 20,000 in two instalments of Rs 10,000 each (*The News International* 2011). In this case, while all of my informants in Badin and Tharparkar had received the first instalment, no one had received the second one.

People who had not received money in Phase II of the Watan Card in Thatta were visibly more affected by this and not always clear about why they had been left out. In Badin and Tharparkar, however, no one seemed to have received, or even made aware, that a second instalment or round of payments was due. In Thatta, people seemed to be more aware, and also expectant, because everyone knew of a distant acquaintance who had received money in Phase II. There was discontentment on this issue and people were generally unsure about why they had not received this money. It is significant, however, that this was not seen by my informants as echoing the injustice of social citizenship but rather as the state over-committing on promises it could not deliver. People in all three districts were able to see that with the Watan Card and the Pakistan Card, opportunities for elite capture and leakages through corruption were limited, so that even when no one, or very few people, got the next tranche of money there was a sense of acceptance that this was a universal woe and not the injustice of class, caste or kinship. Despite the obvious limitation with the Watan and Pakistan Cards, where they were unable to dispense as much money as was initially pledged for flood-affected citizens, there is little doubt that this disaster response resulted in transforming citizenship in Pakistan. In fact, the transformation itself was partly intended and partly accidental, thereby falling between the intentional and accidental spectrum of transformation.

Citizenship transformation: More demands from citizens

This book begins by constructing the popular argument in literature on the 'absence' of the state in Pakistan (Kabeer, Mumtaz and Sayeed 2010) and the 'gap' that exists between the state and its people (Lall 2012). Scholars who have worked on citizenship in Pakistan have tended to conclude either that citizenship does not exist because people confuse it with other identities, such as religion, or that social structures such as caste and kinship networks have fragmented society, making it very difficult for a meaningful citizenship framework to emerge in most parts of rural Pakistan such as lower Sindh. Evidence from the field, however, has overwhelmingly illustrated that when people in Pakistan felt particularly vulnerable in the face of the flooding disaster, they immediately turned to the omnipresent state for service provision such as disaster rescue and relief.

I have emphasised in the previous chapter that in the many months I spent in lower Sindh, perhaps the only question to which I received a near universal response was when I asked my informants who they believed should have had helped them in the face of this natural disaster; every single individual (barring two) indicated the state or the government. Despite literature suggesting that people in these non-cosmopolitan parts of Pakistan only interact with the state through their patron, a tribal or kinship leader, during the floods my informants did not expect help from tribal leaders or local patrons; they wanted help from the larger entity, the *sarkar* (state). This illustrated a very alive and direct connection between the state and its citizens in Pakistan, not always captured in the various accounts of fractured and fragmented citizenship in Pakistan. My research further shows that the Watan and Pakistan Cards were critical in making vulnerable people demand more of the state and push this relationship forward.

Some of my informants expressed surprise that I would ask the obvious, such as the interviewee I mentioned earlier, who said: 'This is Pakistan right? So obviously it is the government of Pakistan that is *responsible*, not the Indians or Americans.' Even those who emphasised that it was because they pay the government tax or because they voted their political representatives into office that they expect a disaster response service from the state, all illustrate that they were not even considering any other intermediaries or alternatives to the state. They broadly understood disaster response as a state-oriented activity and also believed that, as they were citizens, it was the government's responsibility to provide service to them. While these informants may not have used the words 'rights' or 'entitlements', it was evident in these multiple conversations that people believed that because they had cast a vote in the 2008 elections, often for the incumbent party or political representative, expectation of disaster relief was part of the wider set of empowerments that this new political liberty was meant to provide. This was the citizenship guarantee that Ignatieff (2005) refers to in his essay when he emphasises that citizenship ties are not bound by charity but by a right to claim resources from the government at a time when the citizen simply cannot help him/herself. The flooding disaster in Pakistan in 2010 and 2011 were an unprecedented moment when those rights were often being exercised.

Rawls (2009), in his work on the justification of civil disobedience and dissent, makes an important contribution by linking it to the 'derivation' of the principles of justice in the social contract. His work on the justification of civil disobedience suggests that civil disobedience is in fact a political act attempting to achieve those established principles of justice (Rawls 2009). Legally, too, the refusal to comply or withhold assent to unjust requirements is 'implicit in a proper understanding of the ideal of the rule of law' (Allan 1996, 90). Given that civil disobedience is a recognised prerogative of a citizen in the face of injustice, it was significant that, in one particular town, citizens demanding their Watan Cards repeatedly blocked the highway between Thatta and Badin districts. Some sort of administrative error had resulted in people from an area close to the town of Sajawal from being left out of the Watan Card initial distribution. In the four months between May 2012 and September 2012, I found it a challenge, during fieldwork, to cross this part of the highway because these residents would regularly emerge onto the Sajawal road and block vehicular access. These roadblocks rarely, if ever, turned violent, though I did see some men burn tyres on one occasion. With time, it became clear that much like the DCO and the MPA and other government functionaries, citizens too understood the Watan Cards as an entitlement, and saw the protests and civil disobedience to access this card as their legitimate right as citizens. Along with illustrating people's understanding of Watan Cards as a right worth fighting for, such performance of political rights is transformative in its own right, transmuting a passive citizenry into to an active one.

It is important to point out that the language and the words for 'rights' and 'entitlements' were not yet being employed by citizens when they spoke of the Watan or Pakistan Cards, even though the understanding and wider construction of citizenship clearly included that idea. Shakeel *bhai*, who, as I explained, was engaged in a small scale political and legal struggle to get drinking water to his village, commonly used the Urdu term for 'fundamental right' (*bunyadi haq*) when referring to access to drinking water. He was all too aware that his fight was one for a basic 'fundamental right'. Those who had been left out of the Watan Card allocation[11] were not using the word for fundamental right but still utilising the same instruments to fight for what they believed was their right – petitions in the courts (Mujahid 2011) and civil disobedience in the form of road blocks and sit-ins. Even if the language of disaster response had not evolved enough for this to be called a 'right', it was still evident that, even without using the words, people's understanding and construction of cash transfers in the aftermath of a disaster very closely resembled the understanding of a 'fundamental right'. It seemed to me that a certain minimal disaster response was already being conceptualised as an important part of citizenship in Pakistan.

My research in the field revealed that citizens affected by the disaster in Pakistan repeatedly exercised agency and demanded more from state functionaries whom they had voted into office. While at a narrative level people often articulated thoughts such as 'I am a poor man what can I do?' they would also explain how they went to see the local politician or walked into the DCO's office, demanding disaster relief provisions. Often, informants had bought into the narrative of their own disenfranchisement at a discursive level, but my

[11] As with any large-scale social intervention targeting millions of people, there is no doubt that there were some errors in the system and also in distribution, albeit proportionally very small, that remained unresolved to the end.

findings supported those made by Semple (2011), and reveal that rarely – if ever – did they act as passive victims. Rather, they behaved as active agents who were exercising some degree of citizenship, a citizenship that was now also beginning to have a minimum amount of disaster response built into it. Also, people did not expect this disaster response or relief as charity but demanded it as a responsibility the state should fulfil. De Waal's work on famines and the social contract, discussed earlier, makes a powerful argument in stating 'freedom from famine (disaster) arises within a specific form of social contract, developed through political struggle' (1996, 199). In the post-disaster context of lower Sindh, too, it seemed that socio-political struggles were taking place, challenging the nature of the interaction between the state and its citizens. Forces of change, particularly the flooding disaster, were encouraging people to demand more of the state and its agents, whom they helped into office. The flooding disaster, therefore, helped a progressive transformation in citizenship and the way in which it was experienced in Pakistan.

Drivers of Change

Social transfers and the Citizen Damage Compensation Programme (CDCP)

The floods in 2010 and 2011 catalysed a critical juncture in state–citizen relations in Pakistan. The disaster resulted in regular questions being asked about the responsibilities of the state and the role of citizens as well. It is, however, imperative to place this moment of transformative change within the wider context of political contestations that were taking place in Pakistan at the time. The flooding disaster acted as a significant catalyst because other drivers for change had already been in place leading up to, and continuing after, the moment created by the disaster had passed. Principal among these 'emergent' drivers was Pakistan's return to democracy in February 2008, after nine years of military rule, and the Sindh-based PPP forming the ruling coalition in parliament.

Gazdar (2011) identifies this 'party of the poor', the PPP, forming the majority in the parliament as being an important reason behind Pakistan's 'irreversible paradigm shift' in pro-poor social protection policy being implemented in the country, even before the flooding disaster of 2010 and 2011. His study revealed that in the financial year 2008/2009, fiscal allocation for cash-transfer programmes increased almost six-fold. The large cash-transfer programme called the Benazir Income Support Programme (BISP) is of particular significance as it has been protected by a law that was passed unopposed in parliament and, in 2011, reached more than 7 per cent of all households in a country of 180 million people, coverage that has only increased over the years. It has managed to positively impact 'the nature of interactions between state and citizen' and give 'primacy' to women as beneficiaries in a patriarchal society (Gazdar 2011, 65). The BISP cash transfers were the first to be linked to the NADRA database, and, after some trial and error, with recipients initially receiving transfers through money orders, beneficiaries eventually began to receive cash transfers through a smart card. The lessons learnt from this programme were instrumental in the design and implementation of the Watan and Pakistan Cards-based disaster response programme officially called the Citizen Damage Compensation Programme (CDCP).

It is critical to state that this paradigm shift did not occur in an unsystematic, entirely coincidental, way. In fact, using 'social protection for nation building' was an explicit goal in the strategy paper 'Final Report of the Panel of Economists' prepared by the Planning Commission, Government of Pakistan, in April 2010, just months before the first flooding disaster in 2010. In writing about the conflict-affected areas of the country, the document clearly stated, 'Social protection must be part of the strategy to reclaim the space and legitimacy for the state in Pakistan, through protection to the basic entitlements of people in the conflict-affected areas' (Planning Commission 2010, xvi). This policy statement is particularly significant when looking at the role such state interventions played after the flooding disaster in lower Sindh. Pelling and Dill (2010) emphasise that some earlier literature sees disaster outcomes as path dependent. For instance, one of the earliest works in disaster politics by Albala-Bertrand notes, 'Responses to disasters vary according to the political visions of the major power holders (endogenous and exogenous) and tend to reveal dominant political philosophies' (Pelling and Dill 2010, 24). Hence, it logically follows that because the state in Pakistan had already begun to conceptualise and implement (with geographical limitations) a policy of citizenship through social protection, the disaster response after the flooding disaster in 2010 and 2011 was able to push that objective along.

Historically, this framework for large-scale social transfers, particularly in the case of emergency management, existed in Pakistan. Additionally, cash transfers being used universally by the state to reach out to affected citizens had first taken place in the aftermath of the Kashmir earthquake in 2005. After this, cash transfers were also disbursed to IDPs affected by military operations against the Taliban insurgency, from the northern parts of Pakistan in 2009 (NDMA and UNOCHA 2015). These cash-transfer programmes, however, were not linked to people's citizenship number in the same way. For instance, a database of all households who applied for the earthquake cash-transfer programme was created and then verified against the information available on individuals by the NADRA. Earthquake-affected residents did expect a cash transfer from the state, but not as a right of citizenship. The cash-transfer programmes implemented after the floods were not only better constructed, and also incorporated lessons learnt from earlier programmes, but also actively set out to use the NADRA system to reach out to affected households. This goal was partially even reflected in the choice of name for the programme: 'Citizen Damage Compensation Programme'. The World Bank and other development agencies have also highlighted the benefits of using this database system in the CDCP (Ovadiya 2014). Even though making disaster response a right of citizenship was not a stated benefit, these 'technologies of development' created an enabling environment for this to occur (Corbridge et al. 2005).

At the narrative level, it was often difficult for citizens to link bank cards, and cash-transfers, to the state and see it as evidence of the state reaching out to them. Especially, as I mentioned earlier, seeing an individual as a manifestation of the state remains important. Hence, for a number of my informants who had been affected by the flooding disaster in lower Sindh, it was common to describe the state as having done 'nothing at all (*kuch bhee nahin*)' for them after the disaster. I have discussed this *kuch bhee nahin* narrative regarding the state, in the aftermath of the flooding disaster, in greater detail elsewhere (Siddiqi 2013). For now, however, it is important to point out that despite this narrative, one that was often created or reinforced by the media, the wider state–social intervention policies were recognised by even some of the most marginalised of its citizens.

One of my informants from Thatta, whom I will call *chachajee,*[12] was admittedly a PPP voter but also belonged to one of the most deprived villages I spent time in. Large parts of lower Sindh also suffer from longer-term environmental challenges as a result of large infrastructural projects upstream on the Indus River, ranging from sea-intrusion to environmental degradation downstream (Mustafa 2010). In many of the villages where I undertook

[12] The literal meaning of the word is 'uncle', but it is respectful to refer to an elder person as such.

fieldwork, residents were struggling to adapt to a new reality of non-agrarian livelihoods and even fishermen were having to get used to different fish stocks in different seasons.[13] *Chachajee* and his family were struggling to make a living even before the flooding disaster and had to leave their homes and live in relief camps for a month after the disaster. The level of deprivation in their village was therefore very visible and obvious. Yet when talking about the government he says:

> They assisted us in a difficult time. In fact, their assistance far exceeded our expectations ... It was in the first 3–4 years of Mr Bhutto's government[14] that the poor people were able to breathe a sigh of relief; after that it is only now during Mr Zardari's tenure[15] that the poor people have been provided assistance. Something or the other is being done to help the poor, whether it is in the form of Watan Card, Pakistan Card or the Benazir Income Support Programme (BISP). We were never aware of such programmes in the past, we had never even heard of them. The people in our village had never even seen an ATM. They did not know what an ATM card was.

As stated earlier, *chachajee* may well be conflating the PPP state and the democratic state, like many of my other informants, but the wider point he makes remains valid. The state was following a policy of reaching out to address the vulnerability of its citizens, whether they had been affected by the disaster or poverty, more generally, and this was not only being recognised by citizens such as *chachajee* but also strengthening citizenship in the region.

Contextualising the state's disaster response policy, particularly the CDCP, within the wider environment for social interventions in Pakistan helps explain the path-dependent nature of this strengthened social contract in the region as well. The context also makes it possible to see that the citizens' expectations of the state in the aftermath of the flooding disaster of 2010 and 2011 – the increased citizen activism and mobilisation for access to Watan and Pakistan Cards, much of the fight for rights and entitlements – was possible in this climate in Pakistan.

---

[13] A study on environmental change in one sub-district of Thatta, called Keti Bunder (Salman 2011).

[14] Zulfiqar Ali Bhutto was the founder of the Pakistan People's Party (PPP) and the Prime Minister of Pakistan from 1973 to 1977.

[15] Asif Ali Zardari was the PPP President of Pakistan from 2008 to 2013.

Social protection beyond Pakistan

At the same time, there was some degree of economic acquiescence for large-scale state interventions that was driven by international momentum as well. The Pakistani economy has a history of being dependent on International Monetary Fund (IMF) loans (with World Bank policies and conditions attached) that goes back to the first few years of the country's existence as an independent state (McCartney 2011). Pakistan's limited economic independence has meant that the IMF and the World Bank had to be on board with a social intervention programme that, in 2010/2011, cost US$875 million from the state budget,[16] without a direct return on expenditure. Here, the international climate with regard to social spending in recent years, particularly in the Global South where social protection policy has had a serious impact, played an important role.

Hulme and Barrientos (2008) have noted that the increased focus and importance given to social protection for vulnerable citizens has changed the composition of poverty reduction strategies in the Global South. They argue that the scaling up of such social interventions has resulted in economic growth, human capital development and social protection. These are increasingly seen as elements of national development strategies: a three-pronged approach that they see as 'increasing national levels of welfare, raising economic productivity and strengthening social cohesion' (Hulme and Barrientos 2008, 4). Notable examples include South Africa's Child Support Grant, implemented in 2003, reaching 7.2 million children by 2007/2008; India's National Rural Employment Guarantee Scheme, reaching out to 26 million households in 2008, and various well-known programmes in Latin America such as the Oportunidades (Mexico) and Bolsa Familia (Brazil) (Hulme and Barrientos 2008). Pakistan's social protection strategy, drafted in 2006, specifically refers to Pakistan's low social spending when compared to countries in Latin America and also mentions Mexico's Oportunidades programme by name and suggests that its selection criteria should be emulated by the programme design in Pakistan (Barrientos 2006).

Many, though not all, of these large-scale social interventions were implemented when left-of-centre governments were voted into office in these countries. The Bolsa Familia, for example, was a central feature in Lula's political campaign in the Brazilian presidential election of 2006 (Kingstone

---

[16] Benazir Income Support Programme (available at http://www.bisp.gov.pk/).

2006). In particular, the federal government in Pakistan does seem eager, at least to some extent, to implement the lessons learnt from the Brazilian experience of social protection. Even a cursory look at Pakistani newspapers over the last few years reveals articles titled (Naeem 2012; *Pakistan Today* 2014):

> 'Seminar: Fighting Malnutrition, Poverty the Brazilian Way'
>
> 'BISP, Brazil to Share Expertise on Social Protection'[17]

The World Bank and other international financial institutions (IFIs) that generally hold great sway in Pakistan's fiscal policy have also looked favourably at these social interventions and have provided support for the BISP and the CDCP in particular, touting them as success stories (The World Bank 2013b). The World Bank played a central role in the design of the BISP targeting mechanism, and in designing a cash transfer that is run in a transparent and technocratic manner to allow minimum leakages from the total allocation. In fact, the World Bank website on social safety nets illustrates the ways in which the bank has taken a more progressive and all-encompassing approach to social protection:

> In the context of the World Bank's new strategy for Social Protection and Labor, the Bank has made an important *shift* from supporting the delivery of social assistance projects to helping countries build safety net systems and institutions that respond to country-level poverty, risks and vulnerabilities. With a growing evidence base on the positive impacts of safety nets – from low- and middle-income countries – there has been an explosion of interest in safety nets. Adding to the flagship examples such as Mexico, Brazil, Ethiopia, and Bangladesh, there is a new generation of countries emerging with robust safety net systems, for example, Niger, Cameroon, Rwanda, and *Pakistan* [emphasis added]. Country aspirations are supported at a global level by the G20 process, with growing calls to consider social protection as part of the post-2015 development agenda. (The World Bank 2013c)

This enabling environment for large-scale government assistance, which was then extended to include a disaster response programme, such as the Watan and Pakistan Cards, based on the same principles as the BISP, was also driven in part by the international environment and momentum for social protection in the developing world.

---

[17] This article also discusses mutual cooperation between Brazil and Pakistan on BISP and the Bolsa Familia among other social protection and agriculture schemes.

The social space beyond social interventions

General Pervez Musharraf was the military dictator who ruled Pakistan for nine years between 1999 and 2008. He was forced to resign as the president of the country and had to call for elections because of popular public demand. This was driven in no small part due to a protest movement led by lawyers in the country, now colloquially referred to as the Lawyers' Movement of 2007. Lawyers and judges had turned against General Musharraf when he unconstitutionally suspended the Chief Justice of the Supreme Court earlier in 2007. The lawyers' movement was problematic for various reasons, such as its dependence on dangerous ideologues, and its socially regressive and religiously conservative leanings. At the same time, however, it was a successful non-violent social movement that changed the political process in the country significantly. By 2009, writes Hasan Abbas, 'it was well known that things had changed and that the judiciary was now independent and powerful' (2009, 24). The battle for an independent judiciary, the supremacy of the constitution and rule of law is far from over, and the justice system in Pakistan leaves a lot to be desired. It would, however, be fair to say that some faith has been restored in this broken system as a result of the events of the last few years.

One of my informants was an almost-eighty-year-old man in a small village in Badin who had severe mobility challenges. He told me that he always voted for the opposition candidate in provincial elections, despite knowing that his candidate would lose and the local power brokers in the area would harass him and his family by filing false police cases against him and having him arrested. I asked him why he continued to vote for the losing candidate when it clearly caused so many problems; he replied, 'Because now I can go to the courts and they give me justice.' The fact that the justice system worked for this old man does not mean it works in all cases but it is very significant that the justice system is now sometimes able to work for the poorest and most dispossessed as well.

In my meeting with two members of the JuD at their *markaz* (centre) just outside of Thatta district, I was informed that I could 'friend' them on Facebook to keep myself informed of their activities. I also had the option of following the activities of one of their 'brothers' on Twitter. Also, when writing about the 2007–2008 lawyers' movement Abbas notes that 'the movement's leading activists were connected through Twitter.com' (2009, 7). Saeed, Rohde and Wulf (2008) examined the role of information and communication technologies (ICTs) in the anti-government protests of 2007–2008. They point out that social networking websites (Facebook and Orkut) and video sharing websites (YouTube and Google Videos) were used to mobilise and disseminate information on organised protests. While 'blogs, online petitions, emails, Yahoo groups, SMS and wikis' were also part of the coordination and mobilisation process. They conclude that 'an initial impression of this protest movement suggests that modern ICTs were used optimally' but that more research on this subject was necessary (Saeed, Rohde and Wulf 2008, 3). It has often been noted that Pakistan has embraced the digital age at a faster rate than many other countries at comparable levels of income. Almost 90 per cent of Pakistanis live in parts of the country that are now covered by mobile networks, mobile usage is over 130 million people – well over 75 per cent of the total population – and in 2008, Pakistan was the world's third fastest growing telecommunications market (*The Nation* 2013).

Writing in 2012, Pirzada and Husain (2012) state that 'Pakistan's electronic media has made huge strides in the last one decade'. Until General Musharraf took over as President in 1999 there was just one terrestrial channel, Pakistan Television, which was state owned and operated. According to one estimate, there are now 90 TV channels and 106 licensed FM radio channels operating in Pakistan (Haq 2010). The authors point out that, in breaking the state monopoly on information and its dissemination, the Musharraf regime not only helped liberalise Pakistan's social and political discourse but also contributed to its own eventual demise (Pirzada and Husain 2012). Political battles, such as allegations of corruption against the powerful Chief Justice of Pakistan by a property tycoon, were fought in a very public sphere due to this free media. During the floods of 2010 and 2011 as well, live media broadcasts were informing people of government responses to the disaster and what rescue and relief were being provided by other non-state actors. My conversations with flood-affected communities also revealed that their expectations of the state, and frustrations over inaction, or acknowledgement of government support, were often framed by what *Geo-wallay* (people from the TV channel Geo[18]) reported.

At the juncture when the flooding disaster took place in 2010 and 2011, it was no longer possible for the state to either manage the public narrative through control of media or ignore the voices of the most vulnerable and affected. People had struggled for a free and empowering democratic process

[18] Pakistan's largest private TV corporation.

and, in return, expected to see a more responsive state. In such an internal environment the way the disaster response was designed and implemented helped to establish a direct connection between the state and its citizens, transforming citizenship in the region.

Strengthening the Social Contract through Rights-based Citizenship

This chapter emphasises the transformation in citizenship that took place in lower Sindh in the aftermath of the flooding disaster in 2010 and 2011. Popular accounts and media narratives had been suggesting that the state–citizen relationship was 'damaged' and 'breached'. Instead, I illustrate that the transformation taking place in the flood-affected districts of Pakistan was considerably different from that dominant story. My evidence systematically demonstrates that the state and the citizens were able to evolve a more progressive citizenship in the aftermath of the disaster. I also emphasise that this transformation went beyond what was instituted legislatively by the state in the aftermath of the disaster. The National Disaster Management Act (NDMA) of Pakistan, for example, shied away from declaring disaster response an entitlement or a right of citizenship. Yet the framing and implementation of state interventions, particularly the cash transfers linked directly to people's citizenship numbers, in the post-disaster context, were commonly being constructed by people in lower Sindh as a right.

Ethnographic evidence from three districts that were amongst the worst-affected by the flooding disaster in 2010 and 2011 in Pakistan illustrates that the lived experience of the disaster response on the ground was more complex and unplanned. Both actors, the state and the citizens, were not unitary forces that were behaving in tandem with each other. The federal state formalised a conservative NDMA but then, in the Citizen's Damage Compensation Programme (CDCP), operationalised a disaster response strategy that was based on progressive principles. It included universality, direct connection to citizenship number and card, and minimum scope for elite capture and leakages, all of which helped people and state officials to construct this disaster response discursively as an entitlement of citizenship, even if they were not using the words to refer to it as such. In particular the wider political climate in Pakistan enabled a greater amount of citizen activism and mobilisation, resulting in people demanding more of the PPP state as well. In a truly unique and exciting moment in the country's political history, the climate disaster in 2010 and 2011 interacted with a number of social and political processes, in both informal and formal spaces, to create a lived reality in which people were demanding disaster response as a 'right' of citizenship, and the state, for its part – without explicitly stating it as such – was trying its best to deliver.

This transformation in citizenship, on the part of the state at least, fell somewhere between 'accidental' and 'intentional' but it was profound because it is difficult to reverse or turn back. On the one hand it created an opportunity for disaster response to be formalised by law as a right of citizenship, a momentum that has so far not been fully exploited. On the other, this transformation was also driven, in part, by local socio-political processes at a time and place when society was demanding, and the state was providing, that change. Hence, to some extent, regardless of whether it is codified by law, the response has now been socially sanctioned; it would be extremely difficult for the state to not respond in a similar, or even more effective manner, when another disaster strikes. Because citizens and state officials have begun to construct the Watan and Pakistan Cards cash transfer as a right of 'every citizen ... having a national identity card', not doing this in future could result in serious backlash for any elected government in power.

The rhetoric around *azaadi* (freedom), the discursive framing of disaster relief as a right, and the disaster response policy that was implemented in a socially just and humane manner have resulted in a transformation of citizenship in Pakistan that is not easy to reverse. This has been acknowledged by the state at a limited level because, based on the experience of the CDCP, a wider action plan known as the Action Plan for Early Recovery in Future Disasters has been established, in collaboration with the World Bank and other local and international agencies involved in the CDCP (Ovadiya 2014). The state is aware that in times of future disasters citizens will have an expectation for a basic minimum amount of 'rights-based' disaster relief. An expectation that is unlikely to be satisfied with less than what was done for affected citizens in 2010 and 2011.

CHAPTER 5

The Failing 'Islamist Takeover' in the Aftermath of the Indus Floods

This analysis has so far demonstrated that beyond social relations or 'mixed up' ideas of citizenship, people in Pakistan have a relationship with a larger entity, 'the state'. The ethnographic social contract may include a construction of the state that has elements of kinship and hereditary structures but it very tangibly also includes an understanding of citizenship and the responsibility of the *sarkar/hakumat/riyasat* to these citizens, particularly during difficult and trying times. In the aftermath of the flooding disaster in 2010 and 2011 a more rights-based understanding of citizenship emerged, helping to push these progressive aspects of the social contract along. This final chapter will address the issue of 'dominant' political agents that theory suggests might, and popular narrative insists did, emerge in the aftermath of the flooding disaster in Pakistan. I engage with this idea to dismiss any remaining doubt on the existence of the social contract, one that has progressive elements, in the lower Sindh region of Pakistan.

The construction of the 'disaster discourse' affects the social contract between the state and its citizens as the prior contract is reassessed and negotiated in the wake of the crisis (Warner 2013). Pelling and Dill highlight that they are particularly interested in the extent to which this post-disaster 'space is politicised whether it is populated by new or existing social organisations and how quickly and in what manner the state and other *dominant social actors* respond' (2010, 27; emphasis added). Their analytical framework emphasises (*a*) the state's use of this political space, discussed in significant detail in the previous chapter, and (*b*) the way other social organisations instrumentalised this post-disaster political space.

This research has revealed (*b*) to be entirely connected and dependent on (*a*). Rather than being constructed in opposition to the state, the social organisation I study, the Jamaat-ud-Dawa (JuD), illustrates that it was only able to capture as much political space as the state allowed it to, and that it was not very interested in presenting itself as an 'alternative' paradigm to the state. The existence and very visible presence of the JuD in the aftermath of the disaster in 2010 and 2011 only served to illustrate that dominant position of the state in lower Sindh.

In order to interrogate the impact of the JuD on people's relationship with the state in Pakistan, I examine the JuD not primarily as a religious movement with a specific Ahl-e-Hadis ideology, but rather as representing a 'moment' in the post-disaster context – a moment that is referred to by Pelling and Dill as 'the mobilisation of *non-state* and state actors to champion, direct, counter or *capture* evolving critical discourses' (2010, 22; emphasis added). This moment can be fully exploited if the state has failed its people and these non-state actors are able to instrumentalise that opportunity. It is particularly relevant because the post-disaster context is one where people are critical of the incumbent government. The shortcomings of the government are what actors such as the JuD, or even NGOs with alternative paradigms for development, are able to use to mobilise and construct themselves as the dominant force opposing the state. This chapter is, therefore, an examination of the extent to which a dominant social and political actor, the JuD, was able to *capture* an evolving post-disaster political space, critical of the status-quo.

The Jamaat-ud-Dawa and the Indus Floods

The Marmara earthquake in Turkey in 1999 opened political space for faith-based development groups to reach out to affected communities, in the aftermath of the disaster, in a vehemently secular Turkish political landscape. While these dominant social or political organisations could well be NGOs or other providers of post-disaster development services, in this chapter I examine a militant Islamist group, the JuD. This is because the 'master narrative' constructed after the flooding disasters of 2010 and 2011 was along the following lines, as reported in by a TV news channel:

> The people of Sindh are in a desperate situation, they have not had any help from their government and the only help they have received is from the organisation, the Jamaat-ud-Dawa.[1]

[1] *Al Jazeera English* coverage of the floods of 2011, available at http://www.youtube.com/watch?v=nlMrBmYV1ZU.

The narrative could also be seen in a more international and less nuanced story that was broadly based on the 'Islamists' taking control of flood-hit areas.

> Unless we (in the West) act decisively, large parts of flood stricken Pakistan will be taken over by the Taliban. (Rashid 2010)

This idea that Islamist groups were 'taking over' as a result of state failure in the aftermath of the disaster was powerfully constructed in words and in images on media and in the testimonies of people who were visiting the worst-affected areas. The Islamist group considered to have the widest outreach in Sindh, and believed to provide disaster relief and assistance even where the state could not, was the JuD.

This analysis of Islamist groups such as the JuD was not based on rigorous empirical evidence and it was also premised on the notion of state 'absence'. The JuD was reportedly making advances in 'winning the hearts and minds' of flood-affected people. This was primarily because they were seen to be working tirelessly to provide flood relief and aid in areas where the state was believed to have had abrogated its responsibilities and retreated. According to one report, even where there was not 'a United Nations pick-up or Pakistani government official in sight' it was possible to see the JuD's humanitarian label, the FIF (Falah-e-Insaniyat Foundation[2]) operating relief camps (Crilly 2010). This chapter challenges both aspects of this construction of the JuD. Evidence and analysis in the previous chapter have shown that the state was not 'absent' in the aftermath of the disaster, and, in fact, the interaction of supply-driven and demand-side disaster response interventions helped to strengthen the progressive elements of the social contract in this area of Pakistan. Further, it will disprove the second part of this construction, one that sees state weakness as the main reason for this dominant social and political actor to present itself as a competitor or challenger to state authority in the aftermath of disaster in Pakistan. My evidence, instead, shows that framing the JuD as a challenger was itself incorrect as the group was neither able nor willing to construct itself as such. Citizens' social contract with the larger entity of the *sarkar* remained strong even in the aftermath of the disaster. People in the flood-affected areas, for their part, were also not readily convinced into following political agendas based on simply flood relief.

[2] Roughly translates as 'foundation for service to humanity'.

On one of my early days in Badin, when I was just getting to know the city, I came across a wall with graffiti scrawled on it that said 'No America No India' (in English) signed with a 'Jamaat-ud-Dawa' (in Urdu) underneath the message. Similar political slogans were visible on walls in fairly central parts of the city with a Jamaat-ud-Dawa signature or flag underneath. When I enquired about the appearance and visibility of these messages and signs a number of my informants suggested that these slogans had become more visible since the JuD reached out to affected communities in the aftermath of the flooding disaster in 2011.

Figure 5.1 A wall graffiti in English with a Jamat-ud-Dawa signature in Urdu, in Badin city. Photograph taken by author.

One of these informants was Feroze, a primary school teacher from a village on the boundary of Badin and Tharparkar districts. He had personally not been affected by the flooding disaster that had completely submerged some of the other *goth*s in his *taluka* in 2011. Feroze also did not believe in the Ahl-e-Hadis tradition of Islam followed by the JuD and was not personally convinced by their political ideals vis-à-vis *jihad* and the liberation of Kashmir. Yet he impressed upon me that the JuD's effective disaster relief campaign has resulted in it making *dilon main jagah*, literally translated as 'space in the hearts' of people, in the post-disaster context of Pakistan.

His words echoed those I heard just three months earlier. Before going to my field site in lower Sindh, and while still doing preparatory work in Karachi in early 2012, I had interviewed the *Al Jazeera English* correspondent for Pakistan, Mr Kamal Hyder. Mr Hyder's reporting on the floods in Sindh in both 2010 and 2011 had been very influential in constructing the national and international story on this disaster in Pakistan. I have mentioned one of his famous news reports that he filmed while sitting on a JuD boat in Badin district at the height of the floods in August 2011. During our telephone interview, I asked Mr Hyder about the role of the JuD in Pakistan in the aftermath of the flooding disaster in 2010 and 2011. After criticising an 'incompetent and inefficient' state that had chosen to remain 'absent' in the wake of a calamitous disaster, he said:

> In the battle for 'hearts and minds' they (the JuD) have already won.

In my early days in the field, I also began to accept the narrative around state 'absence' and collapsed citizenship that had allowed the JuD to construct itself as a dominant social actor and make political headway amongst affected communities. The physical geography that included JuD graffiti on walls and remnants of their relief camps in public grounds, as well as the testimonies from my early informants, all pointed in that direction. It seemed possible for the JuD to demonstrate to people in Thatta, Badin and Tharparkar that it was better at delivering basic human security, an important aspect of the ethnographic social contract, than the state. In the subsequent months that I spent in these three districts doing detailed ethnographic work, however, a more complicated relationship between the JuD and the state began to unravel. The JuD in lower Sindh had, in fact, only been as successful as the larger entity, the *sarkar*, had wanted it to be, reaffirming the presence of certain 'state effects' in the aftermath of the disaster rather than its publicised 'absence'.

The work of anthropologist Alpa Shah (2013) makes a strong case for why my findings run counter to the general perception of the JuD in the aftermath of the flooding disaster in 2010 and 2011. Her work on the Maoist insurgency in India explains that there has generally been a 'shortage of field level data and analysis' on the revolutionary mobilisation of the Maoists in India. It has, therefore, been 'reasonable to assume' that the neglect of the state in these areas combined with uneven economic opportunities resulted in those living in the Maoist guerilla zones to become part of the struggle. Her work based on ethnographic research and extended amounts of time spent in an insurgent area reveals that there is far more to the story than captured by these popular accounts. She highlights that beyond grand narratives used to theorise this struggle, much of the movement's appeal can be explained by 'the development of relations of intimacy between the mobilising force and the people in its area of expansion' (2013a, 486). Similarly, my field research in lower Sindh in the aftermath of the disaster revealed a more complex interaction than 'the JuD versus the state' binary that has been the subject of most post-disaster grand narratives on the JuD so far.

In the seven months that I spent doing fieldwork in Pakistan, it became clear that the JuD was most visible in the public narrative and in the physical geography of Badin compared to the other two districts where I undertook fieldwork. Just outside the main city there is a large JuD *markaz* (centre) that was used to manage all its disaster relief services in 2011 and also used to coordinate efforts in other districts during the floods of 2010. In particular, the JuD's presence was far more noticeable and appreciated in Badin as compared to Thatta. In the latter district, few people outside of one *taluka*, Jhatti, where the JuD was still doing some reconstruction work when I did fieldwork in 2012–2013, knew about them. This had little to do with the JuD filling a 'vacuum' or 'void' left by the state in Badin. Despite authors such as Tankell (2011) overemphasising the role of JuD's vast network of social services, the group had not established a 'parallel administration which cared for all local needs that were neglected by the authorities', as the Agha Khan Development Network is said to have successfully done in the area of Gilgit-Baltistan in northern Pakistan (Soekefeld 2012, 203). Rather, the JuD encountered a more favourable environment in Badin, as compared to Thatta, in the aftermath of the flooding disaster in 2010 and 2011, and this was in large part due to the support of the 'state effect' of the larger entity of the *sarkar*.

The Jamaat-ud-Dawa and the State

The role of support groups, access points and state repression in creating or limiting the 'structure of political opportunities' available to social and political movement has been established in classic texts on the subject. In particular, scholars such as Tarrow, Kitschel and McAdam clearly explain how such 'environmental factors' open up political opportunities for social and political movements, or are able to restrict them significantly (Tarrow 1998). One such definition of political opportunity structures states:

> The configuration of forces in a (potential or actual) group's political environment that influences that group's assertion of its political claims. (Brockett 1991, 254)

In the case of the JuD in lower Sindh it became obvious that the political environment influencing JuD's assertion of political claims was almost directly linked to its level of support or co-option by the local state (and also to some extent whether rival politico-religious groups were tolerant of its activities or not). The JuD, as an independent actor challenging the state, was far less influential or powerful than most general narratives on its post-disaster activities seem to suggest. As I argue later, in fact, it did not attempt to do so either.

The JuD was able to capitalise on political momentum in the aftermath of the disaster in Badin but not in Thatta. In the summer of 2017, the JuD announced, for the first time ever, its intention to contest national elections taking place in Pakistan the following year. Until this point, and definitely not in the aftermath of the flooding disaster in 2010 and 2011, the JuD did not see itself as a political party and has not had any institutional standing within government. In its literature,[3] and in interviews with its higher-level members used to public interfacing, its goal was always described as purely humanitarian or charitable. Despite this, the JuD was able to use its humanitarian goals to remain politically active. Tankell states that the JuD was not a political party but it 'was and remains a political player. Its vast social welfare offerings and high public profile translated into influence with the population and some politicians depended on it to help deliver the vote banks they needed to remain in office' (2011, 243; also see Iqtedar 2011). To some extent this also reveals that the JuD remains an operator within the system,[4] and is directly influenced by the level of 'state repression' or 'access points' provided by state affects.

In the post-disaster context of lower Sindh, it was evident that if the local state system, including not only the local politicians but also the wider district administration, DCO, law enforcement, and so forth, allowed it space to operate, it created an enabling environment for the JuD to successfully mobilise. This also made it possible for the latter to access communities and coordinate efforts with the local government. In such situations, primarily in Badin, the JuD's ground level activities were able to flourish. On the other hand, where it did not encounter a welcoming and accessible local leadership and faced hostility, the JuD was unable to continue operations for too long. Its activities were, therefore,

[3] They publish separate magazines for men and women. The men's magazine I was able to peruse was the Urdu *Hafta roz* (weekly) *Ahl-e-Hadis* and the women's was called *Mahana* (monthly) *Al-Safaat*.

[4] Also suggested in the works of Tankell, Fair and others.

curtailed in those regions and it could not exploit the full opportunity created by the post-disaster moment. This made it possible to conclude that instead of capturing any political space as a consequence of a fractured social contract between the state and its citizens in Pakistan, it was, to a large degree, the state that determined the scale of JuD's success at a local level.

I now present an ethnography that helped emphasise this role of the local state as an enabler for the JuD, rather than fearing a 'take over' by the latter. In May 2012, I shadowed the JuD Director for Sindh for three days and continued to meet with him frequently during the course of my fieldwork. During one such meeting, he specifically mentioned the name of a local NGO in the town of Sajawal in Thatta and told me that this NGO had asked the JuD to come in and mobilise disaster rescue and relief in the first few months after the 2010 floods. I got in touch with this NGO independently, through a local contact, because I did not want them to think I was associated with the JuD in any way, and went to see them about two months later in July 2012.

Three male employees[5] greeted me when I went into the NGO office in Sajawal town in Thatta. All three were part of the management and administration team and performed different duties relating to the main operations of the NGO, in vocational training for women and provision of water and sanitation (WATSAN) programmes to selected communities in Thatta. During our discussion of the floods, they informed me that they 'invited' and then 'hosted' the JuD after the entire town had been devastated during the 2010 floods. All three informants firmly believed that the situation at the time was dire, government capacity was overwhelmed, and that it was necessary to call in people who were experienced with carrying out rescue, relief and eventually even rehabilitation services. It soon became clear that, unlike in Badin, and to some extent Tharparkar, where the JuD had some meaningful access points within the political system in the form of local politicians, in Thatta they did not.

The JuD did find support groups and allies in the form of this NGO staff but it faced considerable opposition and some degree of state 'repression'

[5] The three included: Manzoor *chacha*, a middle-aged man who had a beard and a mark on his forehead (*mehraab*) that is the result of praying frequently in the mosque; Sarwar, a non-bearded man in his mid-twenties who, two weeks after our meeting, got married and went on an atypical middle-class honeymoon to the hill station of Muree in Pakistan; and Aleem, a non-bearded, single man in his mid-twenties who admitted to being a Sufi poet and philosopher.

from the local government. The district government and local politicians did not give the JuD physical space, in terms of land, to set up a relief camp nor was it allowed to register an office in its own name; it faced a generally hostile and unwelcoming environment. By using such official channels, the local government was able to curtail the JuD's activities and influence quite significantly in Thatta. The employees at this NGO also repeatedly told me of the political pressures they faced to throw the JuD out of their Sajawal office.

> Sarwar: When no one gave space to the JuD to work in district Thatta, we provided them our office and made different arrangements for them.
>
> Aleem: I will be honest, the government did not want them to work here. Our Madam (chairperson of the NGO[6]) was in Saudi Arabia at the time and she was being pressured (remotely by government officials in Thatta) while there, to throw the JuD out from our office. But they entered Thatta because we invited them so we also protected them to the last day.

Interestingly, the local state was unwilling to give the JuD a physical space to operate in Thatta. The building that the JuD was eventually given by this NGO was one that was being rented using money from USAID funds. The American aid agency was funding one of the NGO projects on 'safe drinking water' and this building was rented for that project using the USAID grant. Subsequently, however, the JuD took over the entire building to manage their flood relief activities, and the 'safe drinking water' programme had to be relocated elsewhere. Once USAID staff in Karachi became aware of this situation they obviously demanded that the JuD be vacated from this office. Even then, I was told, negotiations ensued, with the NGO staff eventually being allowed to let the JuD remain in the office rented using USAID funds for another month. It was, however, on the condition that the JuD would not use its humanitarian label of the Falah-e-Insaniyat Foundation (FIF) and use an alternative name, which I will withhold to keep this NGO anonymous. This camp continued to be operated by the same JuD Sindh chapter but under

---

[6] Local NGOs in Pakistan do not need to operate under a very formal charter or memorandum. It is quite common for women from wealthy or middle-class backgrounds to start some sort of community outreach programme that evolves into a larger NGO-type organisation dispensing large quantities of aid monies. The *madam* of this NGO was described to me as a wealthy, non-Sindhi woman based in Karachi. It also seemed that she was very religiously inclined and had partly established the NGO to gain favour with Allah.

a different name and the JuD agreed to not use any of its banners and logos. This also in fact highlights the USAID programme's inability to control situations on the ground, revealing that, in Pakistan, it is perhaps less politically influential than many have suggested (Miller 2012).

These men further told me that I would struggle to find any ongoing projects of the JuD in this area as it had more or less withdrawn from the city of Sajawal after the floods. When I asked why, Manzoor *chacha* gave a very succinct description of meaningful access points and state support being missing in the Thatta context but being available for the JuD in Badin.

> In Badin they have their base for the last 20 years. Unfortunately they have no such existing support base in Thatta. In Badin it is also true that some influential people, politicians support them, social activists support them, and local people support them. Here, however, the community and the state are not supportive of their activities. In the cities of Badin and Golarchi (city in Badin district) their religious activities mean that they have the support of many thousands of people already.

The interviewees were unanimous in the view that the JuD needed state support to remain operational, something that they repeatedly struggled to find in Thatta. It was also interesting that none of the men believed that the JuD had political aspirations. Sarwar even sounded irritated by my question and said, '*How can they have a political motive when they do not even contest elections?*' At the same time, the interviewees also pointed out that even if it did have political ambitions, the JuD would not find political space in the town of Sajawal as the townspeople already overwhelmingly supported a different political Islamist organisation (Jamiat-e-ulma-e-Islam, JuI-F).[7] This discussion helped me understand that the relatively visible and well-entrenched position of the JuD in Badin, particularly in the post-disaster context, is partly because of the local state and not in spite of it. It also helped clarify another important issue of political influence: it would be difficult for the JuD to dislodge an existing Islamist group's dominance in one village, town or city, in order to

[7] The JuI-F, unlike the JuD, contests elections, and while it still has a deeply theocratic ideology it is one that people can vote for at the polls. Also, unlike the JuD, the JuI-F is a part of the Deobandi movement in South Asian Sunni Islam and are patronising towards the Ahl-e-Hadis followers because they do not follow any of the Sunni schools of jurisprudence.

establish its own. Given that the JuI-F existed and operated in this area, the JuD was unlikely to get any support at the town-level either.

The time that I spent with this NGO staff in Sajawal, Thatta, on two different occasions did help me make sense of different observations I had made in the field. The 'environmental variables' in Badin were more supportive for the JuD when compared to those in Thatta. The Pakistan Army has a base just outside the main city of Badin and, during my fieldwork, people often mentioned the role of the army in disaster rescue operations after the floods. The army had also set up a large relief camp hosting 1,700 displaced people and seemed to have considerable visibility on the ground in the early days after the floods. When I was finally allowed to interview the Commander of this base,[8] I gradually brought the JuD into our conversation after over two hours of talking about the floods and the details of what the army provided in what numbers and to whom. He said: '*Bibi*, the JuD did not come here (to provide disaster rescue and relief services).' 'Ok, then the FIF,' I press on. The commander gives me a half-smile and says, 'You are very well-conversant.'

Without acknowledging or denying their presence the commander goes on to say that the army is not concerned that these groups might capture political space in this area ('this is something the civilian government should be worried about') before quickly changing the subject. Given that the JuD (not FIF) *markaz* in Badin, on main Gularchi road, is less than 5 miles from the army base, and the way in which the commander reacted, provide further evidence for arguments that the army is, at the very least, aware, or perhaps even supportive, of JuD activities in the area. Additionally, my time in the field enabled me to draw some more connections. These links between the military establishment and the JuD on the ground began to get more obvious after I had spent about four months around the districts of Badin and Tharparkar. It is evident from my community-based work that the military is not part of the ethnographic social contract in lower Sindh, and is never referred to as the *sarkar*. Officially, too, it was fairly clear that the men in uniform and the local state system stayed out of each other's way. That said, however, the military went about its business of 'security', and even disaster relief around the base. Their presence was an enabling factor which made it possible for the JuD to have a local visibility in Badin and Tharparkar in a way that it clearly did not in Thatta.

[8] I will withhold his rank and name for anonymity.

I had been working, and was visible, around Badin for many months, yet I only received a threatening phone call, from someone who identified themselves as 'Inspector Naseem, from the Inter-Services Intelligence (ISI)', on my personal mobile the day after I visited the JuD *markaz*. This made me believe that there was fairly direct communication between the JuD and the military in Badin. In fact, the physical proximity of the JuD *markaz* and the army base in Badin was itself a telltale sign. It would be difficult for the commander to make his weekend visits to Karachi without crossing the *markaz*. One of my informants from Badin, who repeatedly said to me that the army and the local authorities are supportive of the JuD in the area, took me to see graffiti on a wall minutes away from the army base that was signed as '(FIF) *fauji* (army) brothers'. Since the JuD has been banned by the Musharraf government in Pakistan, it had been operating under the official brand of FIF (Falah-e-Insaniyat Foundation). There have since been some reports that the government in Pakistan was 'mulling' (Mukhtar 2016) over a ban on the FIF as well, but no official announcement to that effect has been made. The FIF website and humanitarian missions are live and expanding.

Figure 5.2 Graffiti on a building showing some Urdu text with '(FIF) fauji [army] brothers' signed underneath. Photograph taken by author in Golarchi city.

In the aftermath of the flooding disaster as well, the JuD was easily able to access land and space to set up a relief camp in a central location in Badin city. Its centre itself is a large renovated building that is continuing to operate long after the flood-affected have returned home, and my local informants believed that it was being used to recruit new cadre. The JuD reconstruction work that I was able to witness, in flood-affected communities around Badin, was all labelled with FIF banners and was extensively branded with their logos and slogans. When compared to Thatta, where the district-level hostility resulted in the JuD leaving within a couple of months after the disaster, the JuD encountered a much more favourable structure of political opportunities in Badin. This again illustrates that the JuD is only able to operate, and have an impact, in places where the larger entity, the *sarkar*, gives them space or, at the very least, turns a blind eye, allowing them to operate.

Even with regard to access to entry points in the political system, the JuD enjoyed much better terms with the Mirzas in Badin than with the Sheerazis in Thatta.[9] The JuD Director of Sindh made it a point to tell me that during the worst days of the disaster, he was in regular phone contact with Dr Fehmida Mirza, MNA from Badin and, at the time, one of the most politically influential women in the country as the Speaker of the National Assembly. Even if speaking everyday was a stretch, it was common knowledge that the JuD did have access to the Mirzas when necessary. On the other hand, the JuD Director for Sindh, and the head of relief operations in charge of Thatta district after the 2010 floods, made absolutely no mention of the Sheerazis of Thatta. Locally, in and around Thatta city as well, I did not meet a single person who knew of the JuD's flood relief activities. One of my informants, a local community activist from Thatta, was politically opposed to the domination of the Sheerazi family in National and Provincial Assemblies. Yet he maintained that the local administration in Thatta, including the Sheerazis, have a zero-tolerance policy towards Islamist groups such as the JuD. The city of Thatta, in particular, is a hotbed of Sindhi nationalism and various kinds of smaller leftist parties, and seems to hold little traction for Islamist groups as well. This was also supported by my informants from the NGO in Sajawal, who said that access to meaningful entry points in politics for the JuD is far more limited in Thatta when compared to Badin.

The presence of the army, a district administration including officials such the DDO (Deputy District Officer), and the local political family that included one MNA and one MPA in Badin – an entire local state structure that was supportive of JuD activities on the ground – resulted in their greater visibility

[9] The political families in Badin and Thatta, see Chapter 2.

in Badin. In comparison, in Thatta district the local DCO and DDO, the political family that had one member in the National Assembly and multiple in the Provincial Assembly, the existence of a vibrant political opposition that included the JuI-F in the city of Sajawal along with Sindhi nationalists and other smaller political parties in Thatta city, all made it very difficult for the JuD to gain any significant access into the district.

Tharparkar, too, revealed a similar but more ambiguous pattern of JuD support, due to the polarised nature of state politics at a local level. Broadly speaking, in areas with Arbab support, some of which as I have explained earlier comes from Ahl-e-Hadis and more religiously conservative factions of society, it was more likely to hear of some JuD presence after the floods. That said, however, Tharparkar also has the largest Hindu population as compared to any other district. The push on citizenship to move towards minimum rights and entitlements beyond just social relations or hereditary structures of power and privilegehas resulted in the emergence of small political forces such as the Bheel[10] Ittehad Party and the Pakistan Hindu Panchiyat (PHP), exercising great influence at a local scale. In these areas the JuD was not visible in the aftermath of the floods.

In all three districts of Pakistan where my study is based, it was evident that the JuD was most operational and functional, and able to have a significant impact in the post-disaster context, where it was provided an enabling environment and supported by the state. It is important to highlight that in this situation, the Sheerazis, the Mirzas and the Arbabs are acting as state representatives, who are part of the state architecture, rather than simply as powerful patrons. As the work of Robins, Cornwall and von Lieres (2008) tells us, they too are adept at moving 'seamlessly' between these differing roles.

The JuD was not a dominant social actor, presenting an 'alternative' in the aftermath of the flooding disaster in Pakistan, in the way faith-based NGOs were in Turkey in the aftermath of the Marmara earthquake (Pelling and Dill 2010). Not only did people's social contract with the larger entity, the *sarkar*, remain strong, but the discussion so far has also further emphasised that even the JuD was only able to exert as much influence, in the post-disaster context of lower Sindh, as the *sarkar* allowed it to exert. The next section will now illustrate that the JuD itself was not interested in constructing itself in opposition to the state.

---

[10] The Bheels are a Hindu scheduled caste.

The Jamaat-ud-Dawa Does Not Try to Be the Larger Entity, the *Sarkar*

Pelling's work (2011) on disasters and transformative change emphasises the instability caused by development failures made obvious at the point of the disaster. This opens scope for change, particularly creating opportunities for alternative narratives and discourses that challenge prevailing ruling practice (Pelling 2011). In his examination of the case of the Marmara earthquake in Turkey, Pelling highlights the obvious ideological distance between the Kemalist state, which maintains a paternalistic, secular Turkish polity, and the NGOs and civil society organisations that seem to be comprised of more conservative and religious elements in the predominantly Muslim country. It was the latter, however, that were the first to provide disaster rescue and relief in the early days after the earthquake in 1999. Interestingly, until this civil society was being presented in popular narrative as an extension of a paternalistic state, they were allowed to operate with relative freedom. Once the media discourse changed to one of inadequate state capacity resulting in NGOs doing the job of the state, there was a serious crackdown on the relief operations of civil society groups. The state feared that loss of legitimacy in the wake of the disaster could disturb a delicate balance between the secular and Islamic forces in the country, not only due to the activities of a conservative civil society but also because their political loss would be the gain of an Islamic party very active after the disaster and with strong grassroots-level support. This case study gives a clear sense of 'competition over discourse' between the secular Kemalist state and the Islamic NGOs and parties in the post-disaster political space in Turkey.

My fieldwork gave me a clear sense that no such competition existed in the post-disaster context of lower Sindh, partly because the JuD was only able to function effectively with state support and not in opposition to it. In my field area it was evident that the state allowed the JuD to operate with impunity in the district of Badin and in parts of Tharparkar; so in these areas the JuD encountered an enabling environment after the floods. In Thatta, where there was opposition to the JuD at a district government level, it was only able to have a marginal presence for a few months before being completely pushed out. The JuD, for its part, maintained a pro-state narrative.

In my interview with the Director of the Sindh chapter he repeated the word 'anti-state' (in English, in our Urdu conversation) twice. The point he took pains to make was: 'We have never said we are an anti-state organisation.'

In much the same way, he repeated the phrase *shana bashana* (shoulder to shoulder) four or five times when talking about the *fauj* (army), acknowledging that the army personnel worked with them when providing rescue and relief to flood-affected people. The Director also maintained his position that he was in regular telephone contact with the army commander in the area, and with Dr Fehmida Mirza, the MNA from Badin. The JuD never positioned itself as an alternative force of development and change.

Once again this fact was brought home to me when I was having a conversation, this time not with a member of the JuD cadre or leadership but with someone who operates along opposing lines to the JuD. When I interviewed a local head of a Sipah-e-Sahaba (SeS) *madrassa*, his response was very different. The SeS is a banned Sunni extremist group with a very militant history of targeted violence against Pakistan's Shia minority. Unlike the JuD, however, it does contest elections in Pakistan and is part of the electoral process under the name of Millat-e-Islamia Party (Party of the Islamic Nation). The militant outfit of the SeS has been subjected to state repression at various points since its creation,[11] and is also now part of the anti-state Tehreek-e-Taliban Pakistan rebellion (Abou Zahab and Roy 2004). The way the SeS (and its militant wing, the Lashkar-e-Jhangvi) constructs itself, therefore, was in stark opposition to the JuD.

I visited an SeS *madrassa*, based just outside the town of Khoski, run by a well-known SeS leader, Abdullah Sindhi. Sindhi's fiery hate speech on Shias can be found on YouTube, and my local informants were fully aware of his political views. He has also been contesting elections against the Mirzas in recent years and is trying to establish himself as a political force in this part of Badin.

While I was able to interview him on a separate occasion, when I first asked to meet with the head of this *madrassa*, I was introduced to Sindhi's younger brother. I will refer to the younger brother as Mufti sahab because he expressed a preference for remaining behind the political scenes and chose to lead a quiet life of teaching children instead.[12]

[11] Most famously, the Chief Minister of Punjab Province and brother of Prime Minister Shahbaz Sharif instituted a crackdown against the organisation in 1998 in which many high level SeS/LeJ leaders were killed in extra-judicial 'encounters' with law-enforcement agencies.

[12] It also seemed to work well in terms of management of the *madrassa* because Sindhi spent a lot of time in Jhung where the SeS are widely known to be based.

Figure 5.3 Abdullah Sindhi's election campaign poster on a wall in Khoski city. While he was officially standing as an 'independent candidate', the poster has a picture of Maulana Mohammad Ahmed Ludhianvi (a prominent leader of the SeS) in the background and the SeS's electoral symbol of a glass in the foreground, so that voters know Sindhi's unstated affiliation. Photograph taken by author.

In our interview, as soon as the conversation turned to the floods that devastated Badin in 2011, it became clear that Mufti sahab and the JuD Director did not share a common platform. Mufti sahab almost raced to tell me of a '*gayab riyasat*', which quite closely translates to 'absent state'. Then, perhaps because he is less used to giving interviews and answering people's questions than his brother, he gave me a surprisingly honest and direct response when I asked about their motivation for providing disaster relief services:

> Look, our main motive is always *Allah ki raza* [*sic*[13]] but there was another motive. Our other motive is to teach people a lesson. We want people to know that in all the difficulties and pain (*dukh dard*) that you face, we are standing right by you, supporting you. Hence if we are the first to arrive during your hardest ordeals then the 'background' thinking we want to 'provide' to people is that politics is also our right (*haq*). We are not in government, we have no,

[13] The phrase *Allah ki raza* is being used incorrectly by the interviewee. He means to say 'to please Allah'; instead he ends up saying 'with the will of Allah'. This was a common grammatical error made by various people in this particular context of disaster relief.

> uh, 'support' of government, and we have nothing. The point we are trying to convey is – look, when we have nothing we are able to do so much for you, bring us into power then see how we will do everything for you … It is about resources (*vasail*); those who have resources are doing nothing – give us these resources and then see what happens.

The essence of Mufti Sahab's message was radical. He believed that the 'absent state' needed to be replaced by the SeS taking control of the government. My interview with Abdullah Sindhi was not as eventful and I received fairly scripted answers, though in one part of the conversation he also slipped up and said, 'Obviously, we want to strengthen our foundations in the communities as well.' While the political head of this local SeS movement seemed to know how to manage interviews and narratives, upon slightly deeper inspection, it becomes clear that the organisation does in fact set itself up to be an alternative to the existing state. They emphasised that the 'absent state' needed to be replaced by a new order and paradigm of development, one they believed the SeS could provide. Such views were never expressed at any level among the rank and file of the JuD. The lower level cadre at JuD did on occasion express disdain for an inefficient state that was very ineffective during the disaster, but always maintained that their *amir* (leader) is not seeking political power or capture of the state.

It is necessary to highlight at this time that neither the JuD's political ideology nor its militant wing[14] is supportive of the Tehreek-e-Taliban Pakistan (TTP) armed rebellion raging against the state at the time and, while less deadly, still active today.[15] The message to the flood-affected people they were helping was never framed as 'the JuD versus the state', implying that,

[14] During my fieldwork it became clear that referring to the LeT as the militant wing and JuD as the humanitarian wing might be useful for understanding the undertones within the organisation but it is not representative of the reality on the ground. The JuD cadre actually move freely between militant, humanitarian, even political, rallying, while calling themselves JuD or FIF. The identities of the two or three groups being managed by Hafiz Mohammad Saeed are much more fluid than they have been made out to be.

[15] The Tehreek-e-Taliban Pakistan (TTP) is a movement with a 'local and nuanced' Pakistani focus that is 'definitely distinct' from the Afghan Taliban, though divisions and differences exist even within the group. The TTP is broadly based on three ideological principles: enforcing Sharia in Pakistan, uniting against coalition forces in Afghanistan and performing a defensive *jihad* against the Pakistan Army. The group has been fighting an armed insurgency against what they call the '"infidel" state of Pakistan' since the TTP was officially formed in December 2007.

because they were reaching out to people where the latter was failing to do so, they were a force more competent and compassionate than the state. The JuD did not present itself as an alternative to the state. The people, too, showed no signs of interpreting them as such. Comparing the JuD narrative with the one presented by the SeS made their opposing agendas obvious. While the SeS's support to the TTP and a history of fighting the state, sometimes even being violently repressed by it, explain why the SeS is anti-state in its political agenda, the JuD with its obvious links to the Pakistani military establishment is clearly not. Sindhi and his brother made clear the fact that they did see themselves and their political ideology as an alternative to the state. The JuD leaders and members of the cadre on the other hand were extremely careful to mention that they were not anti-state agents; rather, that they had very good relations with the military and civilian administration in the aftermath of the flooding disaster in Pakistan in 2010 and 2011 – contrary to the popular narrative constructed after the floods in Sindh that presented a struggle between the JuD and the state competing to win 'hearts and minds' of the affected population. My evidence clearly illustrates that this was a false dichotomy; the JuD had no interest or desire to be the state in the aftermath of the flooding disaster in Pakistan and people's relationship with the larger entity, the *sarkar*, remained intact.

The Jamaat-ud-Dawa's Limited Ability to 'Win Hearts and Minds'

One final point on this issue of 'winning hearts and minds' deserves attention because it relates to the omnipresence of the state and illustrates that the social contract between the larger entity of the *sarkar* and the citizens remained intact in the aftermath of the flooding disaster in Pakistan in 2010 and 2011. This idea that Islamists would 'take over' parts of disaster-affected Pakistan, not militarily but politically, through the provision of disaster aid, is built on the same premise as the US counter-insurgency policy on 'winning hearts and minds'[16] of hostile populations using humanitarian aid and assistance

[16] Phrase taken from US President Lyndon B. Johnson's statement on Vietnam that 'the ultimate victory will depend upon the hearts and minds of the people who actually live out there. By helping to bring them hope and electricity you are also striking a very important blow for the cause of freedom throughout the world'; made at a Dinner Meeting of the Texas Electric Cooperatives, Inc., 4 May 1965. Available at http://www.presidency.ucsb.edu/ws/index.php?pid=26942#axzz1uDRuoCji

(Williamson 2011). The fact that American bilateral aid in Pakistan is an established 'vehicle towards that end' is now well documented (Andrabi and Das 2010). The way that this has been operationalised on a ground level is through the prolific use of branding. All US-funded aid carries the logo of USAID and the words 'From the American People' in the vernacular language (Yu 2010).

The American aid agency was, in fact, convinced that state 'absence' in flood-affected areas, in the aftermath of the flooding disaster in 2010 and 2011, was resulting in groups such as the JuD increasing their political popularity at a ground level and 'gain(ing) recruits'. So, tens of millions of dollars were diverted from other aid funds given to Pakistan and turned towards flood relief (Anthony 2010). Such policies were based on a flawed understanding of 'absent' state and collapsed citizenship that were not very representative of the situation on the ground.

First, I have argued elsewhere (Siddiqi 2014) that people exercise agency and, even in the aftermath of the flooding disaster in 2010 and 2011, people in lower Sindh were vulnerable but they were still unlikely to allow flood relief or bags of food aid stamped with 'USAID: From the American People' to dictate who they would support politically.

Second, the role of the state in the aftermath of the disaster, and the way it reached out to affected citizens strengthening aspects of the social contract, also explains in part the relative inability of the JuD to 'win the hearts and minds' of people they helped in lower Sindh. Across the three districts, and over the seven months that I undertook fieldwork, I was able to spend time with a total of 23 different families who had spent time in JuD relief camps or been assisted by them in some capacity after the flooding disaster in 2010 and 2011. Of all of these people only one community, surprisingly of Hindu *haris* (landless tenants) in the *taluka* of Tando Bagho in Badin district, seemed to be affected enough by the JuD's relief activities to politically support it in an electoral context. We talked about how the JuD did not at the time contest elections but then I asked them if they would feel compelled to vote for the JuD in the event that the JuD did contest for the next election. Vijay *chacha*, one of the older men in the community with greying hair, emphasised that it was not just the fact that the JuD provided them with much-needed relief, but that they were particularly grateful that the help came to them and they did not have to abandon their homes and livestock to go to *sarkari* (state-run) relief camps. He then carried on:

> If those *maulvis*[17] come to us (to campaign and ask for support), why not? We will vote for them. They cooked food for us and carried it all the way from Jhuddo;[18] it is not something we will forget easily.

Vijay *chacha* belonged to a community of about 15 *hari* families living on a vegetable farm[19] they had been working on for many years. These *hari*s were Hindus and belonged to the scheduled caste known as Kohlis. A conversation with one of the young women, a twenty-something-year-old mother of three, earlier that week, had already revealed that in August 2011, at the height of the floods, they were struggling to find any food or water but were still reluctant to leave their homes. These families suffered from social exclusion, economic dispossession and nebulous legal safeguards and guarantees, given that they were non-Muslim landless tenants living and working on land that belonged to a local businessman–landlord. They feared that if they left during the floods it was possible that the landlord would not allow them back on the land, or that if their possessions were stolen from their abandoned huts they would find it difficult to get any law enforcement officials to take them seriously. Despite speaking to this informant almost a year after the floods, I was able to hear and feel a very palpable sense of insecurity that this range and mix of vulnerabilities raised.

The root of Vijay *chacha*'s support lay in his belief of his own economic and food insecurity. These *hari*s truly believed that if the JuD had not brought them cooked food to eat they would have starved to death in their homes. This level of food insecurity, however, was the exception and not the norm in flood-affected areas of Sindh. A study conducted by the Agha Khan University in flood-affected regions of Sindh and Punjab after the 2010 disaster analysed

---

[17] *Maulvi* in Urdu refers to the religious cleric in charge of a mosque. In this case the informant is referring to the JuD men he met as 'maulvis' possibly because of their appearance.

[18] The closest small town where the JuD camp was based.

[19] In the season I was there I could see red chillies, cabbage and salad leaves. The owner of this farm was a Urdu-speaking man from the Rajput tribe (descendants of Hindu warrior classes in north India who were the overwhelming majority in the princely states of Rajasthan and Saurashtra), who owned approximately 200 acres of land and voted for the candidate from Pakistan Muslim League–Quaid (PML-Q), a centre-right party close to the military establishment. He had a lot of family in Rajasthan in India but was still vehemently anti-India and nationalist (in a way most Sindhis are not), which partly explained his political choices.

data from nutrition surveys of children across 70 clusters and 786 households in Sindh and 1,200 households across 60 clusters in Punjab. It revealed that the scale of the 2010 disaster had negatively impacted Pakistan's ability to make progress on malnutrition indicators as part of its Millennium Development Goals (MDGs) pledge. This, however, remained consistent with the general trend at the time: 'the 2010 flood clearly revealed what has always existed and there was no evidence that the floods had induced acute malnutrition' (Hossain et al. 2013). Sindh's record on under-nutrition was already abysmal but it was significant that it had not worsened as a consequence of the floods. According to one estimate, the floods of 2010 alone resulted in loss of crops to the value of half a billion dollars. Similarly, at US$233 million, the loss in livestock was greatest in Sindh as compared to any other part of Pakistan (Dorosh, Malik and Krausova 2010). Despite the enormous scale of the loss, large-scale hunger and scenes of famine were not part of the wider narrative on the floods.

My qualitative work on food security in the three districts where I undertook fieldwork broadly supports these findings. In my paper on this issue of food security, I use Sen's entitlement approach – 'individuals face starvation if their full entitlement set does not provide them with adequate food for subsistence' (Devereux 2007, 67) – to illustrate that the state response to the flooding disaster in 2010 and 2011 was enough to prevent what Devereux refers to as 'new famines'. His work argues against received wisdom that famines have 'receded into history' or that they only occur in countries that are dictatorships or at war. Through case studies of 'peaceful democracies' in Europe, Asia and Africa he illustrates how entitlement failures experienced in the wake of crises, such as an HIV/AIDS epidemic or international sanctions, resulted in 'new famines' in these situations (Devereux 2007). It is clear, however, that despite the large-scale loss in livestock, crops and general food production, the flooding disaster in 2010 and 2011 did not culminate in a climatic disaster–based famine. My informants reveal that even when they were in relief camps, whether run by NGOs or the state, they were able to maintain basic subsistence. Even when state assistance was not easily acknowledged by my informants, two interviewees, independently of each other, said that if the state had not intervened in the manner that it did (one explicitly stated, 'with bank cards and rations'), 'we would have starved to death'. I conclude that, to some extent, it was possible to credit 'state interventions for preventing large-scale food insecurity during the disaster' (Siddiqi 2013, 97).

It, therefore, seems that the situation of exclusion and vulnerability faced by the Hindu *haris* on the vegetable farm was unique. It was made up of a range of factors: they were a relatively small community of only 15 households; their landlord was an absentee landlord, and the farm would have been deserted had they left; they belonged to a Hindu scheduled caste; and were landless with no title to anything they owned. All of which together, but particularly their immobility, made them particularly food insecure, and their fear of starvation was real. This level of food, and by extension, life insecurity made them more vulnerable to the JuD's political message than any of my other informants in lower Sindh in the aftermath of the disaster. The latter were relatively food secure and able to access basic subsistence, partly because of an active state involved in the delivery of basic services after the floods of 2010 and 2011. Even in this exceptional situation of the Hindu *hari*s feeling compelled to vote for the JuD, it is important to note that the JuD was never conflated with the larger entity of the *sarkar*. In fact, the words of my interviewee earlier in the conversation had suggested that he believed it was the relative obscurity of the JuD that allowed it to provide a tailor-made relief service for him and his community. As one PPP comrade from Badin explained to me, it was not possible to compare state disaster relief and recovery with the efforts of anyone else in the disaster-affected areas: 'I tell you, sister, (evidence that) the *gornment* was working (was) everywhere. After all it goes without saying, it is the *gornment*; it has the greatest reach and it can get, everywhere, everywhere.'

Contextualising the Narrative on the Jamaat-ud-Dawa

In a paper published on the 'Changing Tactics of Jihad Organisations in Pakistan' (Rana 2006), the author, a well-known journalist reporting on Pakistan's milieu of *jihadi* outfits, explains that in the post-9/11 crackdown on these groups by the government of the then-President and Chief of Army Staff, General Musharraf, the JuD was a relative 'exception that realised the gravity of the situation just after the shift in Pakistan's pro-jihad policy' (Gul 2010, 18). The JuD's leader, Professor Hafiz Saeed, publicly announced the dissolution of its militant wing,[20] the Lashkar-e-Taiba (LeT), and invested hundreds of millions of rupees in other 'departments' of operations such as education, health transport and the like (Rana 2006). At the same time other groups were also rebranding their militant groups, dropping the use of words

[20] In December 2001, Hafiz Saeed held a press conference in which he declared that the Pakistan chapter of the LeT had been dissolved (Rana 2006).

such as '*lashkar*, *jaish*, *mujahideen*'[21] in order to appear more political than militant, and '*jihadi* leaders' joined religious–political parties and contested the national elections in 2002 (Rana 2006). This 'mainstreaming' of *jihadi* politics is compounded by the fact that the JuD has thus far not contested an election in an open and relatively transparent platform; rather, it chooses to operate through what is considered to be a 'vast network' of social services. This has resulted in the general perception of the JuD as a group that is capable of taking over the state, particularly in times of crises and in areas where the state is seen to be absent.

This is especially true during times of humanitarian disasters beginning with the earthquake that affected Kashmir and other parts of northern Pakistan in 2005. Local and international media was running stories on the role of the JuD (Gall and Jamal 2005) in helping survivors and this led to the group's increased popularity at home and raising concerns about the scale of their operations abroad (Lancaster and Khan 2005). The earthquake in 2005 was the first time that the JuD's humanitarian activities got widespread attention, but its history of reaching out to populations in Sindh, through social services and welfare activities, goes back to the early 2000s. This was a time when the organisation was becoming more political, and was searching for new operational areas, due to the Afghanistan chapter being dissolved and difficulty with infiltrations into Kashmir (Rana 2006).

Interviewees during my fieldwork, such as Mr Kamal Hyder from *Al Jazeera English* or interviewees who had primarily witnessed the disaster and the JuD relief activities, were always more likely to say that they were 'winning hearts and minds' of flood-affected people in Pakistan. Those who had actually been affected by the disaster, and also received JuD aid and support, did not have such a clear answer and, with the exception of the Hindu *hari*s, did not express any desire to politically support the JuD. The flood-affected people I spent time with in lower Sindh had a measured approach to this question of JuD and political support, primarily one that seemed to suggest that neither did they see the JuD as an alternative to the state nor did they wish to engage with them at an electoral level in the future. Those who had only witnessed the JuD's flood relief efforts were much more impressed by the political impact of their disaster response activities. The JuD, it seems, was very effective at making itself look more successful and efficient than it arguably was.

---

[21] All different Urdu words for militants.

My evidence from the field, therefore, comes to similar conclusions as other researchers on the JuD but for different reasons than theirs. Fair (2011), for instance, argues that during the earthquake in 2005, and also during the floods in 2010, the JuD did not have as large a presence on the ground and that they were not as successful in reaching out to people as represented by popular media accounts. Her analysis suggests that the media accounts deliberately exaggerate the JuD's disaster operations to foster support for them under direction from the notorious Inter-Services Intelligence (ISI) of Pakistan. Fair then goes on to state that 'many journalists are explicitly on the ISI's payroll and routinely plant stories on behalf of the ISI or shape stories to suit the ISI's interests' (2011, 14).

Findings from my research on the JuD instead indicate that, regardless of whether the ISI is planting stories aggrandising the JuD or not, the JuD itself is very mindful of public opinion. It has a sophisticated PR machinery and knows how to weigh the scales of spectators and journalists in their favour.[22] Abbas Nasir, a well-known journalist in Pakistan and former editor of *Dawn*, also supports the idea that the JuD is 'media-savvy'. In a piece he published on this subject, he states, 'While at public meetings Hafiz Saeed and other leaders of his organisation unmistakably breathe fire, his TV appearances are marked by a measured tone and a fairly plausible line of argument. But it is social media where JuD's sophistication becomes apparent' (Nasir 2012). The JuD is, in most instances, able to successfully play the media and represent itself in a very positive light. This does not mean, however, that it is either able to or interested in presenting itself as an alternative to the state in Pakistan.

[22] The JuD was often compared to the political party MQM (Mutahida Quomi Movement) by journalists who were familiar with both groups. The MQM is well known for having efficient and effective spin doctors and propaganda machines.

Conclusion

Disasters and the State–Citizen Relationship

This book opens by presenting both the scholarly literature and the popular media narratives around the 'absence' of the state and the lack of a social contract in what is colloquially known as 'interior' Sindh. After clarifying the theory and methodology employed by this research it deconstructs the idea that the state is non-existent and that citizens in non-urban parts of Pakistan, such as lower Sindh, define the very terms of the social contract as a social interaction between themselves and their local *wadera*, *pir* or some other hereditary leader. It emphasizes that while traditional forms of leadership remain important, there is a wider, more comprehensive understanding of state–citizen relations, one that increasingly includes a more rights-based understanding of citizenship.

The focus in later chapters on the flooding disaster that affected Pakistan in 2010 and 2011 also reveals that the state reached out to its citizens in an unprecedented manner, and that citizens made increasing demands of this state, helping to push the citizenship framework forward. Evidence from the field demonstrates that despite increased attention to, and alarmist accounts of, Islamist groups such as the JuD reaching out to people where the state had 'failed', the construction of the state remained intact. In the aftermath of the floods of 2010 and 2011 in Sindh, people made demands on the state as the primary political actor and the larger social entity, the *sarkar*. The state, for its part, attempted to deliver disaster rescue and relief that began to be increasingly interpreted as a right by the people. My work, therefore, makes a case for greater attention to be paid to understanding and explaining concepts of the state and citizenship in non-urban parts of Pakistan, such as lower Sindh, rather than accepting the existing broad and generalised narratives, particularly around social structures.

As the discussion of the political families of Thatta, Badin and Tharparkar in Chapter 2 has illustrated, while social and hereditary relations around *wadera*s and *biraderi*s might be intuitively appealing, they are also analytically frustrating and theoretically limiting frameworks to theorise the state within them. This is particularly true in light of the work done by ethnographers who have attempted to study 'the state' in Pakistan and for years have been trying to say something different. For instance, Verkaaik argues that the 'notion of the state as a benevolent parent' amongst the Muhajirs in Hyderabad (Sindh) is prevalent and 'expect(s) the impossible' (2001, 364). His ethnography on young men from this ethnic group reveals that to them the state in Pakistan is meant to represent 'a truly transparent and democratic state sincerely devoted to the ideas of Muslim fraternity' (Verkaaik 2001, 364). Similarly, Soekefeld's ethnography on Attabad in Gilgit-Baltistan states that there is an apparent contradiction where even if confidence in the state is low it is still expected to meet unreal expectations and is 'held responsible for almost everything' (2012, 203). These authors are, in fact, arguing that the state is bigger than it is thought of and all-pervasive in the political imagination of Pakistan's citizens, not 'absent' or 'damaged'. While one could argue that these ethnographic observations are based on other parts of Pakistan, it is important to note that Khan's (2007) anthropological work on upper Sindh is also not convinced that the *wadera–hari* interaction is the central political relationship in the village where she did her fieldwork in Shikarpur. She argues that this relationship is changing significantly, resulting in a dissipation of associated 'social capital'. Her work in fact illustrates that 'with the reduction in the role and the subsequent predicted reduction in the power of the landlord, there are (other) emerging institutions that may foster positive social capital' (Khan 2007, viii).

This body of literature is based on ethnographic study of politics and society in different parts of Pakistan. Even research that is not strictly ethnographic but intensive and based on one region, Sahiwal in Punjab (Mohmand 2011), illustrates that there is more to the state–citizen relationship not adequately captured in frameworks used by social structuralists to study the state in Pakistan. Instead of using '"traditional" categories of analysis for non-Western societies: tribes, notions of honour, transactions and exchange and kinship' (Maqsood 2012, 171), and then extending them to explain concepts of state and citizenship in Pakistan, this body of work makes it amply clear that it is important to understand the state–citizen relationship beyond such social relations. The state is also understood to mean a democratic entity that might sometimes be seen as being unable to provide basic services but is still held responsible for everything. Traditional asymmetrical power relations between a *wadera* who has all the political, economic and social power and his disempowered and disenfranchised *hari*s also no longer represent an accurate picture of either social relations or political relations in much of Punjab and Sindh. These frameworks which argue that there is no social contract or citizenship framework in Pakistan needs to be revisited.

This book, therefore, set out to address the following research question:

> Do hereditary relations and social structures define the nature of the social contract between the state and the citizens in lower Sindh?

It systematically argues that while social structures along caste and kinship lines remain important in lower Sindh, they do not encompass the complete state–citizen interaction. People in parts of Pakistan such as lower Sindh have a relationship with the wider social and political entity, the *sarkar*, and this is what they invoke during difficult times, such as during natural disasters. Equally, while people living in lower Sindh may not have a vernacular word that accurately encompasses all the ideals of liberal citizenship, they still have an understanding of rights they are entitled to by the state. This analysis, therefore, clearly establishes the fact that a tangible social contract, and a framework for citizenship beyond caste and kinship relations, exists in parts of Pakistan such as lower Sindh. I further argue that this was pushed along in the aftermath of the flooding disaster in 2010 and 2011.

Empirical Findings

Each chapter in the book builds the central argument that people in Pakistan have a tangible relationship with a larger social entity of 'the *sarkar*' in order to answer the main research question stated above.

The state–citizen relationship is defined by more than people's personal interactions with political patrons. In Chapter 2, 'The State as a Complex Web of Social Relations', I argue that a popular and historical narrative sees 'interior' Sindh as a rigid and static society operating within the confines of asymmetrical power relations between the masses in the countryside and the Sufi *pir*, *wadera* or other caste or kin leader. While it is commonly believed that these powerful political patrons are able to use their social and economic position to gain and remain in political power, defining people's entire spectrum and construction of a state, my research argues that these notions need to be updated and contextualised for greater understanding. Arguing in the tradition of other scholars on Pakistan who see society as changing and not rigid, I contend that in the three districts of lower Sindh, there was more to people's relationship with the state than just a relationship with the main political families.

Thatta illustrated the importance for people of seeing a caring, personable individual as a manifestation of the state, while Badin illustrated, to some extent, the importance of party politics and ideologies; Tharparkar provided the perfect illustration of changing politics and political constituencies. Not only was the Arbabs' constituency showing signs of change to include more religiously conservative voters but their number of seats in the National and Provincial Assemblies was equally changing and not static. All three districts may have pointed towards differing political trends but there was little doubt that the trends presented in classical texts on 'interior' Sindh are changing. The idea and complexity of the state in lower Sindh is defined by far more than people's interaction with the Sheerazis, Mirzas, or Arbabs as kin, *hari*s, or clients.

A social contract exists between the omnipresent social entity, 'the *sarkar*' and local constructions of citizenship based on rights and entitlements. In Chapter 3, 'The Ethnographic Social Contract', I extend this idea that the state is *more* than just social relations with political patrons. I construct an ethnography of the state and citizenship in lower Sindh, in an effort to show that people in my study area did not see the state as an extension of their relations with *wadera*s through their *biraderi*s, and instead saw a wider social and political entity, the state, and themselves as citizens of this state. 'The state' is understood to be omnipresent and pervasive in lower Sindh, responsible for providing basic rights and security to everyone and everything. Citizenship is a more slippery term than the state, with more normative values associated with it, and a more limited vernacular vocabulary with which to discuss it, but my informants in lower Sindh illustrated a lived experience of citizenship that included notions of rights and entitlements. Some of these were in fact a consequence of supply-side interventions from the state.

Supply-side state intervention and demand-driven citizen action overlapped with an enabling environment to strengthen progressive aspects of citizenship in the aftermath of the flooding disaster in lower Sindh in 2010 and 2011. I also clearly map out the way this social contract was pushed along in the aftermath of the disaster. In Chapter 4, 'Advancing "Disaster Citizenship"',

I systematically argue that the rights-based elements of citizenship in lower Sindh were transformed after the floods of 2010 and 2011. This was the result of a messy overlap between supply-driven policies and interventions by the state that interacted with the demand-side activism of citizens – an interaction that took place within an enabling environment that included internal drivers such as greater democratisation on the ground and external drivers such as development agencies supporting and even funding large-scale social protection programmes. While the state may not have intended to declare disaster relief a right of citizenship by connecting direct cash transfers to people's citizenship numbers, it was soon being interpreted as such on the ground in lower Sindh.

The state remained at the centre of people's political imagination and the main actor for providing entitlement bundles even in the aftermath of the flooding disaster in lower Sindh in 2010 and 2011. Chapter 5, 'The Failing "Islamist Takeover" in the Aftermath of the Indus Floods', strengthens my argument that the state as the larger social entity, 'the *sarkar*', remains intact even in the aftermath of the flooding disaster. In order to do this I engage with the construction of the 'absent' state that was presented at the start of this analysis. In particular, I engage with popular accounts that suggested that the 'vacuum' or 'void' left by the state had been filled by Islamist actors, one of the largest and most visible of whom was the JuD. I deconstruct this popular narrative on two substantial grounds: first, illustrating that the JuD was only able to be as successful in politically motivated disaster relief as the larger social entity, 'the *sarkar*', allowed it to be; second, that the JuD had no ambition to present itself as an alternative to the state in disaster-affected areas of lower Sindh. Finally, I argue that the significant disaster management and policy implementation of the state did not allow large-scale entitlement failures to occur which had the potential to delegitimise the state and empower other political actors.

To address the primary research question, it is important to directly state that social and hereditary relations remain important in lower Sindh, and 'client-ship', in some cases, may even be a part of citizenship. The social contract is neither entirely defined nor subsumed by these social networks nor do they form the only basis of a citizenship framework in lower Sindh. The social contract in Pakistan has elements of 'client-ship' but also progressive elements of rights and entitlements of citizenship, including citizens demanding an interaction with a responsive state. Aspects of the state–citizen relationship that came to a head in the aftermath of the flooding disaster provided an exciting analytical window through which part of this study could take place.

Theoretical Implications

Before writing about the contribution this work has made to citizenship or disaster studies I want to briefly discuss its contribution to an understanding of the post-colonial state of Pakistan. As I argue in Chapter 1 of this book, while theorising the state and political systems, scholarship on Pakistan has tended to look at the 'over-developed' state apparatus, state 'patronage', 'kinship–*biraderi*' and other clientalistic networks, and more recently, the 'security/garrison' state as well.

One of the leading figures within the Subaltern Studies movement in South Asian history defines this movement within Indian history as 'the contributions made by people *on their own*, that is, *independently of the elite* to the making and development' of Indian nationalism (Guha 1988, 39). There are, of course, those who critique Guha and particularly his idea of an 'autonomous domain', one where subaltern politics were taking place independently of elite struggles for domination. At the same time, it is important to note that this tradition was instrumental in opening the door for a serious examination of individual agency and subaltern constructions.

It is, therefore, all the more surprising that this movement within South Asian history seems to have skipped Pakistan entirely. One historian points out that the Subaltern Studies Collective failed to make any real mark in Pakistani historiography, which continues to be dominated by elite movements within history. At the same time, Marxist readings of the Pakistani state fail to engage with cultural differences, without simply dismissing it away as structure, or even superstructure (Ahmed 2013). The voice of the individual, the agency exercised by the 'masses' and their construction of their reality are absent in any serious examination of state-building or nationalism in Pakistan. Instead, scholarship has retained its focus on the structures that dominate the state. A post-structuralist moment in Pakistani historiography, giving agency to the proverbial common man, has been seriously neglected.[1] Much of the scholarship on the state and political relationships continues to construct, define, and redefine, with further improvements, structures of patron–client relationships, kinship–*biraderi* networks, military–*mullah*[2] alliances, and so on.

Despite not situating myself strictly within a Subaltern Studies tradition, in this study I contribute to an understanding of the Pakistani state and society

[1] Different reasons for this neglect have been suggested, from methodological difficulties to the role of Islam.

[2] Pejorative word used for Muslim religious cleric.

beyond these structures. While it is possible to come across a range of studies examining the state through different structuralist narratives, attempts to move beyond these social relations and political nexuses have been relatively few to date. This book contributes to the burgeoning body of scholarship that is attempting to contribute to our understanding of political agency and exercise of citizenship beyond social structures that we know are important but do not define the sum total of all political interactions between state and society in Pakistan.

Citizenship, client-ship or both?

Citizenship is a universally recognised concept but one that is context specific as well. It is a consciously loaded term that carries, on its proverbial shoulders, ideals such as liberty, community, sovereignty, or even contradictory ones such as subjecthood, depending on the social and political struggles of the time and context where it evolved. Literature on the sociology of citizenship in Europe has normally delineated clear typologies of citizenship; those that were passive because they evolved from 'above' or those that were more active and radical and were the result of political struggle from 'below'. It has also normally tended to chart a somewhat linear path from medieval subject to modern citizen – a journey that involved the erosion of 'particularistic' forms of kinship, to equality and universality as citizens. Finally, this work has also streamlined the type of state that made this evolution possible as stuck between capitalist ideals and the need to provide political freedoms. Modern forms of European citizenship may, therefore, have cultural variations but, by and large, the similar social processes through which they emerged also ensure their consistency.

The analysis presented herein muddies some of these neat lines drawn around the boundaries of citizenship evolution. While scholars in development studies have recognised and discussed the various 'hybridised' versions of citizenship in the post-colonial world, this has not made its way into citizenship studies as yet. I am hesitant to use terms such as 'hybridised' because I am not sure of the value they add to our understanding, but my analysis also takes the work of these scholars of post-colonial citizenship forward by illustrating and arguing that 'citizenship' and 'client-ship' are, in fact, not mutually exclusive. This research has shown that some elements of political patronage remain part of the way the social contract is interpreted between the state and its citizens in this region. This contract equally includes ideas of *bunyaadi haq* (fundamental rights), basic human security and other rights-based constructions of citizenship as well. Despite the former getting much attention, scholarly work on the latter in the context of Pakistan has been limited and underdeveloped to date, something that this book has tried to address.

Rights, entitlements and famines

Entitlements include the full range of options – economic, social and legal – that an individual is able to employ to prevent starvation. The 'entitlement approach' emerged out of Amartya Sen's work on famines and has been used to explain the situation in other complex emergencies (Devereux 2007) over the course of the last three decades as well. Examining state–citizen relations, particularly in the aftermath of the flooding disaster in Pakistan 2010 and 2011, has contributed to a deeper understanding of entitlements in two fundamental ways.

First, it supports the thesis of Dreze and Sen's work (1991), emphasising absolutely the role of the state in large-scale public works programmes and social transfers as critical in preventing starvation-related deaths during food security crises. Also, it furthers an understanding of the 'political' geography surrounding famines, something that Sen's work is often critiqued for not doing because of its very economic and legalistic 'entitlements approach'. My study of the post-disaster context in Pakistan in 2010 and 2011 suggests that if the state had not stepped in with a large-scale social intervention programme, the Citizen Damage Compensation Programme (CDCP), greater entitlement failures would have been far more likely. As my ethnography of the Hindu *haris* in Badin has illustrated, such failures would also have resulted in people actively pursuing alternative political options able to provide them with the minimal human security that they needed. What this research has revealed instead is that people in fear of starvation, related to 'entitlement failures', were the exception rather than the rule and for the most part state interventions were able to prevent such failures from occurring. The post-disaster context of Sindh actually displayed characteristics of what de Waal (1996) considers to be exceptional in the Indian social contract, where 'freedom from famine' was enshrined as a right that must be provided by the state and failure to do so would delegitimise the foundations on which the social contract has been built.

Second, it is important to note that my work on the transformation of citizenship in the post-disaster context of Pakistan also supports the idea of 'socially sanctioned' entitlements in literature on the entitlements approach. De Waal (1996) proposed in his analysis of the Famine Codes of 1901 that while they were 'superficially similar' to the codes that came before them, once implemented they were considerably more comprehensive, resulting in making 'freedom from famine' a political right in India. My analysis of the National Disaster Management Act (NDMA) of 2010, and the way it was implemented and interpreted on the ground, resulted in more and more people seeing a basic amount of disaster relief as a right, part of the entitlement bundle of citizenship. While this may have been accidental, once such a transformation takes place it is difficult (though not impossible) to push back.

Disasters and the social contract

Pelling and Dill's (2010) framework provides a good foundation for exploring issues around transformation in the aftermath of a disaster – in particular, the politics that emerge in the aftermath of a disaster and the way in which it affects the social contract between the state and the citizen. Sections of this book develop these ideas further by examining the flooding disaster in lower Sindh in 2010 and 2011 in detail. In particular, it is able to shed light on the question of 'path-dependency' versus 'critical juncture' when examining transformation in the aftermath of a disaster. Based on literature reviewed by Pelling and Dill, they state that existing work 'may suggest a correlation between regressive political outcomes and an accelerated status quo, and progressive political outcomes and a critical juncture' (2010, 22). My empirical analysis, however, reveals that an accelerated status quo and progressive political outcomes are also a likely possibility, only confirming Pelling and Dill's assumption that 'political direction' is difficult to predict. This research illustrates that because the ethnographic social contract was already showing signs of movement towards more universal and rights-based ideals of citizenship, the post-disaster moment was able to help push this aspect of citizenship and its transformation along. Additionally, there were external political drivers that also created an enabling environment, making this push possible.

Pelling and Dill's work also suggests that if the 'social contract is contested post-disaster by the state, citizenry or subgroups, regime instability opens up' (2006, 27). This was also further emphasised in the case study of Cyclone Bhola in East Pakistan presented in Pelling's book (2011) that discussed how it was the final nail in the coffin for the West Pakistan regime that had lost all legitimacy in its handling of the disaster. The argument in this book, however, demonstrates that the reverse is also possible. In reaching out to citizens affected by the flooding disaster in Pakistan in an unprecedented manner, the state was able to strengthen progressive elements of the social contract. In particular, by connecting CDCP to citizenship numbers and instituting an NDMA that took some amount of disaster relief as a minimum, the state did not allow instability to set in, and instead strengthened people's connection to 'the *sarkar*'. Equally, it is important to emphasise that the framework utilised by Pelling and Dill (2010) uses the case study of the Marmara earthquake in Turkey and pits the conservative and religious civil society groups against the secular Kemalist state. This research shows that even where other political agents are being pitted against the state in popular media narratives, one must still exercise caution in assuming that this is actually the case.

Policy Implications

The main finding of this study is that a larger social entity, 'the state', exists outside of urban metropolises of Pakistan, such as lower Sindh. People have a relationship with this 'state' that is based on more than just social relations, and includes some elements of rights-based citizenship as well. On the one hand, the direct policy implication of this finding is almost banal; it simply reasserts what has been said by a number of development experts and actors before – that instead of using foreign aid related interventions to undercut the state, international intervention should support aspects of the state that are trying to reach out to its citizens. A particularly promising example of this has been seen through the CDCP, which has received considerable support from the World Bank and its second phase was funded through bilateral aid from European governments. In particular, Pakistan's efforts at digitising G2P (government to person) transfers, in a way that increases efficiency, reduces leakages and makes the exchange of money more transparent, have been hailed as a revolution in state–citizen relations by various private and public sector enterprises (Parker, Kumar and Parada 2013). It is necessary to continue to support such initiatives rather than working towards bypassing the state altogether.

At the same time, this policy implication is radical. As I mention in the introduction, immediately in the aftermath of the floods in 2010, the US aid agency in Pakistan was diverting tens of millions of dollars towards disaster relief, using its own political brand 'From the American People'. My ethnography on the NGO operating in Sajawal (in Thatta) also illustrates how some part of this money was clearly helping to keep groups such as the JuD in the business of relief provision, in the aftermath of the flooding disaster in lower

Sindh. Despite problems with the way the state operates, and limitations in the exercise of citizenship, the state remains at the centre of political imagination in Pakistan. This is particularly true during trying and challenging times such as disasters. It is important for development interventions to utilize the moment the disaster creates to strengthen rather than delegitimise the larger social entity, the *sarkar*.

In 2012, while I was still doing fieldwork in lower Sindh, one of Pakistan's foremost security experts was quoted in an article as saying, 'Sindh has failed to produce an alternative narrative to feudalism, and so (Islamist) radicalism has grown' (Rehman 2013). Statements like these are still regularly bandied about without being based on any recent scholarship on this region. This analysis has illustrated 'the danger of a single story'[3] on Sindh, which is commonly extended to include the whole of Pakistan. Because, as my research reveals, there are many stories running parallel to and also intersecting with each other on the ground in Pakistan and the state remains the central character in most of these narratives.

[3] Quoted from Chimamanda N. Adichie's Ted Talks demonstration, 'The Danger of a Single Story' in July 2009, available at http://www.ted.com/talks/chimamanda_adichie_the_danger_of_a_single_story?language=en

References

Abbas, H. 2009. 'Can Pakistan Defy the Odds: How to Rescue a Failing State'. Washington DC: Institute for Social Policy and Understanding (ISPU), available at http://www.ispu.org/files/PDFs/ispu-pakistan_can_defy_the_odds.pdf (accessed on 16 August 2016).

Abou Zahab, M. and O. Roy. 2004. *Islamist Networks: The Afghan-Pakistan Connection*. London: Hurst & Company.

Adeney, K. 2007. 'The "Necessity" of Asymmetrical Federalism?' *Ethnopolitics* 6 (1): 117–120.

———. 2009. 'The Federal Election in Pakistan, February 2008'. *Electoral Studies* 28 (1): 158–63.

———. 2012. 'A Step Towards Inclusive Federalism in Pakistan? The Politics of the 18th Amendment'. *Publius: The Journal of Federalism* 42 (4): 539–65.

Ahmad, I. 2004. 'Islam, Democracy and Citizenship Education: An Examination of the Social Studies Curriculum in Pakistan'. *Current Issues in Comparative Education* 7 (1): 39–49.

Ahmed, M. 2013. 'A Methodological Footnote', *Chapati Mystery*, 13 May, available at http://www.chapatimystery.com/archives/univercity/a_methodological_footnote.html (accessed on 16 August 2016).

Ahmed, Z. 2013. 'Disaster Risks and Disaster Management Policies and Practices in Pakistan: A Critical Analysis of Disaster Management Act of 2010 of Pakistan'. *International Journal of Disaster Risk Reduction* 4 (June): 15–20.

Akhtar A. 2013. 'Indus Basin Floods: Mechanisms, Impact and Management'. Manila: Asian Development Bank, available at http://adb.org/sites/default/files/pub/2013/indus-basin-floods.pdf (accessed on 16 August 2016).

Akhtar, A. S. 2012. 'The Military Myth', *Dawn*, 16 February, available at http://www.dawn.com/news/696055/the-military-myth (accessed on 16 August 2016).

Alam, M. S. 1974. 'Economics of the Landed Interests: A Case Study of Pakistan'. *Pakistan Economic and Social Review* 12 (1): 12–26.

Alavi, H. 1972. 'The State in Post-colonial Societies: Pakistan and Bangladesh'. *New Left Review* 1 (74): 58–81.

———. 1983. 'Class and State'. In *Pakistan: The Roots of Dictatorship – The Political Economy of a Praetorian State*, edited by H. Gardezi and J. Rashid, 40–93. London: Zed Books.

———. 1986. 'Ethnicity, Muslim Society, and the Pakistan Ideology'. In *Islamic Reassertion in Pakistan: The Application of Islamic Laws in a Modern State,* edited by Anita Weiss, 21–47. Syracuse, New York: New York University Press.

Albala-Bertrand, J. M. 1993. *The Political Economy of Natural Disasters: With Special Reference to Developing Countries.* Oxford: Oxford University Press.

Allan, T. R. S. 1996. 'Citizenship and Obligation: Civil Disobedience and Civil Dissent'. *The Cambridge Law Journal* 55 (March): 89–121.

Amer, K. 2013. 'Population Explosion: Put an Embargo on Industrialisation in Karachi', *The Express Tribune*, 6 October, available at https://tribune.com.pk/story/614409/populationexplosion-put-an-embargo-on-industrialisation-in-karachi/ (accessed on 16 August 2016).

Andrabi, T. and J. Das. 2010. 'In Aid We Trust: Hearts and Minds and the Pakistan Earthquake of 2005'. Policy Research, World Bank, working paper no. WPS 5440, available at http://documents.worldbank.org/curated/en/509101468284076977/In-aid-we-trust-hearts-and-minds-and-the-Pakistan-earthquake-of-2005 (accessed on 16 August 2016).

Ansari, S. 1992. *Sufi Saints and State Power: The Pirs of Sind, 1843–1947.* Cambridge: Cambridge University Press.

Anthony, A. 2010. 'US to Give More Flood Aid to Pakistan', Reuters, 25 August, available at https://www.reuters.com/article/us-pakistan-floods/u-s-to-give-more-flood-aid-to-pakistan-idUSTRE66T3RS20100825. (accessed on 16 August 2016).

Ashwill, M. and A. Norton, eds. 2011. *Building Citizenship through Social Policy in the Eastern Caribbean: the Role of Social Guarantees.* London and Washington DC: Overseas Development Institute and World Bank, available at http://www.odi.org.uk/sites/odi.org.uk/files/odi-assets/publications-opinion-files/7399.pdf (accessed on 16 August 2016).

Ayson, R and B. Taylor. 2008. 'Carrying China's Torch'. *Survival: Global Politics and Strategy* 50 (4): 5–10.

Bachmann, C. and C. Staerkle. 2003. 'Re-inventing Citizenship in South Caucasus: Exploring the Dynamics and Contradictions between Formal Definitions and Popular Conceptions'. *Final Research Report JRP 7AZPJ062373* SCOPES: Scientific Co-operation between Eastern Europe and Switzerland, available at http://www.cimera.org/files/reports/rr1/tableofcontents.pdf (accessed on 16 August 2016).

Bamberg, M. 2004. 'Considering Counter-narratives'. In *Considering Counter-Narratives: Resisting Narrating and Making Sense*, edited by M. Bamberg and M. Andrews, 351–71. Amsterdam: John Benjamins.

Barrientos, A. 2006. 'Social Protection Strategy for Pakistan'. *DFID-Pakistan PK 0337*, available at http://www.ids.ac.uk/files/dmfile/TOFinal20ReportPK0337A02MAY06.pdf (accessed on 16 August 2016).

Barrientos, A. and D. Hulme. 2008. 'Social Protection for the Poor and Poorest in Developing Countries: Reflections on a Quiet Revolution'. Brooks World Poverty Institute, The University of Manchester, Working Paper no. 30, available at https://www.unicef.org/spanish/socialpolicy/files/Social_Protection_for_the_Poor_and_Poorest_in_Developing_Countries.pdf (accessed on 16 August 2016).

BBC News. 2011. 'Agencies Warn of Acute Pakistan Flood Relief Shortfall', 9 November, available at www.bbc.co.uk/news/world-asia-15643468 (accessed on 16 August 2016).

Becker, H. S. 1996. 'The Epistemology of Qualitative Research'. In *Ethnography and Human Development: Context and Meaning in Social Inquiry*, edited by R. Jessor, A. Colby and R. A Shweder, 53–71. Chicago: University of Chicago Press.

Briscoe, J. and U. Qamar. 2005. 'Pakistan's Water Economy Running Dry'. Washington DC: World Bank, available at http://documents.worldbank.org/curated/en/989891468059352743/Pakistans-water-economy-running-dry (accessed on 16 August 2016).

Brockett, C. D. 1991. 'The Structure of Political Opportunity and Peasant Mobilisation in Central America'. *Comparative Politics* 23(3): 253–274.

Bryman, A. 1984. 'The Debate about Quantitative and Qualitative Research: A Question of Method or Epistemology?' *The British Journal of Sociology* 35 (1): 75–92.

Burke, C. 2005. 'Comparing Qualitative Research Methodologies for Systemic Research: The Use of Grounded Theory, Discourse Analysis and Narrative Analysis'. *Journal of Family Therapy* 27 (3): 237–62.

Capoccia, G. and R. D. Kelemen. 2007. 'The Study of Critical Junctures: Theory, Narrative and Counterfactuals in Historical Institutionalism'. *World Politics* 59 (3): 341–69.

Chandhoke, N. 2003. *The Conceits of Civil Society*. Delhi: Oxford University Press.

Chatterjee, J. 2012. 'South Asian Histories of Citizenship, 1946–1970'. *The Historical Journal* 55 (4): 1049–71.

Cheeseman, D. 1997. *Landlord Power and Rural Indebtedness in Colonial Sind, 1865–1901*. Richmond: Curzon Press.

Chhotray, V. 2014. 'Disaster Relief and the Indian State: Lessons for Just Citizenship'. *Geoforum* 54: 217–25.

Cole, Shawn, Andrew Healy and Eric Werker. 2012. 'Do Voters Demand Responsive Governments? Evidence from Indian Disaster Relief'. *Journal of Development Economics* 97 (2): 167–81.

Corbridge, S., Glyn Williams, Manoj Srivastava and René Véron. 2005. *Seeing the State: Governance and Governmentality in India*. Cambridge: Cambridge University Press.

Cornwall, A. 2000. 'Beneficiary, Consumer, Citizen: Perspectives on Participation for Poverty Reduction'. *SIDA Studies* no. 2. Stockholm: Swedish International Development Cooperation Agency (SIDA), available at https://www.sida.se/contentassets/4bae59ebedb74236a9339c2b61e34123/15609.pdf (accessed on 16 August 2016).

Crilly, R. 2010. 'Pakistan Flood Aid from Islamic Extremists', *The Telegraph*, 21 August, available at http://www.telegraph.co.uk/news/worldnews/asia/pakistan/7957988/Pakistanflood-aid-from-Islamic-extremists.html (accessed on 16 August 2016).

Crotty, M. 1998. *The Foundations of Social Research: Meaning and Perspective in the Research Process*. London: Sage Publications Ltd.

Dagnino, E. 2007. 'Citizenship: A Perverse Confluence'. *Development in Practice* 17 (4–5): 549–56.

Davis, M. 2001. *Late Victorian Holocausts: El Nino and the Making of the Third World*. London and New York: Verso.

Dawn. 2007. 'Contract System Abolished: Inland Fishing', 19 January, available at https://www.dawn.com/news/228645 (accessed on 16 August 2016).

———. 'LBOD Design Blamed for Sindh's Woes', 15 September, available at http://beta.dawn.com/news/659285/lbod-design-blamed-for-sindhs-woes (accessed on 16 August 2016).

———. 'Left Bank Outfall Drain: Friend or Foe?', 15 July, available at http://beta.dawn.com/news/734548/left-bank-outfall-drain-a-friend-or-foe (accessed on 16 August 2016).

De Waal, A. 1996. 'Social Contract and Deterring Famines: First Thoughts'. *Disasters* 20 (3): 194–205.

———. A. 1997. *Famine Crimes: Politics and the Disaster Relief Industry in Africa*. Oxford and Bloomington: James Currey and Indiana University Press.

Dean, B. L. 2005. 'Citizenship Education in Pakistani Schools: Problems and Possibilities'. *International Journal of Citizenship and Teacher Education* 1 (2): 35–55.

Delanty, G. 1997. 'Models of Citizenship: Defining European Identity and Citizenship'. *Citizenship Studies* 1 (3): 285–303.

Devereux, S. 2001. 'Sen's Entitlement Approach: Critiques and Counter-critiques'. *Oxford Development Studies* 29 (3): 245–63.

———. 2007. 'Introduction: From "Old Famines" to "New Famines"'. In *The New Famines – Why Famines Persist in an Era of Globalisation*, edited by S. Devereux, 1–26. Abingdon: Routledge.

Dorosh, P., S. Malik and M. Krausova. 2010. 'Rehabilitating Agriculture and Promoting Food Security following the 2010 Pakistan Floods: Insights from the South Asian Experience', International Food Policy Research Institute, IFPRI Discussion Paper 01028, available at http://www.ifpri.org/sites/default/files/publications/ifpridp01028.pdf (accessed on 16 August 2016).

Dreze, Jean and A. Sen. 1991. *Hunger and Public Action*. Oxford: Clarendon Press.

Drury, A. C. and R. C. Ohlson. 1998. 'Disasters and Political Unrest: An Empirical Investigation'. *Journal of Contingencies and Crisis Management* 6 (3): 153–61.

Ellick, A. B. and P. Z. Shah. 2010. 'Hard-Line Islam Fills Void in Flooded Pakistan', *New York Times*, 6 August, available at http://www.nytimes.com/2010/08/07/world/asia/07pstan.html?pagewanted=all&_r=0 (accessed on 16 August 2016).

Fair, C. C. 2011. 'Lashkar-e-Tayiba and the Pakistani State'. *Survival* 53 (4): 29–52.

Fuller, C. J. and J. Harriss. 2009. 'For an Anthropology of the Modern Indian State'. In *The Everyday State and Society in Modern India*, edited by C. J. Fuller and Veronique Benei, 1–30. New Delhi: Social Science Press.

Fuller, C. J. and Veronique Benei. 2009. *The Everyday State and Society in Modern India*. New Delhi: Social Science Press.

Gall, C. and A. Jamal. 2005. 'In a Remote Camp, Help from an Unconventional Source', *The New York Times*, 18 October, available at http://www.nytimes.com/2005/10/18/world/asia/18iht-kashmir.html (accessed on 16 August 2016).

Gardezi, H. 1991. *Understanding Pakistan: The Colonial Factor in Societal Development*. Lahore: Maktaba Fikro-Danish.

Gardezi, H. and R. Rashid. 1983. *Pakistan: Roots of Dictatorship*. London: Zed Books Ltd.

Gasper, J. T. and A. Reeves. 2011. 'Make it Rain: Retrospection and the Attentive Electorate in the Context of Natural Disasters'. *American Journal of Political Science* 55 (2): 340–55.

Gazdar, H. 2008. 'Pakistan's Precious Parties'. *Economic and Political Weekly* 43 (6): 8–9.

———. 2011. 'Social Protection in Pakistan: In the Midst of a Paradigm Shift?' *Economic and Political Weekly* 46 (28): 59–66.

Gazdar, H. and A. Khan. 2004. 'A Rapid Assessment of Bonded Labour in Domestic Work and Begging in Pakistan', International Labour Office (ILO), Geneva, Working Paper no. 22, available at http://www.researchcollective.org/researchers_info2.php?val=A_004 (accessed on 16 August 2016).

Gould, W., T. C. Sherman and S. Ansari. 2013. 'The Flux of the Matter: Loyalty, Corruption, and the "Everyday State" in the Post-Partition Government Services of India and Pakistan'. *Past and Present* 219 (1): 237–79.

Government of Islamic Republic of Pakistan. 2003. 'Pakistan's Initial National Communication on Climate Change'. Islamabad: Ministry of Environment, available at http://unfccc.int/resource/docs/natc/paknc1.pdf(accessed on 16 August 2016).

Guha, Ranajit. 1988. 'On Some Aspects of the Historiography of Colonial India'. In *Selected Subaltern Studies*, edited by Ranajit Guha and Gayatri Chakravorty Spivak, 1–8. New York: Oxford University Press.

Gul, I. 2010. *The Most Dangerous Place: Pakistan's Lawless Frontier*. New York: Penguin Ltd.

Gupta, A. 1995. 'Blurred Boundaries: The Discourse of Corruption, the Culture of Politics and the Imagined State'. *American Ethnologist* 22 (2): 375–402.

Haider, E. 2010. 'Eroding the (Vote) Bank: Karachi after the 2010 Floods'. *Jinnah Institute Research Report*, available at http://jinnah-institute.org/publications/176-eroding-the-vote-banks-idps-in-karachi (accessed on 16 August 2016).

Hansen, T. B. 2005. 'Sovereigns beyond the State: On Legality and Authority in Urban India'. In *Sovereign Bodies: Citizens, Migrants and States in the Postcolonial World*, edited by T. B. Hansen and Finn Stepputat, 169–91. Princeton: Princeton University Press.

Haq, Riaz. 2010. 'Mass Communications Boom in Pakistan', 24 June, available at http://www.pakalumni.com/profiles/blogs/1119293:BlogPost:69564 (accessed on 16 August 2016).

Haqqani, H. 2005. *Pakistan: Between Mosque and Military*. Washington, DC: Carnegie Endowment for International Peace.

Haqqani, I. A. 2006. 'Failure of Democracy in Pakistan?' *The Muslim World* 96 (2): 219–32.

Hasan, A. 2009. *The Unplanned Revolution: Observations on the Processes of Socio-economic Change in Pakistan*. Karachi: Oxford University Press.

Hasan, S. S. 2010. '"Hardline" Groups Step in to Fill Pakistan's Aid Vacuum', *BBC News*, 10 August, available at http://www.bbc.co.uk/news/world-south-asia-10925400 (accessed on 16 August 2016).

Hasnain, Z. 2008. 'The Politics of Service Delivery in Pakistan: Political Parties and the Incentives for Patronage 1988–1999'. *The Pakistan Development Review* 47 (2): 129–51.

Hall-Matthews, D. 2005. *Peasants, Famines, and the State in Colonial Western India*. New York: Palgrave Macmillan.

Healy, A. and N. Malhotra. 2009. 'Myopic Voters and Natural Disaster Policy'. *American Political Science Review* 103 (3): 387–406.

Herring, R. J. 1979. 'Zulfikar Ali Bhutto and the "Eradication of Feudalism" in Pakistan'. *Comparative Studies in Society and History* 21 (4): 519–57.

Hopkin, J. 2006. 'Conceptualising Political Clientelism: Political Exchange and Democratic Theory'. Paper prepared for APSA annual meeting, Philadelphia, 31 August–3 September.

Horsburgh, D. 2003. 'Evaluation of Qualitative Research'. *Journal of Clinical Nursing* 12: 307–12.

Hossain, S. M. M, M. Talat, E. Boyd, S. R. Chowdhury, S. B. Soofi, I. Hussain, I. Ahmed, R. A. Salam and Z. A. Bhutta. 2013. 'Evaluation of Nutrition Surveys in Flood-affected Areas of Pakistan: Seeing the Unseen!' *IDS Bulletin* 44 (3): 10–20.

Hull, M. 2012. *Government of Paper: The Materiality of Bureaucracy in Urban Pakistan*. Berkley: University of California Press.

Hussain, I. 1999. *Pakistan: The Political Economy of an Elitist State*. Karachi: Oxford University Press.

Ibrahim, F. 2011. 'Re-making a Region: Ritual Inversions and Border Transgressions in Kutch'. *South Asia: Journal of South Asian Studies* 34 (3): 439–59.

Ignatieff, Michael. 2005. 'The Broken Contract', *New York Times*, available at https://www.nytimes.com/2005/09/25/magazine/the-broken-contract.html (accessed on 16 August 2016).

Iqtedar, H. 2011. *Secularising Islamists? Jama'at-e-Islami and Jama'at-ud-Da'wa in Urban Pakistan*. Chicago: University of Chicago Press.

IUCN. 2006. District Vision Badin. Badin: District Government of Badin. Available at http://cmsdata.iucn.org/downloads/badin_idv.pdf (accessed on 16 August 2016).

Jaan, D. A. 2011. *Sailaab Dairian*. Karachi: Pakistan Studies Centre.

Jalal, A. 1995. 'Conjuring Pakistan: History as Official Imagining'. *International Journal of Middle East Studies* Vol 27 (1): 73–89.

Jayal, N. G. 2013. *Citizenship and its Discontents: An Indian History*. Cambridge, Massachusetts: Harvard University Press.

Jones, E. and J. Gaventa. 2002. 'Concepts of Citizenship: A Review'. *IDS Development Bibliography 19*. Brighton: Institute of Development Studies, University of Sussex.

Kabeer, N., K. Mumtaz and A. Sayeed. 2010. 'Beyond Risk Management; Vulnerability, Social Protection and Citizenship in Pakistan'. *Journal of International Development* 22 (1): 1–19.

Kabeer, N., K. Huda, S. Kaur and N. Lamhauge. 2012. 'Breaking the Multiple Constraints on Poor Women's Livelihoods'. *Development Viewpoint* 73, School of African and Oriental Studies, University of London, available at https://www.soas.ac.uk/cdpr/publications/dv/breaking-the-multiple-constraints-on-poor-womens-livelihoods.html (accessed on 16 August 2016).

Kamal, S. 2009. 'Pakistan's Water Challenges: Entitlements, Access, Efficiency, and Equity'. In *Running on Empty: Pakistan's Water Crisis,* edited by M. Kugelman and R. M Hathaway, 28–44. Washington, DC: Woodrow Wilson International Centre for Scholars.

Keating, C. 2007. *Decolonising Democracy: Transforming the Social Contract in India*. Pittsburgh: Pennsylvania State University Press.

Khan, A. S. 2012. 'Sindh Population Surges by 81.5pc, Households by 83.9pc', *The News International,* 2 April, available at https://www.thenews.com.pk/archive/print/621380-sindh-population-surges-by-81.5-pc,-households-by-83.9-pc (accessed on 16 August 2016).

Khan, F. 2009. 'Water, Governance, and Corruption in Pakistan'. In *Running on Empty: Pakistan's Water Crisis,* edited by M. Kugelman and R. M. Hathaway, 82–104. Washington, DC: Woodrow Wilson International Centre for Scholars.

Khan, M. 2007. 'The Political Ecology of Irrigation in Upper Sindh: People, Water and Land Degradation'. PhD dissertation submitted to Binghamton University, State University of New York, unpublished.

Khan, M. I. 2012. 'Pakistan's Experience with Identity Management', *BBC News*, 8 June, available at http://www.bbc.co.uk/news/world-asia-18101385 (accessed on 16 August 2016).

Khan, M. Z. 2012. 'Almost 600,000 Taxpayers Missing from Tax Net', *Dawn*, 24 November, available at https://www.dawn.com/news/766625 (accessed on 16 August 2016).

Kingstone, S. 2006. 'Brazil Poor Feel Benefits of Lula's Policies', *BBC News*, 18 September, available at http://news.bbc.co.uk/1/hi/world/americas/5301240.stm (accessed on 16 August 2016).

Lall, M. 2012a. 'Citizenship in Pakistan: State, Nation, and Contemporary Faultlines'. *Contemporary Politics* 18 (1): 1–16.

———. 2012b. 'Why Education Matters: School "Choice" and Differing Views on Citizenship in Pakistan'. *Citizenship Studies* 16 (2): 269–86.

Lancaster, J. and K. Khan. 2005. 'Extremists Fill Aid Chasm after Quake', The Washington Post, 16 October, available at http://www.washingtonpost.com/wp-dyn/content/article/2005/10/15/AR2005101501392.html (accessed on 16 August 2016).

Lashari, A. 2011. 'Sindh: Drainage Crisis in Indus Basin', Dawn, 17 October, available at http://unpo.org/article/13342 (accessed on 16 August 2016).

Lau, W. K. M. and K. Kim. 2012. 'The 2010 Pakistan Flood and Russian Heat Wave: Teleconnection of Hydrometerological Extremes'. *Journal of Hydrometeorology* 13 (1): 392–403.

Lazar, S. 2004. 'Personalist Politics, Clientalism and Citizenship: Local Elections in El Alto, Bolivia'. *Bulletin of Latin American Research* 23 (2): 228–34.

Le Billon, P. and A. Waizenegger. 2007. 'Peace in the Wake of Disaster? Secessionist Conflicts and the 2004 Indian Ocean Tsunami'. *Transactions in the Institute of British Geographers* 32 (3): 411–27.

Leach, M., R. Mearns and I. Scoones. 1999. 'Environmental Entitlements: Dynamics and Institutions in Community-Based Natural Resource Management'. *World Development* 27 (2): 225–47.

Leirvik, O. 2008. 'Religion in School, Interreligious Relations, and Citizenship: The Case of Pakistan'. *British Journal of Religious Education* 30 (2): 143–54.

Lieven, A. 2011. *Pakistan: A Hard Country*. London: Penguin Books Ltd.

Loureiro, M. 2012. 'Of the Earthquake and Other Stories: The Continuity of Change', thesis submitted to University of Sussex, unpublished.

Lund, F. 2009. 'Social Protection, Citizenship and the Employment Relationship'. WIEGO Working Paper no. 10, available at http://wiego.org/sites/wiego.org/files/publications/files/Lund_WIEGO_WP10.pdf (accessed on 16 August 2016).

Lyon, S. M. 2002. 'Power and Patronage in Pakistan', thesis submitted to University of Kent, Canterbury, unpublished.

Mann, M. 1987. 'Ruling Class Strategies and Citizenship'. *Sociology* 21 (3): 339–54.

Mansoor, H. 2013. 'Thatta Split to Make Sujawal 28th District of Sindh', *Dawn*, 13 October, available at http://www.dawn.com/news/1049252 (accessed on 16 August 2016).

Maqsood, A. 2012. 'Being Modern in Lahore: Islam, Class, and Consumption in Urban Pakistan'. Phd thesis submitted to University of Oxford, unpublished.

Marshall, T. H. 2009 (1950). 'Citizenship and Social Class'. In *Inequality and Society*, edited by J. Manza and M. Saunder, 148–154. New York: W. W. Norton and Co.

Masood, S. and K. Drew. 2010. 'New Floods Warnings Raise Fears in Pakistan', *The New York Times*, 12 August, available at http://www.nytimes.com/2010/08/13/world/asia/13pstan.html?_r=0 (accessed on 16 August 2016).

McCartney, M. 2011. 'Pakistan, Growth, Dependency and Crisis'. *The Lahore Journal of Economics* 16 (September): 71–94.

Miller, P. D. 2012. 'How to Exercise U.S. Leverage Over Pakistan'. *The Washington Quarterly* 34 (4): 37–52.

Mitchell, T. 1991. 'The Limits of the State: Beyond Statist Approaches and Their Critics'. *The American Political Science Review* 85 (1): 77–96.

Mohmand, S. and H. Gazdar. 2007. 'Social Structures in Rural Pakistan'. *Determinants and Drivers of Poverty Reduction and ADB's Contribution in Rural Pakistan.* Islamabad: Asian Development Bank.

Mohmand, S. K. 2011. 'Patrons, Brothers, and Landlords: Competing for the Vote in Rural Pakistan'. PhD thesis submitted to University of Sussex, unpublished.

Mujahid, Z. 2011. 'Watan Cards: Flood Survivors Petition Against "Discrimination"', *The Express Tribune*, 4 March, available at http://tribune.com.pk/story/127267/watan-cardsflood-survivors-petition-against-discrimination/ (accessed on 16 August 2016).

Mukhtar, I. 2016. 'Govt Mulls Banning Falah-e-Insaniat Foundation', *The Nation*, 16 January, available at https://nation.com.pk/16-Jan-2016/govt-mulls-banning-falah-e-insaniat-foundation (accessed on 16 August 2018).

Mustafa, B. 2013. 'Is Pakistan equipped to manage a natural disaster?' *The Express Tribune Blogs*, 17 April, available at http://blogs.tribune.com.pk/story/16937/is-pakistan-equippedto-manage-a-natural-disaster/ (accessed on 16 August 2016).

Mustafa, D. 2007. 'Social Construction of Hydropolitics: The Geographical Scales of Water and Security in the Indus Basin'. *Geographical Review* 97 (4): 484–501.

———. 2010. 'Hydropolitics in Pakistan's Indus Basin'. *United States Institute of Peace* Special Report 261, available at http://www.usip.org/sites/default/files/SR261%20-%20Hydropolitics_in_Pakistan's%20_Indus_Basin.pdf (accessed on 16 August 2016).

Mustafa, D., and D. Wrathall. 2011. 'Indus Basin Floods of 2010: Souring of a Faustian Bargain?' *Water Alternatives* 4 (1): 72–85.

Naeem, W. 2012. 'Seminar: Fighting Malnutrition, Poverty the Brazilian Way', *The Express Tribune*, 4 December, available at http://tribune.com.pk/story/474770/seminar-fighting-malnutrition-poverty-thebrazilian-way/ (accessed on 16 August 2016).

Nasir, A. 2012. 'A Media Savvy Jamaat-ud-Dawa', *New Age Islam*, 17 November, available at http://www.newageislam.com/islam-and-the-media/a-media-savvy-jamaat-uddawa/d/9340 (accessed on 16 August 2016).

NDMA and UNOCHA. 2015. Presentation on 'Cash Transfer Programming in Emergencies in Pakistan', 4 and 5 November, available at https://reliefweb.int/sites/reliefweb.int/files/resources/20151230_ctp_workshop_report.pdf (accessed on 16 August 2016).

Nielsen, M. 2010. 'Mimesis of the State: From Natural Disaster to Urban Citizenship on the Outskirts of Maputo, Mozambique'. *Social Analysis: Journal of Cultural and Social Practice* 54 (3): 153–73.

Nisbet, R. 1986. *The Making of Modern Society*. New York: New York University Press.

ODI (Overseas Development Institute). 2001. 'Economic Theory, Freedom and Human Rights: The Work of Amartya Sen'. ODI Briefing Paper, Overseas Development

Institute, London, available at http://www.odi.org.uk/sites/odi.org.uk/files/odi-assets/publications-opinion-files/2321.pdf (accessed on 16 August 2016).

Olson, R. S. 2000. 'Toward a Politics of Disaster: Losses, Values, Agendas, and Blame'. *International Journal of Mass Emergencies and Disasters* 18 (2): 265–87.

Ovadiya, M. 2014. 'Building Flexible and Scalable Programs that Can Respond to Disasters'. Social Protection and Labour Technical Note no. 1, World Bank Group, Washington DC, available at http://www-wds.worldbank.org/external/default/WDSContentServer/WDSP/IB/2014/10/23/000470435_20141023125728/Rendered/PDF/917780BRI0P1320SPL0Technical0Note01.pdf (accessed on 16 August 2016).

Pakistan Today. 2014. 'BISP, Brazil to Share Expertise on Social Protection', 18 February, available at https://www.pakistantoday.com.pk/2014/02/18/bisp-brazil-to-share-expertise-on-social-protection/ (accessed on 16 August 2016).

Pantti, M. K., and K. Wahl-Jorgensen. 2011. '"Not an act of God': Anger and Citizenship in Press Coverage of British Man-made Disasters'. *Media, Culture, and Society* 33 (1): 105–22.

Paracha, N. F. 2011. 'The Jiyala: A Political and Spiritual History, *Dawn*, 27 December, available at http://www.dawn.com/news/683564/the-jiyala-a-political-and-spiritual-history (accessed on 16 August 2016).

Parker, S. R., K. Kumar and M. Parada. 2013. 'An Overview of the G2P Payments Sector in Pakistan', CGAP, 31 January, available at http://www.cgap.org/publications/overview-g2p-payments-sector-pakistan (accessed on 16 August 2016).

Pasricha, N. and K. Rezvi. 2013. 'After Watan: The Contributions of a G2P Payments Program to Building a Branchless Banking Industry', Microfinance Gateway, HYPERLINK "https://www.microfinancegateway.org/organization/meda" MEDA and HYPERLINK "https://www.microfinancegateway.org/organization/united-bank-limited" United Bank Limited.

Pelling, M. 2011. *Adaptation to Climate Change: From Resilience to Transformation*. Abingdon: Routledge.

Pelling, M. and K. Dill. 2006. '"Natural Disasters" as Catalysts of Political Action", Chatham House, London, ISP/NSC Briefing Paper 06/01.

Pelling, M., and K. Dill. 2008. 'Disaster Politics: From Social Control to Human Security', Department of Geography, King's College London, Environment, Politics and Development Working Paper Series, paper no. 1.

Pelling, M. and K. Dill. 2010. 'Disaster Politics: Tipping Points for Change in the Adaptation of Socio-political Regimes'. *Progress in Human Geography* 34 (1): 21–37.

Pelling, M., and D. Manuel-Navarrete. 2011. 'From Resilience to Transformation: The Adaptive Cycle in Two Mexican Urban Centres'. *Ecology and Society* 16 (2): 11, available at http://www.ecologyandsociety.org/vol16/iss2/art11/ (accessed on 16 August 2016).

Pirzada, M., and F. Husain. 2012. 'Pakistani Media: Achievements, Failures and Way Forward?', Jinnah Institute Policy Brief, available at http://www.jinnah-institute.org/images/b0312-18%20pdf.pdf (accessed on 16 August 2016).

Planning Commission, Government of Pakistan. 2010. 'Final Report of the Panel of Economists: Medium Term Development Imperatives and Strategy for Pakistan', available at http://www.pide.org.pk/pdf/Panel_of_Economists.pdf (accessed on 16 August 2016).

Preston, D. 1992. 'Restructuring Bolivian Rurality? Batallas in the 1990s'. *Journal of Rural Studies* 8 (3): 323–33.

Qureshi, A. S., P. G. McCornick, M. Qadir and Z. Aslam. 2008. 'Managing Salinity and Waterlogging in the Indus Basin of Pakistan'. *Agricultural Water Management* 95 (1): 1–10.

Raikes, S. N. 1977. *Memoir on the Thurr and Parkur Districts of Sind.* Karachi: Indus Publications.

Rana, M. A. 2006. 'Changing Tactics of JIHAD Organisations in Pakistan'. *The Anatomy of Terrorism and Political Violence in South Asia*, by John T. Hanley et al., Institute for Defence Analysis, Virginia, II-141–II-151, IDA Paper P-4096.

Rashid, A. 2010. 'Pakistan Floods: An Emergency for the West', *The Telegraph*, 12 August, available at http://www.telegraph.co.uk/news/worldnews/asia/pakistan/7941820/Pakistanfloods-an emergency-for-the-West.html (accessed on 16 August 2016).

Ravallion, M. 1992. 'On Hunger and Public Action'. *The World Bank Research Observer* 7 (1): 1–16.

Rawls, J. 2009. 'The Justification of Civil Disobedience'. In *Arguing About Law*, edited by Aileen Kavanagh and John Oberdiek, 244–53. Abingdon: Routledge.

Rehman, Zia Ur. 2013. 'Militant Groups Make Inroads in Sindh', *The Friday Times*, 2–8 August, available at https://ziaurrehman.media/2013/09/02/militant-groups-make-inroads-in-sindh/ (accessed on 16 August 2016).

Rigg, J. 1998. 'Rural-urban Interactions, Agriculture and Wealth: A Southeast Asian Perspective'. *Progress in Human Geography* 24 (4): 497–522.

Ritzema, H. P. 2009. 'Drain for Gain: Making Water Management Worth its Salt: Subsurface Drainage Practices in Irrigated Agriculture in Semi-Arid and Arid Regions', PhD thesis submitted to University of Wageningen, The Netherlands, unpublished.

Robins, S, A. Cornwall and B. von Lieres. 2008. 'Rethinking "Citizenship" in the Postcolony'. *Third World Quarterly* 29 (6): 1069–86.

Rose, N. and P. Miller. 1992. 'Political Power beyond the State: Problematic of Government'. *The British Journal of Sociology* 43 (2): 173–205.

Rubin, O. 2009. 'The Entitlement Approach: A Case for Framework Development rather than Demolition: A Comment on Entitlement Failure and Deprivation: A Critique of Sen's Famine Philosophy'. *The Journal of Development Studies* 45 (4): 621–40.

Saeed, S., M. Rohde and V. Wulf. 2008. 'ICTs, An Alternative Sphere for Social Movements in Pakistan–A Research Framework'. In *Proceedings of the IADIS International Conference e-Society 2008, April 9–12, 2008, Algarve, Portugal,* 523–26. Portugal: IADIS Press.

Salman, A. 2011. *A Coastal Ecosystem and a People in Peril: The Story of Keti Bunder in Pakistan*. Saarbrucken: Lambert Academic Publishing.

Sarwar, M. B. Forthcoming. *Upgrading Programmes in Karachi, Pakistan: A Neopatrimonial Approach to Study Policy Implementation*. Department of Social Policy, University of Oxford.

Semple, M. 2011. *Breach of Trust: People's Experiences of the Pakistan Floods and their Aftermath, July 2010–July 2011*. Islamabad: Friedrich Ebert Stiftung, Pattan Development Organisation.

Sen, A. 1981. *Poverty and Famines: An Essay on Entitlement and Deprivation*. Oxford, New York: Oxford University Press.

Shah, A. 2013a. 'The Intimacy of Insurgency: Beyond Coercion, Greed or Grievance in Maoist India'. *Economy and Society* 42 (3): 480–506.

———. 2013b. 'The Agrarian Question in a Maoist Guerrilla Zone: Land, Labour and Capital in the Forests and Hills of Jharkhand, India.' *Journal of Agrarian Change* 13 (3): 424–50.

Shah, S. 2010. 'Pakistan Floods: Army Steps into Breach as Anger Grows at Zardari President's Tour of West and Perceived Failure to Help Have Damaged Democracy, Say Analysts', *The Guardian*, 8 August, available at https://www.theguardian.com/world/2010/aug/08/pakistan-floods-army-popular-zardari-anger (accessed on 9 February 2014).

Shaikh, F. 2009. *Making Sense of Pakistan*. London: Hurst & Co Publishers.

Sharma, A. 2011. 'Specifying Citizenship: Subaltern Politics of Rights and Justice in Contemporary India'. *Citizenship Studies* 15 (8): 965–80.

Sharma, A., and A. Gupta. 2006. 'Introduction: Rethinking Theories of the State in an Age of Globalisation'. In *The Anthropology of the State: A Reader*, edited by A. Sharma & A. Gupta, 1–42. Malden, MA: Blackwell.

Shefner, J. 1999. 'Pre and Post-disaster Political Instability and Contentious Supports: Case Study of Political Ferment'. *International Journal of Mass Emergencies and Disasters*, 17 (2): 137–60.

Siddiqi, A. 2013. 'The Emerging Social Contract: State–Citizen Interaction after the Floods of 2010 and 2011 in Southern Sindh, Pakistan'. *IDS Bulletin* 44 (3): 94–102.

———. 2014. 'Climatic Disasters and Radical Politics in Southern Pakistan: The Non-linear Connection'. *Geopolitics* 19 (4): 885–910.

Simpson, E. 2013. *The Political Biography of an Earthquake: Aftermath and Amnesia in Gujarat, India*. London: Hurst and Company.

Simpson, E. and S. Corbridge. 2006 'The Geography of Things That May Become Memories: The 2001 Earthquake in Kachchh-Gujarat and the Politics of Rehabilitation in the Prememorial Era'. *Annals of the Association of American Geographers* 96 (3): 566–85.

Soekefeld, M. 2012. 'The Attabad Landslide and the Politics of Disaster in Gojal, Gilgit-Baltistan'. In *Negotiating Disasters: Politics, Representation, Meanings*, edited by U. Luig, 176–204. Frankfurt am Main: Peter Lang.

Solberg, K. 2010. 'Worst Floods in Living Memory Leave Pakistan in paralysis'. *The Lancet* 376 (9746): 1039–40.

Spencer, J. 1997. 'Post-colonialism and the Political Imagination'. *Journal of the Royal Anthropological Institute* 3 (1): 1–19.

Tankel, S. 2011. *Storming the World Stage: The Story of the Lashkar-e-Taiba*. London: Hurst & Company.

Tarrow, S. 1998. *Power in Movement: Social Movement and Contentious Politics*. Cambridge: Cambridge University Press.

Taylor, L. 2004. 'Client-ship and Citizenship in Latin America'. *Bulletin of Latin American Research* 23 (2): 213–27.

The Economist. 2013. 'Pakistan's Waning Feudalism: Gone with the wind', 18 May, available at https://www.economist.com/asia/2013/05/18/gone-with-the-wind (accessed on 16 August 2016).

The Express Tribune. 2011. 'Sindh Floods: LBOD was a Mistake, Experts Finally Agree with Residents', 30 November, available at http://tribune.com.pk/story/299802/sindh-floods-lbodwas-a-mistakeexperts-finally-agree-with-residents/ (accessed on16 August 2016).

The Express Tribune. 2012. 'Left Bank Outfall Drain: "WB Needs to Consult Sindhis before it Sinks Millions of Dollars into Project"', 15 January, available at http://tribune.com.pk/story/321662/left-bank-outfalldrain-wb-needs-to-consult-sindhis-before-it-sinks-millions-of-dollars-into-project/ (accessed on 16 August 2016).

The Nation. 2011. 'Contract System of Fishing Abolished', 14 January, available at https://nation.com.pk/14-Jan-2011/contract-system-of-fishing-abolished (accessed on 16 august 2016).

The Nation. 2013. 'Mobile Phone Users Touch 129.6m Mark', 30 November, available at https://nation.com.pk/30-Nov-2013/mobile-phone-users-touch-129-6m-mark (accessed on 16 August 2016).

The News International. 2011. 'NADRA to Issue Pakistan Card to Flood, Rain-hit Families', 17 September, available at https://www.thenews.com.pk/archive/print/321960-nadra-to-issue-pakistan-cards-to-flood-rain-hit-families (accessed on 16 August 2016).

The World Bank. 2013a. *Pakistan's Citizens Damage Compensation Program (CDCP)*, June 80621, available at http://documents.worldbank.org/curated/en/153031468139211888/pdf/806210WP0P12680Box0379812B00PUBLIC0.pdf (accessed on 16 August 2016).

The World Bank. 2013b. 'Pakistan: Uplifting Lives and Livelihoods through Cash Transfers', 14 January, available at http://www.worldbank.org/en/results/2013/04/15/pakistan-uplifting-lives-and-livelihoods-through-cash-transfers (accessed on 16 August 2016).

The World Bank. 2013c. 'World Bank Support to Social Safety Nets', 11 April, available at http://www.worldbank.org/en/results/2013/04/11/world-bank-support-to-socialsafety-nets (accessed on 16 August 2016).

Thomas, R. H. ed. 1979 (1855). *Memoirs on Sind*. Karachi: Karimsons.

Titus, P. 1998. 'Honour the Baloch, Buy the Pushtun: Stereotypes, Social Organisation, and History'. *Modern Asian Studies* 32 (3): 657–87.

Tran, M. 2010. 'Pakistan Flood Victims Flee Thatta after Another Levee is Breached', *The Guardian*, 27 August, available at http://www.theguardian.com/world/2010/aug/27/pakistan-floods-levee-thatta (accessed on 16 August 2016).

Trouillot, M. R. 2001. 'The Anthropology of the State in the Age of Globalisation: Close Encounters of the Deceptive Kind'. *Current Anthropology* 42 (1): 125–38.

Turner, Bryan S. 1990. 'Outline of a theory of citizenship'. *Sociology* 24 (2): 189–217.

———. 1993. 'Contemporary Problems in the Theory of Citizenship'. In *Citizenship and Social Theory*, edited by Bryan S. Turner, 1–18. London: Sage Publication Ltd.

Tweedie, N. 2010. 'Pakistan Floods: Disaster is the Worst in the UN's History', *The Telegraph*, 9 August, available at http://www.telegraph.co.uk/news/worldnews/asia/pakistan/7935485/Pakistan-floods-disaster-is-the-worst-in-the-UNs-history.html (accessed on 16 August 2016).

Verkaaik, O. 2001. 'The Captive State: Corruption, Intelligence Agencies, and Ethnicity in Pakistan'. In *States of Imagination: Ethnographic Explorations of the Postcolonial State*, edited by T. B. Hansen and F. Stepputat, 345–64. Durham and London: Duke University Press.

Walsh, D. 2010. 'Still Marooned: Plight of Flood-stricken Villagers in Pakistan's Sindh Province', *The Guardian*, 4 October, available at www.guardian.co.uk/world/2010/oct/04/pakistan-floods-plight-sindh-province (accessed on 16 August 2016).

Warner, J. 2013. 'The Politics of "Catastrophisation"'. In *Disaster, Conflict and Society in Crises: Everyday Politics of Crisis Response*, edited by D. Hilhorst, 76–94. Abingdon: Routledge.

Waseem, M. 1994. *Politics and the State in Pakistan*. Islamabad: Quaid-e-Azam University.

Weber, M. 1966. *The City*. Cambridge: The Free Press.

Wedeen, L. 2010. 'Reflections on Ethnographic work in Political Science'. *Annual Review of Political Science* 13: 255–72.

Whaites, A. 1995. 'The State and Civil Society in Pakistan'. *Contemporary South Asia* 4 (3): 229–54.

Whitcombe, E. 1993. 'Famine Mortality'. *Economic and Political Weekly* 28 (3): 1169–79.

Williamson, J. A. 2011. 'Using Humanitarian Aid to Win Hearts And Minds: A Costly Failure?' *International Review of the Red Cross* 93 (884): 1035–61.

Williamson, K. 2006. 'Research in Constructivist Frameworks Using Ethnographic Techniques'. *Library Trends* 55 (1): 83–101.

Yu. S. 2010. 'Flood Relief in the Sphere of Terrorism: The Politics of Humanitarian Responses to the Pakistani Floods of 2010', dissertation submitted to University of Chicago, unpublished.

Zaidi, A. 1999. *Issues in Pakistan's Economy*. Karachi: Oxford University Press.

———. 2003. *Continuity and Change: Socio-Political and Institutional Dynamics In Pakistan*. Karachi: City Press.

Index